REMAINS

Historical and Literary

CONNECTED WITH THE PALATINE COUNTIES OF

Lancaster and Chester

VOLUME XXVII—THIRD SERIES

MANCHESTER:

Printed for the Chetham Society

1980

ACKNOWLEDGEMENTS

The Society is grateful to Greater Manchester Council for assistance towards the cost of publication of this book.

ELIZABETHAN MANCHESTER

by
T. S. WILLAN

MANCHESTER
Printed for the Chetham Society
1980

© The Chetham Society 1980

Published for the Society by
Manchester University Press
Oxford Road, Manchester M13 9PL

British Library cataloguing in publication data

Willan, Thomas Stuart
    Elizabethan Manchester. – (Remains, historical and
literary, connected with the Palatine Counties of
Lancaster and Chester: 3rd series; vol. 27

    1. Manchester Eng. – History – 16th century
I. Title   II. Series
942.   7'33'055   DA 690.M4

    ISBN 0–7190–1336–4

Printed in Great Britain by
Willmer Brothers Limited
Rock Ferry, Merseyside

CONTENTS

PREFACE

This study of Elizabethan Manchester does not attempt to cover all aspects of the subject. There are two omissions in particular which demand a word of explanation. I have said little about the administration of the town because our knowledge of that administration depends almost entirely on the Court Leet records. Those records have been published and have formed the basis for an excellent study of Manchester's administration (A. Redford and I. S. Russell, *The history of local government in Manchester*, 3 vols.). Unless new sources come to light, there is little to be gained by repeating the story already well told by Professor Redford and Dr Russell. The second omission is perhaps more serious. I have made no attempt to deal with the religious life of Manchester. That is largely because the subject has been discussed in a wider context in two recent books (R. C. Richardson, *Puritanism in north-west England. A regional study of the diocese of Chester to 1642* and C. Haigh, *Reformation and resistance in Tudor Lancashire*). Both Dr Richardson and Dr Haigh discuss religion in Manchester within the wider context of the diocese or of the county, and it may be that the township of Manchester, which is my main concern, is too constricted an area to form the basis for a fruitful discussion of religious life. In ecclesiastical matters it would be difficult to separate the township of Manchester from the parish of which it formed only a part.

It remains to thank those who make this sort of study possible by their custodianship of the manuscript sources. I am grateful to the Archivists of the Lancashire Record Office and the Archives Department of Manchester City Library for their help and for the provision of xerox copies of manuscripts in their custody. I must also thank my colleagues Professor J. S. Roskell, for preventing my rusty Latin from disgracing me, and Dr C. B. Phillips, for reading the manuscript and making helpful suggestions for its improvement.

T. S. W.

ABBREVIATIONS

Ch.S.	Chetham Society
C.L.R.	*The Court Leet records of the manor of Manchester*, ed. J. P. Earwaker, 12 vols. 1884–90
D.L.	Duchy of Lancaster
Exch. K.R.	Exchequer Kings Remembrancer
Lowe	N. Lowe, *The Lancashire textile industry in the sixteenth century*, Chetham Society, 3rd series. xx (1972)
L.R.O.	Lancashire Record Office (Preston)
M.C.L.	Manchester City Library (Archives Department)
P.R.O.	Public Record Office
Registers	*The Registers of the Cathedral Church of Manchester*, ed. E. Axon. Lancs. Parish Register Society, 31 (1908)
V.C.H.	*Victoria County History*

Map of the ancient parish of Manchester

CHAPTER 1

THE MANOR

In 1588 William Smith said of Manchester 'it is the cheiffest towne in Lancashire, next to Lancaster, and in many respects passeth the same'.[1] More than a century later Daniel Defoe described Manchester as 'one of the greatest, if not really the greatest meer village in England'.[2] They may both have been right despite the apparent contradiction between 'cheiffest towne' and 'meer village', for Smith was alluding to a centre of trade and industry, with its market and fair, while Defoe was alluding to the fact that Manchester remained under manorial jurisdiction and was ruled by its Court Leet. It was a 'village' in the sense that it was not an incorporated borough despite its size and importance and its charter of 1301, which fell short of incorporation. Much has been written about this rather anomalous method of government and administration, and nothing is to be gained by repeating the story.[3] Nor can much be gained by exploring the complex relationship between the parish, township and manor of Manchester. This was investigated by Tait,[4] and who would rush in where Tait has trod? In the present context this relationship is mainly important in defining what is meant by the term Manchester. The parish of Manchester was very different from the township of Manchester, and both were different from the manor of Manchester.[5] The parish of Manchester covered some sixty square miles, extending from Didsbury and Heaton Norris in the south to Blackley and Moston in the north, and from Stretford and Salford in the west to Denton and Haughton in the east. This vast parish was ultimately to embrace some thirty townships, but it is not clear how many of these places can rightly be called townships in the sixteenth century. Thus the township of Manchester was one of a number of townships within the parish. There is no doubt that it was the most important township, but the distinction between township and parish must always be remembered. It has often been forgotten. In this study Manchester must be taken to mean the township of Manchester and not the parish or the manor. Confusion

between manor and township is as likely as confusion between township and parish, for the government of Manchester 'was manorial,
not burghal',[6] but the manor of Manchester was not co-terminal
either with the parish or with the township. The manor had, however, its centre of gravity in the township of Manchester, and its
records therefore throw some much needed light on the history of
Elizabethan Manchester.

More than a century ago John Harland published a rental of the
manor of Manchester for 1473,[7] but neither he nor other scholars
seem to have known that later rentals existed. There are, however,
a survey and four rentals of Elizabeth I's reign and five rentals of
James I's reign.[8] The survey is dated 14 September 1581 and is
headed 'Mancestre cum membris infra libertatem'. It is practically
confined to holdings within the parish of Manchester and so excludes
the more outlying parts of the manor which are included in the
rentals. The four Elizabethan rentals are for 1589–90, 1592–3,
1598–9 and 1599–1600.[9] They record in detail the rents received at
Midsummer, Michaelmas, Christmas and Lady Day, and these are
summarised in a statement of total receipts and payments for the
year. The rentals have a common form from which it is clear that
they were copied from year to year with any necessary alterations
arising from changes in ownership or from new sources of income.
Such a common form was appropriate, for the rentals very largely
covered property which was subject to fixed and conventional payments to the lord of the manor. Thus the rentals are more useful for
showing the ownership and distribution of property than they are
for showing what that property was worth.

The rentals suggest that the manor of Manchester consisted of a
collection of rights and property scattered over a wide area. Some of
that property lay well outside the parish of Manchester. Thus in
1599–1600 Edward Worthington, gent., paid 3s 8d p.a. for the
'manor of Worthington' near Wigan, which he held 'by halffe a
knight's fee' and 'sute of court at Manchester'; William Orrell, esq.,
paid 12d for lands and tenements in Dalton near Wigan and 18d for
the manor of Turton near Bolton, in each case holding by one-eighth
of a knight's fee; Sir John Radcliffe paid 20d 'for one hole yeres
chieffe rente . . . for the moitie of Flixton'. There were similar holdings as far afield as Anlezargh and Brindle near Chorley, Towneley
near Burnley, and Brocholes near Preston. How these outlying
properties fitted into the manorial structure remains uncertain.
Some of them may have been sub-manors as was Ashton-under-Lyne
which adjoined the parish of Manchester. In 1581 George Booth and
Thomas Haughton, esq., held 'the manor of Assheton under Lyme
and the patronage thereof with a certen howse and lande called

Roddayhouse over agaynste the water of Irke'. They paid an annual rent of a penny and a red rose. In theory the owners of these properties had to do suit and service at the court in Manchester. Their deaths were duly reported to and recorded by the Court Leet, but it is clear that their heirs rarely, if ever, came 'to doe homage and servyce to the Lorde according to the auncyent and laudable custome of this manor'.[10] Perhaps in manorial as in national government the writ grew weaker the further it had to travel.

Naturally much of the manor of Manchester lay within the parish of Manchester. Thus in 1599–1600 Sir John Byron paid a rent of £33 6s 8d for 'Blakeley, Blakeley fieldes and Bothomley' in the north of the parish and £30 11s 4d p.a. for 'the hamells of Gorton and Grenlomarshe' where Elizabeth I held two tenements and fifty acres of former chantry lands and George Birch, gent., forty acres 'called Milkenslade'; Alexander Reddish paid £1 p.a. for 'the hamell of Cromsall' and Edmund Prestwich 5s p.a. 'for the moitie of Hulme nexte Manchester'. In one of the Chorltons (either cum-Hardy or on-Medlock) the heirs of Edward Tildesley, esq., paid 3s 4d p.a. for their lands and tenements while the heirs of Adam Hulton, gent., paid 26s 8d p.a. for the 'hamell' of Harpurhey and 12d p.a. for the mysterious 'Gotherswicke' which has never been identified. Finally Ralph Haughton paid 13s 4d p.a. 'for one oxegange' in Denton, and 12 tenants in Moston, who included Oswald Mosley, paid 3s p.a. 'to the lords of Nuthurste' and 10s p.a. 'to the lord of Manchester' for their lands there. Such holdings, within the parish but outside the township of Manchester, were important to the lord of the manor for they contributed nearly half his total rental, but they are less interesting to the urban historian than is the property within the township of Manchester itself.

In June and July 1596 Christopher Saxton, the cartographer, was in Manchester where he stayed with Dr John Dee, Warden of the College. On 10 July Dee recorded in his diary, 'Manchester town described and measured by Mr. Christopher Saxton'. Four days later Saxton rode away, perhaps taking his map of Manchester with him.[11] No copy of the map is known to survive. This is a great loss, for a map would have shown more of the topography of Elizabethan Manchester than can be reconstructed from rentals and deeds. Nevertheless the main outlines of that topography are fairly clear.

The township of Manchester was bounded on the west by the rivers Irk and Irwell and on the south and south-east by the river Medlock; to the east it included Ancoats, which was never a separate township, and in the north it embraced Collyhurst. This area had originally been part of the demesne of the manor; it included the site of the Roman camp at Aldport and the medieval settlement which lay between the three rivers and centred on the parish church of St Mary (now the Cathedral). This was the nucleus of the modern city, and in the sixteenth century it was a town *de facto* if not *de jure*. Here were the burgages with their frontages onto Millgate, Marketstead Lane, Hanging Ditch, Fennel St., Deansgate and other streets that still exist. Each burgage normally paid rent of 12*d* p.a. to the lord which the charter of 1301 had laid down. There was also much open land in and around the built-up area. Aldport Park, which stretched southwards from Deansgate, covered over ninety acres,[12] much of it apparently woodland. It was divided into Over and Nether Aldport. The latter contained a lodge which was used as a town house by the Derbys, who held the whole Park until the end of the century, paying a rent of £4 13*s* 4*d* p.a. to the lord.[13] In the north of the township at Collyhurst was 'a certen parcell of common or waste ground . . . parcell of the wastes of the manor' on which the burgesses claimed common of pasture. This had originally covered eighty acres, but encroachments and buildings had reduced the area to forty to fifty acres by 1617.[14] Other lands are more difficult to identify. In 1599–1600 Francis Pendleton held tenements and eighteen acres of land 'lyenge on bothe sydes Grundie-lane within Manchester' for which he paid a rent of 25*s* 4*d* p.a., and the heirs of Adam Oldham and others held lands in 'the Heathes adjoyening upon Newton'. Finally in the heart of Manchester were the Nether and Over Acres, which had once been part of the demesne arable. In 1599–1600 Adam Byrom held one acre of land in Nether Acres and the Queen held an acre 'in the Overacres', where the heirs of John Ashton held 'one doale of land', which was also an acre.

The rents from burgages and land formed the main part of the lord of the manor's revenue from within the township of Manchester, but they were supplemented by some manorial dues. Thus the toll on oatmeal and oatmeal groats brought to the market was farmed at a rent of 3*s* 4*d* p.a. In 1599 the farm was held by John Holt, gent., who leased a house in or near Marketstead Lane where he lived and where his goods, utensils and household stuff were said to be worth £70 or thereabouts. He also leased a house in or near the Market Place 'wheare such as were mealemen sould there meale'.[15] The rest of the tolls, described as 'the tolle, tollebothe and stallage of Manchester', were held by the Hunt family who paid 'yerelye at foure severall feastes £4 by even porcions and for relief at the deathe of everye tennante £4'. Richard Hunt, gent., who succeeded his father of the same name in 1573, is not recorded as paying a relief, but as giving a dagger as a heriot.[16] This may, however, have been payable on some other part of his property for he was a man of considerable possessions. In 1581 he held, in addition to the farm of the tolls, a messuage, garden and other lands lately purchased from the lord in Marketstead Lane, Shude Hill and Newton Lane. The lands comprised fourteen acres 'hedged and inclosed', and the total rent was 28s 1d p.a. with a relief of the same amount payable on death. In addition Hunt owned certain 'auncyente burgage landes in Manchester', for which he paid 7s 6d p.a., and a burgage in Millgate. By 1587 he had a house 'new buylded' in Marketstead Lane and was charged with encroaching on the Lane.[17] More seriously, on 4 October 1587, he was charged with taking toll of the inhabitants contrary to the ancient custom and liberties of the town.[18] Presumably he had been taking toll from natives as well as from 'foreigners'. Two months later Hunt was dead. He left considerable property in Manchester, Salford and Ashton-under-Lyne to his eldest son John, then aged twelve. John was 'sworn of the lord' and admitted tenant on 7 October 1597,[19] but unfortunately there is no evidence, either before or after that date, on how profitable the tolls were to him.

There was another manorial right which in a sense involved a toll, namely the compulsory grinding of corn at the lord's mill or mills. The manorial mills in Manchester were on the river Irk, just above its confluence with the Irwell. There seem to have been four such mills, three of them corn mills and one a fulling mill;[20] one of the former was described as a wheat mill, which suggests that the inhabitants did not subsist entirely on oatcakes. All the mills with the rights belonging to them were granted by the lord of the manor in 1509 to Hugh Bexwick, Joan Bexwick his mother, and Ralph Hulme; in 1525 the Bexwicks granted them to twelve feoffees for the maintenance of the Grammar School.[21] In 1599–1600 the property consisted of the mills, Walkers Croft, 'certen lands in Ancotes' and 'one burgage beinge the usher's house'. It paid a rent of £9 14s 4d p.a. to the lord. Little is known of the men who held the mills in farm from the Feoffees. In 1596 one mill was in the occupation of Jervis Travis and another, the 'narmylne' or nearer mill, in the occupation of Robert Langley.[22] Langley was described as a gentleman; he was a man of some property for he had a burgage in Millgate and an intake there, two gardens which were intakes in Withy Grove, a field called Clement Croft and a 'chamber at the nether mylne', for which he paid a rent of 4s 5d p.a. to the lord. It is curious that the chamber at the nether mill, which was described as 'late Sir Hughe Bexwickes', should not have formed part of the grant to the Grammar School.

The grant of the mills to the Grammar School included the obligation on the inhabitants of Manchester to have their corn ground at the mills. It is clear that there were attempts to evade this obligation. In 1561 the Court Leet reminded 'all the inhabitants of the towne of Mamchestre' of this obligation and imposed a fine of 20s on George Bowker and on anyone else who in future had their grain ground elsewhere. Another reminder followed in 1577 because many 'not regarding their common wealthe and good educatyon of theire children in the said school', wilfully absented themselves and ground at other mills. If this were not stopped it would lead 'to the greate overthrowe of the saide schoole, which only ys founded and maynteyned by suche comoditye'. There was some suggestion that the school mills were being avoided because of 'defaulte' in the millers. If those who had avoided the mills now brought their corn to them and found such default, they were to be recompensed. Later in the same year the jury of the Court Leet reported that they had seen 'a survey booke' of Edward II's time which affirmed the obligation to grind at the manorial mills, but no further action seems to have been taken.[23] Evasion, however, continued. In 1592 Anthony Travis was charged in the Duchy Court with owning a horse mill, regrating corn and giving long days of payment to his debtors to draw them to bring their malt and other corn to his mill. It is not known whether Travis was related to the Jervis Travis who farmed one of the school mills or to George Travis who owned a barn and two closes in Marketstead Lane. Nor is it known how the case ended, but Travis's defence was interesting. He did not deny that there were four manorial mills (three corn mills and a fulling mill) or that he owned a horse mill. His defence was simply that his was one of many non-manorial mills. He claimed that the Earl of Derby had two mills in Cheetham only a quarter of a mile from Manchester, Lady Radcliffe had a water corn mill at Ordsall, Sir Gilbert Gerrard had a 'mill called the Garrett milne', Edmund Prestwich and John Strangeways each had a mill within the town of Manchester, and there was a mill in Bradford. Others added a Smedley mill in Cheetham.[24] Much of this was special pleading. Ordsall was in Salford, the Cheetham mills, which may have included John Strangeways's, were not in the manor, and Prestwich's mill was in Hulme next Manchester. Gerrard certainly acquired a water mill when he got part of the Trafford estate in 1561, and it may have been in Manchester.[25] If it were, its relationship to the school mills remains unexplained. Those mills may not have had a complete monopoly even within the township of Manchester.

While the manorial mills produced the flour or some of it, the manorial oven baked the bread. In 1580 the common oven was held by Richard Fox, and the Court Leet requested 'all lovinge neighbours to come and bake with the saide Richard Foxe, he bakinge their breade and other theire necessaryes duelye as he oughte to doe'.[26] The common oven was attached to a burgage in Millgate which Fox had bought in 1568.[27] He paid a rent of 12d p.a. for the burgage and 6s 8d p.a. for the oven. Four years before his death in 1587, Fox sold the burgage and oven to Lawrence Robinson, a clothier of Salford.[28] Lawrence himself died in 1587 and the burgage 'called the stonehouse nowe newlye buylded' and the oven passed to his son Robert Robinson who was a minor.[29] Perhaps the house had been rebuilt in stone as a precaution against fire, which was a constant danger in bakeries. In 1566 the Court Leet decreed that bakers should 'not laye any gorses or kiddes [faggots] within too bayes of the oven or ovens' under penalty of 20s. This decree was extended in 1590 when no gorse or faggots were to be kept within ten yards of the baker's premises or of any man's houses, barns or stables.[30] These decrees show that the common oven held no monopoly of baking. Other bakers existed. At his death in 1583 George Barlow, baker, had a bakehouse with a bolting tub, a kneeding trough and other treen ware. He also had 'gorss kiddes and wood kiddes and other wood fewell' valued at £3 and 'turves and coles' valued at 7s out of a total personal estate of £15 18s 1d.

The rents from property and the yield of various manorial dues went to the lord of the manor, but it is still difficult to determine how profitable the manor was to him. In 1558 the manor was held by Sir Thomas West, Lord de la Warr, but no accounts have survived for the period of his lordship. He mortgaged the manor in 1579 to John Lacy, citizen and clothworker of London, for £3000. West failed to redeem the mortgage, and the manor passed to Lacy in 1581. It was presumably in connection with this transfer that the survey of September 1581 was made. The earliest surviving accounts of the manor for Lacy's lordship are for the year from Lady Day 1589 to Lady Day 1590. They were drawn up by Charles Leigh, who was both clerk of the Court Leet and receiver. They show that the total receipts for the year were £146 16s 11½d, of which £138 14s 6½d was for rents, £1 7s 1d for arrears of rent and £6 15s 4d for 'Perquisites of courtes'. Perquisites covered miscellaneous receipts. They comprised £2 10s from Roger Bexwick, the borough reeve, in part payment of his account of the perquisites of the Leet Court from Michaelmas 1588 to Easter 1589, and 6s 8d from him for 'allowance of his fee as appeareth by his acquittance but not in money', £1 6s 8d from William Reade 'for the perquisites of the Courte Baron his whole yeres rente', 6d from Thomas Kenyon for his relief and 12d 'for a heriott' payable on the half burgage in Millgate which he had inherited at the age of sixty-five on the death of his father.[31] Michael, the son of Michael Dickenson, also paid 6d as a relief for his half burgage and roodland in Over Acres; as he was under age, the relief was paid by his mother who also paid his heriot, which was 'a dagger praysed by the towne praysers to 6*d*', but which, as the receiver added, 'I shall sell to a better value yf I can'.[32] Finally £2 was collected from John Holland 'for the gorse uppon Colihurst' and 10*s* from William Birch 'for his cupboard and in respect of his obligation', whatever that means.

Payments during the year amounted to £146 16*s* 11*d* 'and so this accompante is clere of all his receiptes and paymentes savinge one halfepeny and therefore craveth your acquittance for his discharge'. The payments included expenses totalling £17 19*s* 4*d* of which £6 15*s* was paid to Sir John Radcliffe, bailiff of Salford Hundred,[33] 'for her Majesties chiefe rente due for the manor of Manchester', £1 16*s* 8*d* to the escheator 'for respyt of homage'. 13*s* 4*d* for 'my fee for the clerkshippe' and £6 13*s* 4*d* for 'my fee as receyvor'; 20*s* to Mr George Elcock, the feodary of the manor, in part payment of his fee; 6*s* 8*d* for the boroughreeve's fee. Apart from these rents and fees, the expenses were small: 13*s* 4*d* for the steward's dinners at Michaelmas 1589 and Easter 1590, 6*d* for 'portage of the chauntrie rent' and 6*d* to William Reade 'that he paid to a joyner for takinge downe, caryenge away and settinge upp William Byrche his cupbord'. The remainder of the payments, namely £128 17*s* 4*d*, was delivered to Lacy through Anthony and Rowland Mosley, who presumably used their trading connections with London to remit it to him. If £128 17*s* 4*d* really represented the clear profit of the manor, it showed a yield of about 4·3 per cent on the £3000 Lacy had paid.

The next accounts, which are for 1592–3, show a similar pattern. Receipts amounted to £144 15*s* 4*d*, of which £138 14*s* 0½*d* was for rents and £6 1*s* 3½*d* for perquisites of courts, reliefs and other profits. The latter were a mixed bag: £1 6*s* 8*d* from George Elcock 'for the rente of the petie amerciaments' and 6*s* for various amercements apparently 'lefte ungathered'; 7*s* 6*d* from George Travis, the late boroughreeve, over and above the 40*s* he had accounted for in the last year's account, and 40*s* from Anthony Mosley, the last boroughreeve, in part payment of his account. Reliefs brought in 15*s* 0½*d*, and arrears of rent (no longer a separate heading) 6*s* 2*d* from John Strangeways, gent., for his burgages and lands in Manchester. Finally William Chorlton, baker, paid 20*s* 'for gorse on Colyhurste'. In 1592–3 the receiver paid out £32 14*s* 10*d* in expenses compared with £17 19*s* 4*d* in 1589–90. The increase was caused by paying the steward a fee of £10, the feodary his full fee of £4, and legal charges of £2 2*s* 8*d*. These expenses left £112 0*s* 6*d* for the lord, who received most of it through Anthony Mosley. The return on £3000 was about 3·7 per cent. Perhaps this meagre return on capital encouraged Lacy to sell, for in 1596 he sold the manor to Nicholas Mosley for £3500.

The Mosleys were a Manchester family engaged in the cloth trade between Manchester and London.[34] Nicholas was the son of Edward Mosley of Hough End in Withington in the parish of Manchester; he lived in London where he managed the metropolitan end of the family cloth trade and where he was lord mayor in 1599–1600 when he was knighted. His brothers Oswald and Anthony remained in Manchester where Anthony bought cloth for export through London. The family had connections with the manor before the purchase of 1596. In 1592–3 Nicholas held lands and tenements of the manor at Harwood and Bradshaw near Bolton and some lands at Prestolee in Pilkington parish.[35] In 1577 Anthony had bought nine acres of land adjoining Collyhurst and two houses and some land in Millgate.[36] By the 1590s the Mosleys were building up their estates in and around Manchester. In 1595 Oswald bought Garrett Hall and lands in Manchester from Sir Thomas Gerrard. Two years later Nicholas Mosley's eldest son Rowland paid £8000 for 'all the manor or manors, lordship or lordships of Withington and Hough' in the south of Manchester parish.[37] It is in this context of increasing possessions and power that the purchase of the manor of Manchester must be seen.

The first surviving rental for Mosley's lordship of the manor is for the year 1598–9. It shows total receipts of £189 14s 0½d, which suggests a marked increase, but this is misleading as the figures include £27 12s for the rent of the lordship of Cheetham which was not part of the manor.[38] If this is omitted, the receipts were £162 2s 0½d of which £139 19s 10½d was for rents, £15 8s for pasturage on Collyhurst and £6 14s 2d for perquisites of courts and other profits. The perquisites and profits included 47s from Thomas Goodyear, the boroughreeve, 'uppon his accompte made by Richard Drone-ffielde his catchpolle', 26s 8d 'for the perquisites of the 3 wekes courte', 35s for amercements and 9s for arrears of rent from George Hulton of Farnworth. Payments for the year amounted to £161 14s 10½d[39] and so the receiver, still Charles Leigh, had to produce 7s 2d to balance the account.

Of the payments £41 16s 1d were for expenses. These included the usual rent to the Queen and the usual fees to the steward, receiver, clerk, feodary and boroughreeve. Legal expenses had risen to £8 6s 2d; they were mostly incurred for charges 'about the fynes and recoveries touchinge Withington', and may have reflected the new lord asserting his rights over the Withington property purchased in 1597. It is perhaps significant that 8d was paid 'to one to fetche the rolle of Edw. the 2', which was presumably either the survey of 1320 or the extent of the manor of 1322.[40] The cost of entertainment had risen too. In addition to the customary 13*s* 4*d* for the dinners of the steward and officers at the two court leets, there was 18*d* 'in wine and to the waytes', 3*s* 6*d* 'paide on the fayre daye for a potle of wine 20*d* a potle of beare 4*d* to the waytes 12*d* to the halberd men 6*d*', and 8*s* 'paide to Henrye Hardye for dynner for 13 persons and for ale morninge and eveninge'. Finally there were some interesting payments arising from the enclosure of the common at Collyhurst. Richard Pendleton was paid 5*s* as the rest of his fee of 20*s* 'for lookinge to Colyhurste besyde the gyffte of his horse grasse, his cowe and calffe', and Hugh Barlow was paid 10*s* as the rest of his fee 'for lookinge to Colyhurste besydes his 2 kyegates gyven him'. Both men were paid small sums for mending gates, including the 'Harperhey Yate' and the 'yate towards Newton lane'. Were they repairing damage caused by disgruntled commoners? All these various payments left £120 5*s* 11½*d* to be handed over to Nicholas Mosley as the profit from his manor; it represented a yield of 3·4 per cent on the purchase price.

The last of the Elizabethan accounts, which covers the year 1599–1600, shows receipts of £145 6*s* 5½*d* omitting those from the lordship of Cheetham.[41] Rents provided £120 6*s* 0½*d* with an additional £4 17*s* 3*d* from butchers' stalls, which was a new item, the pasturage at Collyhurst yielded £16 14*s* 10*d* and 'perquisites of courtes and reliefs' £3 8*s* 4*d*. The perquisites and reliefs included 30*s* from Richard Nugent, the boroughreeve, 26*s* 8*d* 'for the perquisites of the 3 weekes courte', two sums of 2*s* and one of 6*d* for reliefs, and 6*d* for an 'estraye' which Henry Holt paid for 'kepinge his nagge at the Houghe 2 dayes'. The fall in rents from around £140 in 1598–9 to around £120 the following year was caused by the disappearance of rents of lands in the 'hamel' of Horwich near Bolton, which had produced £23 16*s* p.a. The reason for this disappearance is not clear. Some of the lands had been held 'for terme of yeres of the demyse of Sir Thomas West'[42] but even if the term had expired one would have expected Mosley to make a new grant. Expenses in 1599–1600 amounted to about £40, which included the usual rent and fees, legal charges of £3 3*s* 7*d* and an unusual 40*s* 'bestowed uppon the poore in Manchester at Christmas 1599'. Perhaps this last was conscience money for the enclosure of Collyhurst common where Hugh Barlow, Richard Pendleton and others were still busy mending gates and rails at a cost of 2*s* 9*d*. Finally £3 6*s* 8*d* was 'paide to the colyer and for worke about the colepitte' and 18*d* 'to Edw. Bryddocke which he layde downe for a colyer'. There is no evidence where this mining was taking place though it may have been at Collyhurst. After all expenses had been paid, there was just over £105 left for Mosley, and this included £4 13*s* allowed to the

receiver, Charles Leigh, for arrears of rent. Those in arrears included
Oswald Mosley who owed 2s, presumably for his portion of the
Garrett lands on which the rent was 2s p.a. This year the return was
just over 3 per cent on the purchase price of the manor.

These accounts for 1598–1600 show two new sources of revenue in
the payments for pasturage on Collyhurst common and for butchers'
stalls. They suggest that the new owner of the manor was trying to
increase its yield by reviving old rights or inventing new ones. Some
of the inhabitants of Manchester certainly thought that was so.
Their leader seems to have been Adam Smith, a Manchester mercer
who was acquiring property in the parish towards the end of the
century. In 1594 he held on lease from John Strangeways, esq., land
called 'the Hollowe meadowes' in Cheetham, two closes in Strangeways, a parcel of land in 'Middlefield' in Salford, two burgages and
a croft in Millgate street in Manchester and nine acres called 'the
Broades' in Manchester and Cheetham. For these he had paid,
presumably as a fine, £220 with an unspecified remainder secured
by bond. Strangeways then sold the property to Smith, but the sale
does not seem to have been completed for the vendor's title to the
land was disputed.⁴³ Smith also owned a barn in Deansgate, and in
1600 bought half a burgage in Hanging Ditch and in 1601 a parcel
of ground at the Smithy Door.⁴⁴ More significant, perhaps, was the
fact that Smith was in dispute with the Mosleys over Aldport Park.
The details of this dispute remain obscure. The whole area of Over
and Nether Aldport was held by the Derbys when, probably about
1595, William, Earl of Derby, leased sixty-four acres of the Park to
Adam Smith for a term which had seventeen years to run in 1599.
In that year Oswald Mosley, Nicholas's brother, and Edward
Mosley, Nicholas's younger son, entered into an agreement with
Smith for the purchase of the whole of Aldport Park from Derby.
The two Mosleys were to pay Smith what he had paid for his lease
and in return Smith agreed that Oswald and Edward should hold
twenty-four acres and Edward himself ten acres out of the sixty-four
acres of his lease. When Smith detained the twenty-four and ten
acres, the Mosleys brought an action against him in the Duchy
Court.⁴⁵ The outcome is uncertain, but there is no doubt about the
animosity between the Mosleys and Smith. Other 'ringleaders',
according to Nicholas Mosley, were Richard Fox, who had a burgage
in Marketstead and was probably a woollen draper, and Nicholas
Hartley, Fox's brother-in-law and certainly a woollen draper, who
was buying burgages and land in Manchester at this time.⁴⁶

Smith and his supporters apparently began by taking action in
the Court Leet held on 8 April 1602, but there is only Nicholas
Mosley's version of this. According to Mosley, the three ringleaders,

Smith, Fox and Hartley, were chosen as jurors and agreed with the rest of the jurors not to make any presentments to the Steward. Although Charles Leigh, 'a man of greate integritie, knowledge and sufficiencye' had been chosen as clerk at the previous Court, they ignored this appointment and chose William Glover as clerk, to whom they gave the presentments. Richard Fox and Nicholas Hartley as boroughreeves in 1599–1600 and 1600–01 respectively had refused to give account of money raised by fines. Finally Adam Smith, having got possession of certain court rolls purporting to prove that subjects had a right to waste grounds and commons, had enclosed, encroached and taken in 'diverse and severall parcells of the saide waste groundes within the saide manor' in and near Deansgate. He had enclosed waste in Deansgate and built part of a barn there to great nuisance of the highway and had felled timber there and erected rails and stoops so that the highway was strait-ened.[47] In the calmer language of the Court Leet for 20 April 1598, Smith had 'sett certen stoupes and rayles uppon the lord's wast before his barne in the Deansgate and also encroched uppon the lord's wast uppon the south end of his barne by estimacion a full yard at the least'. He was ordered to 'remove the saide stoupes and rayles' and this he did.[48] The stirring events of 1602 find little echo in the minutes of the Court Leet, but they may well be reflected in an order of 8 April 1602 that 'divers incrochements' had lately been made 'uppon the common of Colihurste where the burgesses of Manchester have free common pasture without stinte or number' and that these encroachments were to be laid open. No future encroachments were to be made without the special consent of the lord or his officer and 'the wholle jurie and burgesses all jointlie to gether to geve consente of the takinge in of everie suche inclosure'.[49] That was really the heart of the problem, not Smith's stoops and rails.

There was a higher authority than the Court Leet, and that was the Duchy Court. In June 1602 a group of burgesses acting on behalf of themselves and other burgesses of Manchester brought an action in that Court against their lord of the manor.[50] They claimed that Sir Nicholas Mosley, having bought the manor, went about 'to alter, overthrowe and chaunge all the auncient priviledges, usages and customs' which had been to the benefit of themselves and the good of the town. He did this only 'to inriche himselfe by the ympoverishment of the burgesses and the poore inhabitants of the said towne'. Thus he was claiming that burgages were held by knight service as of his manor and that if burgesses died with heirs within age, such heirs were in ward to him. It is doubtful whether even Mosley could claim that the burgages were held by knight service, but there may be some truth in these allegations. When Ralph Byrom, who held lands and tenements in Little Lever, died in 1599 he was succeeded by his brother Adam who was under age. Mosley claimed that these lands and tenements were held of his manor of Manchester by knight service, namely by a sixty-sixth part of a knight's fee, and sold the wardship and marriage of Adam to Jane Byrom, widow, and Thomas Byrom, clothier of Salford, for £40.[51] There is no evidence in the rentals that this property was held by any sort of knight service.

These general allegations against Mosley are rather less convincing than the complaints about Collyhurst common. The burgesses maintained that they had always had common of pasture for all manner of their cattle at Collyhurst, and had commoned their pigs there. This, they claimed, was the greatest and best commodity belonging to their burgages, for men that lived by trade had small quantities of ground belonging to their burgages. Moreover Collyhurst had been 'a common place to walke into and to shoote and disporte for recreation, the butts being made there'[52], and general musters were taken there. In times of plague the sick were moved into cabins on Collyhurst, which was essential for the health and preservation of the town, 'where they have small ease being hemmed in on everye side to there doores with the lande of gentlemen nere thereto adjoyninge'. All this was threatened because Mosley was attempting to enclose and improve the common and so to destroy their rights of common. Mosley's reply to all this was simply that Collyhurst was part of the demesne arable and pasture of his manor; houses and cottages had been built there, and a quarry there had been used for the purchase of stone. There was no liberty for swine to pasture at Collyhurst. For five or six years he had taken the benefit of Collyhurst and had kept it in several for his own use and had taken 6s 8d for every beast pastured there. He claimed that the burgesses used to have common on the Heathes, some 150 acres between Collyhurst and the town, but they had bought land there and enclosed it. Even if the Acres fields lay open after the harvest, there was no general right of pasture. Finally even Adam Smith had sowed Over Aldport with corn and debarred the inhabitants from it. Much of this was very special pleading. There is no evidence that the Heathes or Over Aldport had ever been subject to common rights. Both sides did some special pleading, but there is little doubt that the burgesses had the better case over Collyhurst.

The survey of 1581 declared 'we fynde the lorde a wast called the common of Colyhurste conteyninge by estimacion a hundreth accres or thereaboutes whereunto the burgesses of Manchester have free common and pasture'. The Court Leet also maintained that there was a right of common on Collyhurst and made repeated orders that pigs should be driven there each day by the swineherd.[53] That right does not seem to have been challenged before Mosley bought the manor. Mosley was correct in maintaining that the common had been encroached upon by building, but that was only possible with the lord's consent. In 1585, when Lacy was lord, James Barlow was charged with enclosing some eight acres 'upon the common of Colyhurst'; two years later he was ordered by the Court Leet to 'laye the same open to the common agayne', but the order was disallowed by the steward.[54] Instead he paid a rent of 4s p.a. for his encroachment which included a house. Most encroachments seem to have been smaller than this. Thus Roger Smith paid 6d p.a. 'for an intacke uppon Colyhurste' and 6d p.a. for 'a lytle mylnested decayed upon Colyhurste'. Similarly Ralph Pendleton and William Rodley had built houses upon Collyhurst which they held by lease at rents of 6d p.a.[55] Despite encroachments there was enough land left to make it worth enclosing and to provide pasturage for twenty-one cows, twenty-four calves and six horses in the summer of 1599.

The enclosure was opposed not only by suit in the Duchy Court but also by more direct action. Between 11 p.m. and midnight on 13 April 1603 some sixty men 'riotously assembled' at Collyhurst where they threw down hedges, broke closes belonging to Anthony Mosley, Thomas Blundell and Richard Pendleton, and assaulted Hugh Ryder and Richard Pendleton, whose thumb was cut by a sword. According to the presentment made at the Quarter Sessions of 11 May 1603, over which Sir Nicholas Mosley presided, the twenty-two named rioters were mostly yeomen, husbandmen, linen weavers and labourers from Manchester, Cheetham, Blackley and Moston.[56] This suggests a more grass roots movement than that of Smith and his allies, though it may have included a hireling element. There seems no evidence that any further action was taken against the rioters, but it is clear that their protest failed. Neither suit in the Court nor action on the ground succeeded in preventing the enclosure. A rental of 1608 shows that by then Collyhurst common was almost entirely enclosed, and in 1617 a final agreement was reached with Nicholas Mosley's son and successor, Rowland Mosley, by which the lord of the manor could complete the enclosure of the common, over which all rights of common were extinguished. In return Rowland agreed that six acres of the common should be used for building cabins in time of plague and that he and his successors should pay £10 p.a. 'for the use of the poore' of Manchester.[57]

The final complaint of the burgesses in 1602 was that Nicholas Mosley had started to charge rents for butchers' stalls. These stalls or flesh boards as they were called were highly valued. When Edward

Dyson, butcher, died in 1598 his 'twoe standinge fleshe-bords in the market' were valued at £4, which must have included the value of his right to the stalls. Butchers, along with other stallholders in the market, were subject to control by the Court Leet and its officers. In 1560 butchers and other 'occupiers' were ordered to make clean their 'stalles or standings from tyme to tyme' or pay a penny quarterly 'to theme that shall be appoynted to make clene the market wekelie'. Seven years later butchers having 'standings and flesh bordes in the market place', who did not occupy them, 'as others doe', were ordered to occupy them 'every monethe once at the least', otherwise the place or standing would be given to such other as would occupy it. More interesting was an order of 30 September 1573 that no butcher or victualler should 'leave any borde abroad which they use comonly to set behinde them, but that the same be placed eyther upon or under there flesshe borde, upon payne to forfeit the bords so beinge lefte abroade to the lorde'.[58] The meaning of this is obscure, but it does suggest that the butchers' stalls were permanent structures which had to be left with no loose boards around them. It was rare for orders to be made against individual butchers, but in 1597 Oswald Mosley, then boroughreeve, was ordered to remove the stall or fleshboard in the occupation of Robert Barlow, junior. This was on the direct order of the new lord of the manor to the steward, but it may simply have meant that Barlow had set up his stall in some unauthorised place.[59]

Though these regulations show an attempt at control, they do not suggest that any rent was payable for the stalls. That was an innovation introduced by Nicholas Mosley in 1599 when he started to charge a rent of ½d per week 'for everye flesheborde of the towne butchers' and 1d per week for every fleshboard 'of the foren butchers'. These rents were charged on forty-six weeks of the year; there was no point in paying rent for a butcher's stall during Lent. They brought in £4 17s 3d in the year 1599–1600. The burgesses, in their complaint against Mosley, pointed out that 'the whole countrey rounde abowte doe weekely repayre for there provision of victualls' at the flesh shambles, and that all butchers, including foreign butchers, had the right to stand there without paying any rent or duty for their 'standes and places'. Despite this, Mosley would not allow butchers to stand in the market without paying rent to him, which amounted to above £4 yearly. Indeed he had threatened to pull down their scales and boards. Mosley's reply to these charges is, unfortunately, barely legible. His defence seems to have been that the fleshboards were being kept up the whole week and so presumably as permanent structures they should pay a rent. He referred to fifty or sixty 'infectious boordes', perhaps implying that control through rents would be a public health measure.[60] He might have pointed out, but did not, that a half-penny a week for forty-six weeks come to 1s 11d, which was nearly twice the rent he got from a burgage. Mosley does not seem to have had a strong case or to have established his right to these rents. There are no receipts for butchers' stalls in subsequent rentals.

Nicholas Mosley's actions over Collyhurst common and the butchers' stalls, and the opposition to those actions, suggest that the new lord was trying to increase the revenue from his manor. His predecessor, John Lacy, is a shadowy figure who does not seem to have had any local connections or to have lived on his manor. Mosley rebuilt the family house at Hough End, but he can hardly have resided permanently there until after his mayoralty of 1599–1600 and his resignation as alderman of London in 1602. This was not important, for his brothers were in Manchester to hold the fort. His brother Oswald was boroughreeve in 1596–7 and his brother Anthony was a frequent juror and office holder of the Court Leet. Despite his local connections and his great wealth, Nicholas had not very much room for manoeuvre as lord of the manor. This arose from the nature of the manor itself which was largely a bundle of defined rights rather than a territorial holding. Both outside the parish of Manchester and within it, the tenants of the manor held by free socage subject to the payment of what was in effect a fixed chief rent. Within this rigid framework there might be some scope for the exploitation of feudal rights in the shape of wardship and marriage, as Mosley's opponents alleged, but there is really not much evidence of this. There is no evidence at all that this was possible or attempted within Manchester itself. In Manchester burgages were subject to a fixed chief rent and sometimes to a relief or heriot. Other holdings were usually subject to similar conditions of fixed nominal rents. In these circumstances there were only two areas open to exploitation, for even the mills had passed out of manorial control. The first was the market, but even there the market tolls were farmed at a fixed rent. Hence, perhaps, the attempt to levy rents on the butchers' stalls which, in the one year when there is evidence, yielded more than the farm of the market tolls. The other area was the lord's waste. This was normally exploited by allowing small intakes or encroachments for which a rent was charged. Some of these were held by lease at small fixed rents, but a fine may have been paid, though there is no direct evidence of this. In a sense the enclosure of the common at Collyhurst was a continuation of this nibbling at the waste on a bigger and more profitable scale. If Nicholas Mosley is to be regarded as an 'improving' lord, his 'improvements' had to be made within the rather frustrating framework of his semi-urban manor.

NOTES

[1] W. Smith, *The particular description of England 1588*, eds. H. B. Wheatley and E. W. Ashbee, p. 47.

[2] D. Defoe, *A tour through England and Wales* (Everyman edition), ii, p. 261.

[3] The best account is A. Redford and I. S. Russell, *The history of local government in Manchester*, i *Manor and township*.

[4] J. Tait, *Mediaeval Manchester and the beginnings of Lancashire*.

[5] There was also the Deanery of Manchester which comprised eleven parishes, but it is not relevant to the present discussion.

[6] Redford and Russell, *op. cit.*, i, p. 29.

[7] J. Harland, ed., *Mamecestre*, iii, pp. 476–513, Ch. S. xlix (1862).

[8] They are in the Archives Department of Manchester City Library (MS.f.333 M 45). It does not seem necessary to give detailed references to these manuscripts which are unfoliated.

[9] See Appendix 1 for the rental of 1599–1600.

[10] *C.L.R.*, i, p. 42.

[11] J. O. Halliwell, ed., *The private diary of Dr. John Dee*, pp. 55–6. Camden Soc., xix (1842), J. Lee, *Maps and plans of Manchester and Salford 1650 to 1843*, pp. 7–8.

[12] These were probably statute acres, but it is not always possible to tell whether the statute or the customary acre was being used. The customary acre was one and two thirds of a statute acre.

[13] 'Aldport Park, Manchester', *The Palatine Note-book*, i (1881), pp. 120–1.

[14] *C.L.R.*, ii, pp. 328–32.

[15] P.R.O., D.L., 1 189/H2.

[16] *C.L.R.*, i, p. 160.

[17] *Ibid.*, ii, p. 11.

[18] *Ibid.*, ii, p. 18.

[19] *Ibid.*, ii, pp. 19, 131.

[20] Railway enthusiasts should note that the site of the fulling mill is below platforms 5 and 6 of Victoria Station (J. A. Graham and B. A. Phythian, *The Manchester Grammar School 1515–1965*, p. 6).

[21] *C.L.R.*, i, 30n. 2.

[22] *Ibid.*, ii, p. 118.

[23] *Ibid.*, i, pp. 62–3, 186, 191.

[24] P.R.O., D.L., 1 158/H12.

[25] *C.L.R.*, ii, 83n. 2.

[26] *Ibid.*, i, p. 211.

[27] *Ibid.*, i, p. 123.

[28] *Ibid.*, i, p. 233.

[29] *Ibid.*, ii, p. 15.

[30] *Ibid.*, i, p. 103, ii, pp. 50–1.

[31] *Ibid.*, ii, p. 40.

[32] *Ibid.*, ii, p. 42.

[33] He seems in fact to have been deputy bailiff (R. Somerville, *History of the Duchy of Lancaster*, i, p. 503).

[34] For the Mosleys see E. Axon, ed., 'Mosley Family', *Chetham Miscellanies*, n.s.i. Ch. S. n.s. xlvii (1902); *V.C.H. Lancs.*, iv, p. 232.

[35] M.C.L. MS.f.333 M 45 (Rental of 1592–3).

[36] *C.L.R.*, i, p. 182.

[37] *Ibid.*, ii, pp. 103–4.

[38] *V. C. H. Lancs.*, iv, pp. 259–60.

[39] Excluding payments arising from the Lordship of Cheetham.

[40] J. Harland, ed., *Mamecestre*, ii, pp. 273–431. Ch. S. xlix (1862).

[41] Including £10 received as part of John Fletcher's fine which seems to relate to Cheetham.

[42] M.C.L. MS.f.333 M45 (Rental of 1598–9).

[43] P.R.O., D.L., 1 166/S14.

[44] *C.L.R.*, ii, pp. 134, 163, 174.

[45] P.R.O., D.L., 1 194/M11.

[46] *C.L.R.*, ii, pp. 152, 174, 251n. 1.

[47] P.R.O., D.L., 1 207/M1.

[48] *C.L.R.*, ii, p. 134.

[49] *Ibid.*, ii, p. 179.

[50] P.R.O., D.L., 1 203/H16; 211/H22.

[51] *C.L.R.*, ii, 152n. 3.

[52] In 1560 the inhabitants 'of the northe side of the churche' were ordered to make a pair of butts 'upon Colyhurste' (*C.L.R.*, i, p. 55).

[53] *C.L.R.*, i, p. 117, 144, 262; ii, pp. 89, 179.

[54] *Ibid.*, i, p. 260; ii, p. 17.

[55] M.C.L. MS.f.333 M 45 (Survey of 1581).

[56] J. Tait, ed., *Lancashire Quarter Sessions records*, i, pp. 170–1. Ch. S. n.s. lxxvii (1917).

[57] *C.L.R.*, ii, pp. 328–32.

[58] *Ibid.*, i, pp. 59–60, 114, 161.

[59] *Ibid.*, ii, p. 123.

[60] P.R.O., D.L., 1 203/H16.

CHAPTER II

THE TOWNSHIP

The survey of 1581 and the rentals are obviously a main source for the history of the manor, but they are also, despite their limitations, an important source for the history of the township of Manchester. One of those limitations is simply coverage; it is impossible to tell how much of the township was held of the manor and therefore how much of the property was recorded in the survey and rentals. It is clear that not all the property in the township was held of the manor. The Collegiate Church, for example, was endowed with land and houses much of which was former chantry property. Some of this endowment lay in Newton, which was adjacent to Manchester but not part of the township. Some, however, lay within Manchester, in Deansgate, and this does not seem to be recorded in the manorial rentals at all.[1] Other former chantry property was still in the Queen's possession, but this she held of the manor and paid rent to the lord for it, as did the Earls of Derby for Over Aldport and three burgages 'beinge chauntrie landes'. The surviving evidence is strongly biased in favour of manorial property and so may exaggerate the extent of that property within the township, but among other sources, which are not strictly manorial, it is difficult to find many cases of the transfer of property which was not held of the manor. Whatever the truth may be, it is clear that the manorial rentals provide the best evidence for the ownership and distribution of real property within Manchester at this period.

According to the survey of 1581 most of the manorial property in Manchester was held in free socage; some of the land there was held in free socage and in fee simple by fine and recovery, but it is not clear what these differences in tenure really meant. Property held in free socage was subject to a fixed chief rent payable to the lord and sometimes to a relief and a heriot. Thus in 1581 John Birch held by free socage in fee simple by fine and recovery three acres of land called Smithy field 'now devided into two closses' at a rent of 6s p.a. and a relief of 2s an acre. Similarly Thomas Goodyear held a

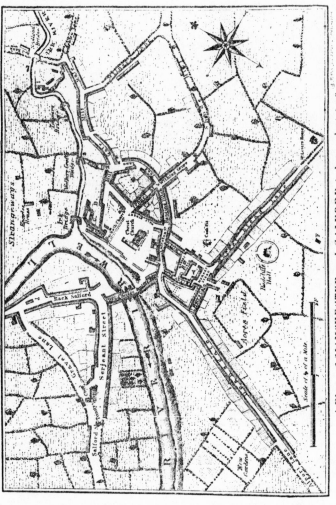

A Plan of MANCHESTER and SALFORD taken about 1650.

'Taken from a Plan in the possession of William Yates, Esq., by John Palmer, Architect, 1822'

A. The Booths, Court House B. The Meal House C. The College (afterwards Chetham's Hospital
D. The Free Grammar School E. Mill Hill F. The Fountain 1. 2. 3. The School Mills
(For the history of this map, originally published in John Palmer's *History of the Siege of Manchester*...
1642, 1822, see Jack Lee, *Maps and Plans of Manchester and Salford, 1650 to 1843, 1957*)

tenement and a field of six acres for which he paid 7s 8d p.a. and a relief of 2s an acre. Henry Pendleton, on the other hand, paid only 12s as a relief for his two tenements and twenty-one acres 'lyenge upon the easte syde of Newton Lane'. Heriots were usually given in the form of a dagger.[2] Thus on the death of Francis Pendleton in 1574 his son Henry was admitted as tenant and gave to the lord a dagger according to custom, which dagger was valued at 12d by the appraisor.[3] The dagger was often described as 'his father's dagger' and given the conventional value of 12d, at which no doubt it was redeemed by the giver so that he could pass it on to his son. It might be wrong to assume that daggers were purely ceremonial. When Roger Bexwick, yeoman, died in 1599 he left to his son-in-law Simon Mallon 'my dagger which I have worne a longe tyme and ys dressed with sylver'. On the death of the father, these manorial holdings normally passed to the eldest son; in the absence of a son, they went to a daughter or, if there was more than one, to all the daughters as co-heiresses. These transfers were recorded by the Court Leet, for the new owner had to come and do his suit and service and to be admitted as tenant of the manor. Despite this emphasis on primogeniture, property could be freely bought and sold. According to the charter of 1301 a burgess could sell property he had inherited provided he had the consent of his heir, but even if that consent were refused he could sell 'if need arises'. A burgess could sell property he had not inherited to anyone he wished, though in theory his heir had a right of pre-emption.[4] It is doubtful whether these rather vague limitations on sale had much force in the sixteenth century.

Burgages could not only be bought and sold but they could, of course, be leased, and they frequently were. These leases made by burgesses must be distinguished from the leases made by the lord of the manor himself. Some property in Manchester was held by lease from the lord, but it is impossible to estimate the amount. These leases seem to have been largely confined to intakes or encroachments on the waste. Thus in 1599–1600 William Radcliffe held an intake in Marketstead Lane by lease for years at a rent of 6d p.a.; it had been 'inclosed betwene the highe waye and Barkehouse field'. Some intakes on Collyhurst were also held by lease for years at a rent of 6d p.a. At 'Tillhill nere Colyhurste' Richard Pendleton paid 2s 6d p.a. 'for a parcell of waste . . . whereon he hathe buylded a house and made a gardyn'. He held by a lease for twenty-one years granted in 1587. Some other leases were for twenty-one years. The smallness of the rents suggests that fines must have been paid, but there are no details of these.

Much of the manorial property was in the form of burgages whose

rent of 12*d* p.a. was fixed by the charter of 1301.[5] The charter
assigned no size to a burgage, though the earlier charter to Salford
defined it as an acre.[6] Manchester burgages could be divided; some
people held half a burgage and one or two held a quarter. This
raises the difficult question of what was really meant in the physical
sense by a burgage in the later sixteenth century. The most reasonable answer is that a burgage was an area of land with a frontage
onto a street, and that what went onto the land in the form of houses,
shops, barns and gardens varied considerably. Thus in 1599–1600
Robert Langley had a burgage in Millgate containing two tenements
and two gardens, while Nicholas Hartley got two tenements and two
gardens into his half burgage in the same street. Thomas Byrom had
'3 tenementes with gardyns' on his burgage in Marketstead Lane.
Sometimes the layout seems to have been more complicated.
William, Thomas and Edward Pilkington paid a rent of 12*d* 'for the
new buyldings in Milnegate and the land upon both sydes the streete
there'. In 1596 this had been described as 'one burgage in the
Mylnegate, to wytte three cottages, one tannehouse and one parcell
of lande'. Perhaps the three Pilkington brothers (of whom Edward
was illegitimate) occupied a cottage each, but this seems unlikely as
they were a Salford family and their father was a gentleman. They
were younger sons who had been left a life interest in the burgage
with reversion to their eldest brother Adam, who inherited half a
burgage at Shude Hill and probably the Salford property.[7] Finally
Thomas Brownsword, a wealthy clothier, owned half a burgage in
Hanging Ditch part of which he sold to his brother-in-law Richard
Tipping in 1587. This part measured fifty-two feet from east to west
on the street side, eighty-one feet from north to south on the west
side, sixty-seven feet from the street to the churchyard on the east,
and forty-five feet from the east to the west along the churchyard.
It was in the several occupation of eight people, which suggests that
even part of a burgage could accommodate some high density
housing.[8]

Much less is known about urban than about rural property,
partly because the former has been less studied and partly because
the sources for its study are less adequate. Thus comparatively little
has been written about who owned urban property and about the
extent of owner occupation. Similarly little work seems to have been
done on the very difficult problem of the capital value of urban
property and of the rent such property could command. Urban
property held within a manorial framework may not be the ideal
type for a study of these problems, but the existence of manorial
rentals provides evidence on the ownership of property which may
be lacking for incorporated boroughs.

In Manchester the manorial property was held by three types of owners: country landowners, large urban landlords and small urban owners who were sometimes owner occupiers. The country landowners were headed by the Queen who had retained a considerable block of former chantry property. This included at least a dozen burgages in Hanging Ditch, Marketstead Lane, Millgate, Toad Lane, Deansgate and St. Mary Gate, an acre of land in the Over Acres and three fields called Blackacres 'lyenge betweene Marketstid Lane and Aldporte'. Most of this was leased en bloc to Sir Edmund Trafford of Trafford at a rent of £4 5s 8d 'beinge the anncyent yerelye rent for the same'. After the lease expired, a new one was granted, on 10 December 1593, to Peter Proby, gent., for twenty-one years at the same rent, but Proby paid a 'good consideration' for the lease and was bound to maintain the premises which were in great ruin and decay. It is clear that the land and burgages were sublet by the lessee, but there is no evidence on what terms this was done.[9] The only members of the peerage to hold manorial property in Manchester were the Derbys. Apart from Over and Nether Aldport, their holdings were not very large: three burgages in Fennel Street, a tenement in Millgate with an orchard and garden and a field adjoining it, two small crofts and two 'little meadoes' and 'the Colledge barne'. Most of this property was tenanted, though Nether Aldport was kept in hand.

Lower down the social scale there were a number of minor country gentry with property in Manchester. George Chaderton, gent., of the Lees near Oldham owned three burgages, a croft 'nexte Aldporte Parke', and 'one parcell of a field lyenge on the southe parte of the Marketstidlane' for which he paid the considerable chief rent of 11s 8½d p.a. Some or all of this property may have been bought by his father, Thomas Chaderton, who left 'all my purchessed landes in Manchester' to his wife for life. Thomas also had lands in the Lees, in Crompton and in Staffordshire.[10] John Culcheth, esq., of Culcheth near Warrington had lands and tenements in Millgate which paid 4s 1d in chief rent. In 1599 these were said to be in the tenure of Robert Langley, but earlier rentals give 'Robert Langley and others' which is more likely. Robert Langley, gent., of Manchester owned a burgage and some land there; in the 1590s he and his son Lawrence each leased a messuage in Culcheth from John Culcheth.[11] The combination of a burgage and some land was also found in the case of William Holland, esq., of Clifton in the parish of Eccles. He held a burgage, consisting of two tenements, and 'one lytle meadow' in the upper end of Marketstead Lane 'nexte the watringe place'. He died unmarried in 1589 and the property passed to his sister Eleanor.[12]

B

Other country gentlemen owned only burgages. Thus Edmund Hopwood, esq., of Hopwood near Middleton, owned six burgages in the Marketstead and at the Smithy Door which he had bought from Ralph Winnington, gent., of Offerton, Cheshire, in 1597. At that time the burgages were in the tenure or occupation of nine men, and three of the burgages and a messuage were subject to unexpired leases.[13] One of the burgages was occupied by Ralph Winnington himself so perhaps it had provided him with a town house. There is little other evidence, except in the case of the Derbys, of such a provision, and indeed most of the country landowners were near enough to Manchester to make a town house hardly necessary. That was truer still of the minor gentry who lived within the parish, but outside the township, of Manchester.

A number of such minor gentry had manorial property in Manchester. Thus John Strangeways, gent., of Strangeways in Cheetham, had lands and burgages in Deansgate, Millgate and the Nether Acres for which he paid 6s 2d p.a. in chief rent.[14] Richard Holland, esq., of Denton had burgages and lands, including a little croft near Aldport Park, for which he paid 5s 6d p.a. in chief rent. He had other property at Sharples near Bolton. Similarly Edmund Prestwich, esq., of Hulme next Manchester, whose father had been keeper of Aldport Park under the Derbys, had two burgages and a parcel of land in the Acres as well as his 'moitie of Hulme'.[15] The holdings of these minor gentry were sometimes quite small. George Birch, gent., of Birch Hall had 'the moitie of three burgages' in Fennel Street, and the co-heiresses of Robert Cleyden of Cleyden had half a burgage, also in Fennel Street. Not a great deal of property in Manchester was owned by men who lived elsewhere in the parish. Their interests seem naturally to have been more concentrated in their own townships.

Within Manchester there was some concentration of manorial property in the hands of burgesses who lived in the township, though ownership of real estate was by no means the sole criterion of wealth. In 1599–1600 there were about a dozen such burgesses with considerable holdings. Thus William Radcliffe, gent., who lived near the Conduit in a house known as Pool Fold or Radcliffe Hall, paid 9s 6d in chief rent for what was described as 'his auncient inheritance'. The earlier rentals show that this consisted of burgages in Marketstead and Oldmarketstead and a little land in and around the Acres. He also paid 6d p.a. for an intake held on lease and 3s 10d p.a. for his portion of Cowopp's lands. The latter was apparently acquired by inheritance through the daughters and co-heiresses of John Cowopp who died in 1559.[16] A moiety of Cowopp's lands was bought by George Birch, mercer, in the 1560s; it consisted of unspecified land and burgages and paid 4s 7d in chief.[17] The final portion of Cowopp's lands, which paid only 9d in chief, went by inheritance to Roger Bexwick, yeoman, who in the 1560s had unsuccessfully claimed Radcliffe's portion as well.[18]

These larger holdings could be acquired by inheritance or built up by purchase or indeed by a combination of the two. The rentals sometimes give information on this, but it is not always very accurate. Thus Francis Pendleton held a tenement and garden in Deansgate, a barn and a yarn croft in Marketstead Lane and a tenement, barn and garden in Withy Grove which together paid 1s 9d in chief rent. He also held lands and tenements 'adjoyninge to Grundylane', which paid 25s 4d p.a. and which were said to be 'latelye purchased'. In fact he had inherited them from his father, Henry Pendleton, who in turn had inherited them from his father, another Francis. It was the grandfather, a merchant who died in 1574, who had bought the Grundy Lane property of some twenty acres from the lord of the manor; its position on the east side of Newton Lane suggests that it was part of Collyhurst common. Similarly in 1599 the heirs of Adam Oldham held two tenements and ten acres of land 'sometyme parcell of the Heathes adjoyeninge upon Newton and latelye purchased'. Again 'latelye' was misleading; the property had been held at least from 1581 by Adam Oldham, a yeoman and dyer who died in 1588.

The combination of purchase and inheritance is well illustrated by John Marler's property. There were a number of Marlers who are difficult to disentangle. A Robert Marler, goldsmith, who died in 1582, left property, some of which descended to the Pendletons through the marriage of his daughter Elizabeth to Henry Pendleton. He also left £20 in trust to his cousin, John Marler, to pay to a nephew, Edward Marler, 'when he comethe fourthe of his prentice-shippe'. The cousin was probably the John Marler under discussion. The latter was certainly the son of Roger Marler and Jane, a daughter and co-heiress of Edmund Bardesley. Jane survived her husband and later married Thomas Hyde, gent. Her son, John Marler, gent., bought six acres, parcel of the Heathes, in 1572 from Robert Shaw, gent.[19] They were charged with a rent of 6s 8d and a relief of 12d an acre. On his mother's death about 1593, Marler inherited her share of the Bardesley property consisting of burgages and lands paying a chief rent of 16s 5d, which suggests that it was a considerable holding. Like his Bardesley grandfather John Marler left no male heir; on his death in 1602 his property passed to his daughter Thomasine and her husband Ralph Hulme, gent.[20] Ralph Hulme already owned a substantial amount of property; he paid 45s 6d p.a. for a house, two barns, four fields and two pastures in the north part of Newton Lane, which he had inherited from his

father, Robert Hulme, in 1584. He also paid a chief rent of 30s 4d
'for his inheritance' which probably refers to burgages in half a
dozen streets and to lands in the Acres which his father was said to
own in 1581. Thus Hulme had accumulated an extensive urban or
semi-urban estate by the painless process of inheritance and marriage
familiar to rural landowners.

These larger owners were outnumbered by the smaller men with
their single burgages or half burgages. Some of these were owner
occupiers. Richard Fox owned a burgage in Marketstead 'wherein
he dwelleth'. William Barlow occupied his own house and garden in
Millgate which he had bought in 1582;[21] though described as a
burgage its chief rent of 4d suggests that it was only part of one. But
small owners were not necessarily owner occupiers. Adam Holland's
half burgage in Millgate had William Leese as tenant, and Richard
Smethurst's burgage 'on the north parte of the Boothes doare' was
in the tenure of Henry Haughton. It is often impossible to tell from
the rentals alone whether property was occupied by its owner.
Sometimes property was described as in the owner's occupation and
sometimes tenants' names were given, but often only the owner was
recorded, and it would be rash in such cases to assume that he was
the occupier. Indeed the bigger owners obviously did not in general
occupy their property, and that was probably true of many smaller
owners. The evidence of wills, deeds and court cases strongly
suggests that much of the property in Manchester was leased and
sometimes sub-leased to the ultimate occupiers.

Less can be learned about this urban leasing system than about
its rural counterpart. In some cases property was leased in large
blocks as the Queen leased a block of chantry property to Peter
Proby for twenty-one years in 1594.[22] Whether Proby re-leased this
en bloc or split it up and leased it to the actual occupiers is not clear.
In 1599 when the Queen leased a smaller block of burgages to
Roger Pilkington he re-leased it to Richard Houghton, who in turn
let the burgages to their occupiers.[23] Similarly when John Strangeways leased lands and burgages to Adam Smith in 1594, they were
all tenanted.[24] Other large owners leased or let direct to the occupiers
of their property, but the whole system was capable of infinite varia-
tions as the case of Thomas Tetlow suggests. In 1599 Tetlow owned
four gardens and four tenements in the tenure of widow Croxton,
who was Cicely, daughter and heiress of George Pendleton, a
Manchester draper, from whom she inherited 'a lytle closse in the
Sousehilles' and a third of his personal estate. She married John
Croxton, gent., of Ravenscroft in Cheshire with a marriage portion
of £200 from her father, which may have been the going rate for the
marriage of a Manchester draper's daughter into the minor Cheshire

gentry. After her husband's death she married Robert Mainwaring, one of the Cheshire Mainwarings and an esquire. It is unlikely that Cicely occupied any of her four tenements.[25] Tetlow had a house, garden and an acre of land in the tenure of Richard Fox, who may have been the Richard Fox who owned and occupied a burgage of his own; a corner house in the tenure of Henry Hardy, who may well have occupied it for, as a younger son, he had inherited only 'one cloughe or close' from his father, William Hardy, the rest of the property, half a burgage and two closes, having gone to the eldest son Robert;[26] a house at the Smithy Door in the tenure of Samuel Tipping, who had inherited a burgage from his father Richard Tipping, a linen draper.[27] Finally there were six tenements in Deansgate and a house where Mrs Alice Hulton lived. Mrs Hulton had succeeded her husband as tenant of the house on his death in 1597; he was Adam, the son and heir of William Hulton, esq., of Hulton.[28]

Other owners showed some variety in the way in which they dealt with their property. Ralph Hulme, whose accumulation of property has already been noticed, leased a small parcel of ground in Deansgate for a term of years to Robert Blomeley, blacksmith, who in turn granted it for twelve years (presumably the residue of the term) to Edward Ellor. This was straightforward enough, but Hulme did not lease out all his property in this way. He owned a messuage or tenement in St Mary Gate which he let to Edmund Smith as tenant at will 'one quarter of yeare to another' at a rent of 10s 'for everye quarter'. On Smith's death his widow Margaret and her two children continued to live in the house on the same conditions and at the same rent until Hulme removed her tables, chests, bedstocks, bedclothes and other goods to the value of £4 10s, on the ground that Edmund had been in arrears with his rent. Margaret claimed in 1599 that if there had been any arrears of rent in the lifetime of her husband, she was sure Hulme owed her husband more than the arrears came to.[29] It does not sound very convincing, but it would be interesting to know how common it was to let houses on the precarious basis of a tenancy at will at what was obviously a rack rent. Land, too, was sometimes let on that basis. In 1597 Richard Thorpe held a close of an acre and two crofts which John Hunt had let to him for one year for a certain sum of money, and John Witton and Christopher Downes held three acres which they had rented, also from Hunt, for one year at a rent of £3 13s 4d.[30] Such cases are a reminder that not everyone enjoyed the comparative security of long leaseholds.

The way men held real property in Manchester, whether as owners or as leaseholders, is important in showing how such men regarded property ownership in an urbanised manorial setting. It is commonly supposed that most men in the sixteenth century wished to own houses and land, and that may be true of rural areas, but was it also true of towns? In Manchester the evidence suggests a preference for leasing rather than owning. The two things were not incompatible; a burgess might own property and hold it by lease. Such a combination was common enough, but wills show that the 'mix' of owning and leasing could vary widely. John Davie, a dealer in flax, linen yarn and cloth who died in 1573, left a daughter Anne as sole heiress. He made a complex will by which he left four burgages recently purchased from Thomas Tetlow to his daughter Anne, subject to a life interest in a third of them to his wife Elizabeth. One of the burgages was 'now in the holding of the Duche man' and another was held and occupied by Davie's brother-in-law Robert Farrington and his wife, who were to hold it for twenty-one years at a rent of 14s p.a. Anne also inherited leases held by her father of two fields, one of them at the head of Marketstead Lane, and a house in Millgate; her mother was to have the lease of a field and two kine gates so long as she kept herself 'soole and unmarried and lyvethe chaste in the feare of God', and to occupy the family house during widowhood.

John Davie probably owned more property than he held on lease, and the same may have been true of Francis Pendleton, a merchant who died in 1574 leaving a personal estate of £218 8s 10d. Pendleton left his lands and tenements in Grundy Lane, which he had bought from the lord of the manor, and half his lands and tenements in Marketstead Lane, bought from Adam Holland, to his wife Cicely for life in the name and recompense of her dower. After her death they were to go to his son and heir, Henry, who also got the other half of the Marketstead Lane property, a house and garden in the same lane 'wherein I now dwell', and a burgage in Deansgate. The leasehold property was similarly bequeathed. Cicely got a lease held from Randal Winnington with reversion to Henry, and she shared with him the lease of a house in Market Street with an orchard and garden, held of the Queen as late chantry land. Henry got the lease of certain lands and tenements in Shooters Brook, held from the heirs of Ralph Trafford. Finally there was a house at the Smithy Door which had been leased to Randal Hurlestone, Steward of Manchester, for ten years and in which he lived; if this lease had not expired at the time of Pendleton's death, then his widow and son were jointly to enjoy the house and garden in Marketstead Lane where Pendleton lived.

This mixture of property owned and property held by lease was found also in Thomas Brownsword's estate, but there the balance had

shifted in favour of leasehold. Thomas Brownsword was a well-to-do
clothier who died in 1588 leaving a personal estate valued at £1109.
His will rather grandly bequeaths the messuages, burgages, lands,
tenements and hereditaments which he had purchased in Manchester to his son and heir Thomas. In fact the lawyer's language was
describing half a burgage in the Hanging Ditch which paid 6*d* in
chief rent and part of which Brownsword had sold to Richard
Tipping in 1587 for £71 13*s* 4*d*.[31] Brownsword's leaseholds were
much more important. He held three leases for a messuage in
Stretford and for certain 'clausures commonly called the yeldhowses'
from Sir Edmund Trafford and Edmund Trafford, esq.[32] He left
his wife Ellen, who seems to have been Francis Pendleton's daughter,
a half-share in the yeldhouse lease and his son the other half. The
lease of the Stretford house, which was held in reversion after the
death of Mr Richard Trafford, was left to his daughter Isabel 'for
her better advancement and preferment in marriage'. Finally a
lease of lands at Shooters Brook went to the widow and son equally,
with reversion to Isabel. In the probate inventory the yeldhouse
leases were valued at £300, the Stretford lease at £80 and the
Shooter's Brook lease at £280, thus accounting for more than half
the personal property. The half burgage in Hanging Ditch could not
compete with that sort of valuation.

In other cases men, some of them well-to-do, seem to have owned
no real property but only to have leased it. Thus John Shaw, a
mercer who died in 1581 with a personal estate of £113, held a
lease of a house in Millgate, which was valued at £8, but there is no
evidence that he owned property. Similarly John Hardman, a
mercer with a shop in Manchester and one in Warrington who died
in 1583 with a personal estate of £451, apparently owned no real
property, but entries in his probate inventory suggest that he leased
both his shops as well as a field in Blackley and two meadows in
Warrington. John Billing was a similar case. He was described as a
glazier in his will of 18 April 1588; his probate inventory of 20 April
1588 (the day before he was buried)[33] shows personal property
valued at £325. This included £4 for the lease of his house, £26 for a
lease of a close in the Acres and £2 for '3 yeares in a close in
Brughton'. Though Billing held a succession of offices under the
Court Leet as scavenger, mise gatherer, market looker etc., there is
no evidence that he owned any manorial or other real property. Nor
apparently did Francis Hough, a clothier who died in 1593 having
personal property valued at £241, which included £3 for the lease
of a field or close from Ralph Hulme 'for one yeare'. He sounds like
another of Ralph Hulme's tenants at will. Finally Edward Dyson, a
butcher who died in 1598 with personal property valued at only £34,

had the reversion of a lease in Millgate held for certain years yet to come from John Strangeways, which was valued at £2 13s 4d, and which at least shows that leasehold was not confined to the better off.

These examples are relatively straightforward in the sense that they simply show men combining the ownership of manorial property with the possession of leasehold or men who owned no manorial property but held by lease. It would be unwise to draw too definite conclusions from them, but the evidence does suggest that leasehold was widespread and that Manchester was far from being a community of burgesses who owned and occupied their burgages. The possible reasons for this are many. Some property was owned by men outside the township and even outside the parish, and this would naturally lead to leasing or letting in some form. Within the township there was some concentration of ownership in the hands of large owners, and this would have the same effect. Moreover the members of a commercial community like Manchester may have preferred to hold their assets in a rather more liquid form than property ownership. Probate inventories often show a good deal of money as being owed to the deceased, and some of this strongly suggests money lending, which may have been as attractive as and more profitable than investment in real estate. Finally investment in real property requires the willing seller and the willing buyer; in other words it requires an active land market. Could such a market exist when so much property was held within a manorial framework which stressed the custom of primogeniture? This is a difficult question to answer for the evidence is conflicting.

In theory property held of the manor descended from father to eldest son or to a daughter or daughters in the absence of a son. There is no doubt that this was the common practice and that it introduced some measure of stability into property ownership. A comparison of the survey of 1581 and the later Elizabethan rentals suggests this strongly, but great changes could hardly be expected in two decades. A longer time span, from the rental of 1473[34] to the Elizabethan rentals, shows families owning their property throughout that period, but this seems commoner in the outlying parts of the manor than in Manchester itself. Within the manor as a whole some forty-six families retained all or part of their property during that period, but only twenty-six of the families had property within the township of Manchester. This implies a considerable change of ownership within the township, but the Elizabethan evidence suggests that the change must have come largely before 1581. Such change could arise from the failure of male heirs, or from migration or from sales. The failure of male heirs did not necessarily bring property onto the market; it could be inherited by daughters or even by other relatives of the deceased. Of migration little or nothing is known. Wills suggest that when a member of a family migrated from Manchester he went to London, but other members of the family remained in Manchester. Sales of property certainly occurred, and indeed the custom of the manor allowed for them with or without an heir's consent, but it is difficult to tell whether they were sufficiently common to indicate an active land market. Both the transfers of property on death and the transfers of property by sale were recorded by the Court Leet, and it is interesting to compare these two types of transfer for the twenty years from the survey of 1581 to the rental of 1599–1600.

In those two decades the Court Leet recorded the deaths of eighty-four people who owned property in the township of Manchester, though they did not all live there, and transmitted that property to their heirs. A few deaths were also recorded of people who do not seem to have owned property and whose heirs in some cases never came to do their suit and service. These have not been included in the eighty-four. Thus transfers on death average 4·2 p.a., but the range was from none in 1592 to eleven in 1593. These years are in effect harvest years for the Court Leet met about Easter and about Michaelmas, and the Easter meeting recorded deaths since the previous Michaelmas meeting. Thus the eleven deaths of 1593 were in fact the deaths from 5 October 1592 to 4 October 1593. There is naturally some correlation between these deaths and the burials recorded in the register of the Collegiate Church, but it should be remembered that some of the property owners lived and died outside the parish and were buried elsewhere. The low burial figures (142 p.a.) of 1581–4 are reflected in the deaths of only half a dozen property owners; the higher burial figures (303 p.a.) of 1585–88 are equally reflected in the deaths of twenty-one property owners. By the 1590s the correlation is less obvious; 1593 produced 230 burials and eleven deaths of property owners, while in 1598 the figures were 433 and ten respectively. Whatever the mortality there was always an heir, or heiress, to take over. These transfers of property by inheritance greatly outnumbered the transfers by sale. Between 1581 and 1600 the Court Leet recorded only twenty-nine transfers by sale of property in Manchester (and hardly any at all outside the township). This average of just under one and a half sales p.a. is low and raises the suspicion that not all sales of property held of the manor were recorded by the Court Leet. There are cases of sales which appear as if they should have been recorded by the Court Leet and were not. Thus John Strangeways sold a messuage, four cottages and land in Deansgate to Adam Chedock in 1595 which is un-recorded by the Court Leet.[35] Such cases seem to be few. Unless the sources are deceptive, which is always possible, they do not show a very active land market in Manchester.

Whatever the state of the land market, some property was bought and sold and much was leased, but to determine the capital or rental value of that property is the most difficult problem of all. Here the Court Leet records themselves are no help, though Earwaker's annotations sometimes are; when the Court Leet recorded the sale of property it never recorded the price. Nor are the survey and rentals helpful; they naturally record rents and not capital values, but the rents are largely quite nominal chief rents. The curious case of Widow Hope, who in 1599–1600 paid a rent of 43s 4d for the house in Hanging Ditch 'wherein she dwelleth', seems to be a unique example of a 'real' rent, and a very high one. In these circumstances it is only possible to find isolated examples of what purchasers paid for their land or house and of what lessees or tenants at will paid for their leases or tenancies. Such examples provide nothing more than a sample, but perhaps a fairly random one.

On 10 April 1572 the Court Leet recorded that Thomas Willott, gent., had bought from Robert Shaw, gent., 'certayn closses or landes' which Shaw had purchased from 'my Lorde Lawarr' to whom 21s p.a. was payable.[36] The property consisted of land, a messuage and a cottage and garden. It had formed part of the Heathes near Newton Lane, and according to the survey of 1581 extended to fifteen acres, on five of which a relief of 12d an acre was payable and on the other ten acres a relief of 2s an acre. Willott paid forty marks or £26 13s 4d for the property, a price which may have been influenced by the high rent of 21s and the liability to relief.[37] Five years later, in 1577, when William Bainbridge of Lockington, Leicestershire, was disposing of his Manchester property he sold two messuages lying between the Irk 'and the highe streete called the Mylnegate' to John Platt, son of Richard Platt of Platt Hall in Rusholme for £17. Though they were sometimes described as a burgage, their chief rent of 5d p.a. and their price suggest that they were less than that.[38] When Roger Bexwick sold what seems to have been a burgage in 1584 he got £40 for it.[39] Even part of a burgage could be valuable. In 1587 Thomas Brownsword sold part of his half burgage in the Hanging Ditch to the brother-in-law Richard Tipping for £71 13s 4d. Tipping was to pay his share of the chief rent and also to pay 13d p.a. to the Henry Earl of Derby, 3s 6d p.a. to Richard Holland and his heirs, and 10s p.a. to Richard Brownsword for his life and 30s 6d to Elizabeth Jepson for her life. Richard Holland and Richard Brownsword were former owners; Elizabeth Jepson seems to have been a former tenant, but her interest remains obscure. Tipping seems to have paid a high price for a somewhat encumbered property, but perhaps it was justified by the presence of eight tenants on the property.[40] Some encumbrance was not uncommon. In 1589 John Whitworth, linen draper of Newton, bought a burgage from Hugh Travis of Ancoats for £80. It consisted of a messuage and shops in the street called Marketstead and was subject to a rent charge of 20s p.a. to the heirs of Thomas Tetlow, late of Chester. There were four tenants, two of whom held leases; John Billing held a lease for twenty-one years and John Whitworth, the purchaser, held two leases, one for fourteen and one for six years.[41]

Sales of property in the 1590s show a wide range of prices. In 1592 Humphrey Haughton sold a burgage in Deansgate to Ralph Haughton for £10. It was subject to a crown rent of 8s p.a.[42] Three years later John Strangeways sold seven acres of land called Great Knowles and a messuage, four cottages and gardens and the 'Little Meadow' in Deansgate to Adam Chedock, feltmaker, for £40 6s 8d.[43] A much bigger sale was made in 1597 when Ralph Winnington of Offerton, Cheshire, sold to Edmund Hopwood of Hopwood his 'syx messuages, burgages or tenements' in 'the Marketstyd nere unto the Shambles' and a rent of 13s 4d issuing from a burgage in the street called the Smithy Door occupied by John Sorocold, who had inherited the burgage from his father Ralph Sorocold. The six burgages, which paid 6s p.a. in chief rent, were occupied by six tenants and Ralph Winnington himself. They were subject to a number of leases; two burgages had been leased by Winnington's father, Randal Winnington, to George Pycroft for certain years still to run. Robert Dickenson occupied one of the burgages which he held on lease from Ralph Winnington for twenty-five years or thereabouts. Hopwood paid £173 6s 8d for the property which was said to have a clear yearly value of £18 over and above all charges and reprises.[44] If that were true, it was a good investment. Finally in 1602 Stephen Pendleton, a linen weaver of Manchester, sold to John Travis, chapman of Little Bolton, a messuage, burgage or tenement in Millgate for £30. Though the Court Leet described it as a burgage, its chief rent of 3d p.a. suggests a lesser property.[45]

These examples show a range of price which is only to be expected, for property is not a standard article. There are not enough of them to judge whether property in the heart of the township was more valuable than property on the fringes or whether prices were affected by the general inflation of the period. Indeed the examples only suggest a certain order of magnitude, which it seems impossible to compare with property values elsewhere. Certainly property was worth fighting for as the cases in the Duchy Court show with their stereotyped claims of forcible entry, dispossession and testamentary villainy. But it was a litigious age in which lawyers grew rich, and the sound and fury of the complainants often seem out of proportion to the value of the disputed property. In an urban setting where so much wealth was held as personal property, it may be easy to exaggerate the importance of owning real estate, just as it is easy to exaggerate the importance of fixed capital in industry.

Men needed a roof over their heads, and if they did not own one they could rent one. In some ways rents are more difficult to determine than are the capital values of property. Much property was held by lease, and under the prevailing system leases usually involved the payment of both a fine and a rent. It is necessary to know both the fine and the rent to determine what a lessee was really paying for his property. Contemporaries sometimes showed a certain coyness about fines, describing them vaguely as a good consideration, rather as twentieth-century landlords and tenants are coy about key money. It is possible, however, to find a few examples of the terms on which property was leased in Manchester.

In 1572 Thomas Herle, Warden of the College, leased a tenement and garden in Deansgate to Edmund Blomeley, smith, for forty years at a rent of 4s p.a. and a fine of £5.[46] This was property belonging to the Collegiate Church, but it cannot be identified with certainty from a list of such property made in 1581.[47] The list shows that Collegiate property in Manchester was let at anything from 1s 8d to 13s 4d p.a., but such rents mean little if the properties were let on beneficial leases. Indeed the complications of leases are well illustrated by the case of Robert Chadwick, esq., of Spotland near Rochdale. Chadwick owned a house in Manchester which he let to John Ashton, clothier, who occupied it at a rent of 15s p.a. and the payment of 12d p.a. to the Warden of the College and 6s 8d p.a. to the heirs of Hamlett Bibby of Salford. On 24 December 1593 Chadwick leased the house to Ashton for twenty-one years at a rent of £3 p.a. and a fine of £3 6s 8d. Ashton was to continue to pay the 12d p.a. to the Warden and the 6s 8d p.a. to the heirs of Bibby. Here the fine was low in relation to the rent because the house was in a ruinous condition, and Ashton agreed to repair the house and then maintain it in good repair during the term of the lease. He claimed to have spent £120 in repairs, which Chadwick denied but which, if true, must have amounted to re-building. Indeed the Court Leet recorded in 1602 that Ashton had 'builded a howse' on the land of Robert Chadwick and had encroached ten inches onto the land of George Birch. In 1601 Ashton claimed that his expenditure on the house entitled him to a new lease for three lives, apparently without any additional fine. He also claimed that this had been a condition of the original lease, which Chadwick denied.[48] Whether Ashton had been promised a new lease for lives remains uncertain, but it looks

very much as if he had done considerable re-building. Other leases
were perhaps less complicated. Thus in 1607 Ellen Cogan, George
Tipping and his wife Mary leased to Richard Holland, esq., of
Denton a messuage on the west side of Millgate with a barn, cow-
house, shippons and half an acre of land on the east of Millgate. The
lease was for eighteen years at a rent of £9 p.a.; this high rent may
well explain the absence of any reference to a fine.[49] Similarly in
1608 Edmund Platt of Rusholme, gent., leased to Edward Massie of
Manchester, gent., a burgage in Millgate for three lives at a rent of
26s 8d p.a.; again there was no reference to a fine.[50] Two years later
George Allen of Manchester, gent., leased to George Clarke of
Manchester, haberdasher, a shop at the Smithy Door with a chamber over and a room behind the shop. The fine was £5 10s, the rent
£2 p.a., and the term ninety-nine years.[51]

   The practice of capitalising part of the rent in the form of a fine
was common in this period, but some property was let at a straightforward economic rent. That was probably true of Richard Holland's rent of £9. Similarly in 1599 when Richard Houghton leased
from Roger Pilkington some burgages belonging to the Crown, they
were occupied by tenants who paid what appear to be economic
rents and who challenged Houghton's lease by withholding those
rents. Thus Anne Buckley occupied a messuage and garden at a rent
of 30s 8d p.a., which was two years in arrears in 1601. She was said
to have caused great decay by pulling down the glass and taking
away wainscoting and doors. William Moss paid 30s p.a., Reynold
Costerdine 20s 8d p.a. and Hugh Battersley 18s p.a. for their messuages.[52] Such rents can be compared with those for corporation
property in Winchester in 1588–89 when eighty-three houses and
cottages paid 10s p.a. or less, thirteen paid 13s to 16s p.a. and fifteen
paid 20s to 25s p.a.[53] Manchester had no corporation and no
corporation property, and the examples of rents paid there are too
few for any really valid comparison. In any case house property is
subject to so many variables of size, quality and location that, even
if the evidence were fuller, comparison would remain difficult and
perhaps misleading.

   It is easier to see the pattern of property ownership in Manchester
than it is to discover what that property was worth. There was some
concentration of ownership, but in an urban setting that may be less
important as an indication of social and economic standing than it
was in rural areas. In the countryside the connection between the
ownership of real estate and the social standing of the owner was
fairly obvious, but it was much less obvious in a town where even the
wealthier burgesses might hold the bulk of their wealth in personal
rather than in real property. The cloth in the warehouse or the goods

in the shop might be much more valuable than a burgage. Urban wealth should be thought of in terms of circulating rather than of fixed capital. That is true whether a burgess was engaged in commerce or in industry, for in both cases the amount of fixed capital required was negligible. The profits of such commerce or industry might be invested in land or houses, but it might equally well be put out at interest or put back into the business. It would be unwise to assume that the Elizabethan bourgeoisie, when they accumulated a bit of money, reacted like peasants by adding acre to acre.[54]

NOTES

[1] M.C.L. MS. Misc. 125. (Rental of lands etc. belonging to the Collegiate Church 1581).

[2] They were sometimes described as reliefs (J. Tait, *Mediaeval Manchester and the beginnings of Lancashire*, pp. 70, 115).

[3] *C.L.R.*, i, p. 167.

[4] Tait, *op. cit.*, pp. 114–15.

[5] *Ibid.*, p. 114.

[6] *Ibid.*, p. 63.

[7] *C.L.R.*, ii, pp. 114–15.

[8] *Ibid.*, ii, 9n. 2.

[9] P.R.O., D.L., 1 208/A49. Peter Proby held a number of posts under the Duchy of Lancaster; in 1591 he was a feodary in Northamptonshire and in 1594 master forester of Amounderness and steward of Ormskirk and the other Burscough manors (R. Somerville, *History of the Duchy of Lancaster*, i, pp. 507, 509, 590).

[10] C.L.R., i, 149n. 1; G. J. Piccope, ed., *Lancashire and Cheshire wills and inventories*, ii, pp. 130–2. Ch. S. li (1860).

[11] L.R.O. DX Ancient Deeds, 349, 350; *C.L.R.*, ii, 221n. 2.

[12] *C.L.R.*, ii, p. 42.

[13] M.C.L. MS. Misc. 224/11; cf. P.R.O., D.L., 1 96/W19 for a dispute of 1572 which seems to concern this property.

[14] For disputes over this property see P.R.O., D.L., 1 161/S2 and 166/S14.

[15] *C.L.R.*, ii, 75n. 1.

[16] There is some doubt whether they descended from John or Peter Cowopp (*C.L.R.*, i, pp. 43, 51; ii, pp. 48, 115). They may have descended through the daughters of Peter Cowopp, John Cowopp's father (P.R.O., D.L., 1 66/B11), but the whole matter is obscure.

[17] *C.L.R.*, i, pp. 67, 72.

[18] P.R.O., D.L., 1 66/B11.

[19] *C.L.R.*, i, p. 150.

[20] *Ibid.*, ii, p. 183.

[21] *Ibid.*, i, p. 231.

[22] P.R.O., D.L., 1 208/A49.

[23] P.R.O., D.L., 1 203/H33.

[24] P.R.O., D.L., 1 166/S14.

[25] L.R.O. Will of George Pendleton (1585); *C.L.R.* i, p. 258; ii, pp. 58, 143.

[26] *C.L.R.* ii, pp. 82–3.

[27] *Ibid.*, 11, 68n. 6, 77.

[28] *Ibid.*, ii, 275n. 2 where Earwaker says Alice was the daughter of William

Baguley who died in 1573, but that Alice seems to have died unmarried in 1580 (*Registers*), p. 229).

[29] P.R.O., D.L., 1 189/H9 and H11.

[30] P.R.O., D.L., 1 204/L28.

[31] *C.L.R.*, ii, p. 9.

[32] The 'yeldhouse' seems to have been in Withington or Rusholme, par. Manchester.

[33] *Registers*, p. 264.

[34] J. Harland, ed., *Mamecestre*, iii, pp. 476–513. Ch. S. xlix (1862).

[35] M.C.L. MS. L1/33/113.

[36] *C.L.R.*, i, pp. 143–4.

[37] M.C.L. MS. L1/28/3/2.

[38] *C.L.R.*, i, p. 183; M.C.L. MS. M 57/1/15/4 and Owen MSS. 79 f. 144.

[39] P.R.O., D.L., 1 194/L8.

[40] *C.L.R.*, ii, pp. 4, 9.

[41] *C.L.R.*, ii, p. 43; M.C.L. MS. M35/1/12/1, 5. The details are drawn from a mortgage of the property by Hugh Travis to John Whitworth in 1587 (MS. M35/1/12/1). Billing's lease was presumably the one valued at £4 in his inventory of 1588.

[42] M.C.L. MS. L1/33/112/1.

[43] M.C.L. MS. L1/33/113.

[44] M.C.L. MS. Misc. 224/11.

[45] *C.L.R.*, ii, p. 188; L.R.O. QDD 14 m.1.

[46] M.C.L. MS. L1/33/111.

[47] M.C.L. MS. Misc. 125.

[48] *C.L.R.*, ii, p. 179; P.R.O., D.L., 1 196/A49, 200/A7.

[49] M.C.L. MS. L1/28/5/10.

[50] M.C.L. MS. M35/1/15/3.

[51] M.C.L. MS. M35/1/16/1.

[52] P.R.O., D.L., 1 203/H/33.

[53] T. Atkinson, *Elizabethan Winchester*, pp. 128–9.

[54] On investment in urban property see W. G. Hoskins, *Provincial England*, pp. 76–8.

CHAPTER III

THE TOWN ECONOMY: AGRICULTURE

The manorial rentals show that Manchester contained a concentration of burgages in the streets around the Collegiate Church and stretching out from there along Millgate, Marketstead Lane and Deansgate. Within this area there was some farm land, and further out there was more of it in places like the Heathes, Aldport Park and Collyhurst. What population this implied, it is difficult to tell. Sir Nicholas Mosley claimed in 1602 that there were 'above seaven or eighte thowsand people' within the jurisdiction of the Court Leet.[1] This was presumably an estimate of the total population of the manor, but even so it seems much too large. It does however point to one of the difficulties in assessing population, namely to what area do the figures relate, is it the manor, township or parish? Thus Professor Hoskins estimated Manchester's population at about 1500 in the 1520s. This seems to be based on the lay subsidy return of 1524, which gives 163 names, and a multiplier of nine to take account of women and children and those exempt from payment.[2] But it is not clear what is meant by 'Manchester' for the return of 1524 seems to relate to the parish. The lay subsidy of 1543 gives 256 taxpayers in the township of Manchester.[3] If the return covered all households in the township it would show a population of 1152 at four and a half persons per household, but presumably some householders were below the exemption limit. There is really no method of telling how many were so exempt, but a multiplier of nine to cover women, children and the exempt would give a population of about 2300.

The lay subsidies after 1543 are useless for estimating population; in 1563 only forty-eight taxpayers in Manchester were recorded as contributing to the subsidy.[4] In that year an episcopal return to the Privy Council gave the number of households in Manchester as 414, but again there is the problem of the area covered by the return. The returns are apparently based on parishes, but the vast parish of Manchester must have contained more than 414 households. Moreover the return has a separate entry of 339 households in the six 'chapels' of Didsbury, Blackley, Newton, Denton, Chorlton and Stretford, which were all in Manchester parish. The 339 households could not have been included in the 414, for that would have left only seventy-five households for the rest of the parish.[5] Logically the return should mean that the parish of Manchester had 753 [414 + 339] households, or perhaps some 3300 people, but it is not clear how many of these were in the township of Manchester. It is tempting to assume that all the 414 households were in the township, giving it a population of perhaps 1800.[6] Such an interpretation is not very logical, but the result seems plausible, especially as the estimate of 1152 people in 1543 should obviously be raised because of exemptions from the subsidy.

After 1563 information on Manchester's population becomes even scantier. The Elizabethan registers of the Collegiate Church very rarely distinguish between those who lived in the township and those who lived outside it. From 1607 they normally give the place of domicile in the case of baptisms and burials, but not in the case of marriages. Thus from 1607 to 1611 total burials averaged 188 p.a. of which seventy p.a. were of people who lived in the township. If the death rate lay within the band of thirty to forty per thousand, and migration is ignored, this would give the township a population in the range 2333 to 1750. In the same five years baptisms within the township averaged about 114 p.a.[7] The figures would suggest that Manchester was replenishing its population after the great mortality from the plague of 1605. They also suggest that inward migration played some part in that replacement. Whether that was true or not, the population certainly increased in the next thirty years. In 1642 the inhabitants of Manchester were called upon to sign the Protestation to maintain the established religion, and to protect the King's person, the freedom of Parliament and the rights and liberties of the subject. The Protestation was to be taken by householders and others being eighteen years of age or over. In practice it was taken in Manchester township by 1157 men and one woman. Allowing for females over eighteen and for children under eighteen, this must have represented a population of over three thousand.[8]

The Elizabethan township of Manchester may have had a population of about two thousand. If that were so, it was a respectable size for a market town. Even an old and important city like Worcester had only 4250 inhabitants in 1563; Winchester had about 3120 in 1604.[9] Such towns had some bucolic features, and these were naturally more pronounced in the smaller than in the larger places. Manchester's economy was based on agriculture, industry and trade, but it is difficult to assess the relative importance of these activities. This is largely because the sources are inadequate for any quantitative assessment. Thus neither the Court Leet records nor the parish registers of the Collegiate Church normally give a man's occupation in this period, though they may do so to distinguish between two men of the same name. The registers often describe a man simply as 'householder', but that is not very helpful. Moreover even when occupational descriptions are given, they can be misleading when they ascribe a specialised occupation to a man who was not, in practice, so specialised. Even so, the task of describing Manchester's economy would have been much easier if more occupations had been recorded; if in fact those who compiled the Court Leet records and the parish registers had shown a finer regard for the needs of future historians.

The question of specialisation arises in connection with agriculture. There was obviously farm land and farming in Manchester. On 6 October 1586 the Jury of the Court Leet presented that the Over and Nether Acres (which lay to the east of Deansgate) had until recently lain open to the street from such time as the corn had been gathered until Candlemas.[10] The Acres appear to have been open field arable divided into 'doles' of an acre and subject to right of common after the harvest.[11] John Bradshaw, who had '1 acker of ottes' at his death in 1588, may have had such a dole. Others died possessing quantities of barley, oats and wheat, which they may have bought rather than grown, though William Sandforth, a linen draper who died in 1598, had oats and barley 'unthreshed' valued at £3 10s 8d. Inventories give the impression that arable farming was less important than animal husbandry; they rarely record the possession of the implements necessary for arable cultivation. It was otherwise with pigs and cattle. The Court Leet, which had a morbid obsession with pigs and privies, showed little interest in the misdeeds of cattle, though in 1576 it complained that cattle had broken down the rails protecting 'one paire of butts in our townes ende in a lane there called Alporde lane'. As this 'maye be an occasion to hinder artillerie' the rails were to be repaired 'att the costs and chargs of the whole towne'.[12]

Pigs were a different matter. They were kept, or were supposed to be kept, in the 'backsides' of their owners' houses. In 1587 it was decreed that 'no inhabitor within this towne shall keepe any swyne within theire howse havinge not a backsyde belonginge to the same'.[13] Those who had no such backside or were unwilling to use it for their pigs, built swine cotes 'in the streets or towardes the streetesyde', which, in 1595, they were ordered to remove under penalty of 20s. At the same time they were forbidden to allow their pigs 'to goe at large either in the churche or churcheyarde, Markytte place or in the streetes of this towne unringed and unyoked' under penalty of 12*d* a pig. As an alternative to this nomadic foraging, pig owners were either to keep their pigs 'within theymselves' or to have them driven by the swineherd to Collyhurst common each day.[14] The battle against the pig can be traced back to 1554; it was still being waged in 1603.[15] For probate purposes pigs were valued at anything from 6*s* to 24*s* apiece in the 1580s and 1590s. They were sometimes kept by men who had no other animals; Robert Wharmby, a butcher who died in 1592, had only three swine valued at £2 and Edward Dyson, another butcher, had swine valued at £4 in 1598. On the other hand men with cattle quite often had no pigs. Perhaps backyard pigkeeping was more common among those whose inventories have not survived.

Horses and cattle appear more frequently in inventories than do pigs. Of sheep there is little sign at all, but sheep are unsuitable animals for a semi-urbanised existence. The possession of a horse, or even of a horse and a few pigs, hardly made a Manchester burgess into a farmer, especially as the horses rarely had anything of an agricultural nature to pull. It was natural enough that Edward Hanson, a mercer who died in 1584, should own a gelding for he had a shop in Bolton as well as one in Manchester. Indeed it is rather surprising that quite wealthy burgesses like James Bradshaw, saddler and yarn dealer, and Robert Walshman, goldsmith, should have owned no horse. Presumably they could hire one when necessary. Those who owned horses could pasture them on Collyhurst common, but at the end of the century they had to pay Nicholas Mosley for such pasturage. In 1599–1600 five men had summer pasturage for their horses on the common, at a rate of 13*s* 4*d* per quarter for a horse and 10*s* for a colt. They included Roger Ryder and Roger Smith, who each had an intake on Collyhurst. In the same year twenty men and one woman paid summer pasturage for their cows and calves at 6*s* 8*d* per quarter for a cow and 3*s* 4*d* for a calf. They included Anthony Mosley, Edward Briddock, who paid a rent of £27 19*s* 2*d* for the lordship of Cheetham, Richard Rothwell, who paid a rent of 30*s* p.a. for half the quarry at Collyhurst, and Francis Pendleton, who owned tenements in Deansgate and Withy Grove and lands and tenements near Newton Lane. This does not suggest that Collyhurst common under the new regime was catering for the poorer cowkeepers, but perhaps the poorer Mancunians confined themselves to pig keeping.

There is no doubt that agriculture played its role in Manchester's economy, but it is difficult to see exactly what that role was. It may be that the sources are not only scanty but deceptive, for they rarely reveal anyone whose sole occupation was farming. Thus Roger Bexwick was described as a yeoman in his will of 1598 and in his inventory of 1599. His will showed that he owned or held on lease considerable property; there were houses in Fennel Street, Millgate, Deansgate and Over Ardwick; there was a messuage at Grindlow in Gorton; there was a barn in Shude Hill which he left to his son-in-law Simon Mallon, who was to get the great garner, the bowses and crutches and other implements in the barn, but not the corn and hay. The inventory reveals that Bexwick was indeed a farmer. He owned five pigs valued at £2, a brown cow, a black pied cow and a calf valued at £5 13s 4d, a heifer in calf and two other black heifers valued at £4 6s 8d, twenty thrave of oats and an old garner valued at 18s, and corn and hay at Shude Hill valued at £8. There were cheese boards and a cheese stone in the kitchen. Bexwick's personal estate was valued at £110 1s 1d, which did not include any of the real estate which he owned or even which he held on lease. He looks like a well-to-do yeoman whose farming was on a fairly modest scale, but in 1590 when he was charged with breaking down a paling in Randal Beck's land, he was described as an innholder.[16] A closer look at his long inventory suggests that Bexwick was in fact an inn-keeper. His house had thirteen rooms. There was a parlour above the hall with a bed and fourteen yards of 'celinge' [panelling or wainscoting], a parlour on the backside with a standing bed, a truckle bed, two framed tables, three forms and thirty-four yards of 'celinge and benchinge', a parlour between the doors, a new cham-ber over that parlour with fifty-two yards of 'celinge' and a standing bed, another little chamber, the cloth chamber with two standing and two truckle beds and a warping stock, a chamber next to it with bedding but no bed, the 'Ockepen' chamber which contained only 'od trumperye', the chamber over the parlour over the hall, which shows that this part of the house at least was three-storied, another chamber which held a loom and an old bed, the hall with its '9 yardes of ceiling with two celed cupbordes att eyther ende', a long table and a square table, four stools and fourteen cushions and 'a hanging light of brasse', a buttery, a tavern or cellar, a kitchen, a brewhouse and a stable. It all seems a bit excessive for a yeoman; so too do the 461 pounds of pewter, the 144 pounds of 'brasse pan metle', the 192 pounds of 'brasse pot metle', the silver valued at £18 14s and the linen valued at £4 7s 10d. The combina-tion of farmer and innkeeper was a natural one, and Bexwick's inventory suggests that he followed both occupations.

At the other extreme from Bexwick was Arthur Kershaw, a yeoman who died in 1588 leaving a personal estate of only £1 13s. This was made up of 10s for his apparel and 23s owing to him. There were no household goods which suggests that Kershaw was a lodger, perhaps with his sister Alice, wife of William Birch, who lived in a house called Pursgloves which Kershaw left her for life subject to the payment of 4d p.a. to his heirs. According to his will, Kershaw had owned lands in Manchester worth £40 and had been forced into conveying them to Thomas Brown of London, who had married Kershaw's sister Anne. The will is obscure; Kershaw had apparently reserved to himself 'a state for terme of my naturall liffe' in the lands, but 'the premisses' had never been performed. Perhaps as a result of this knavery, he died a poor man for whom yeoman was a rather meaningless description.

Much of the farming that can be traced in Manchester was done as a side-line by men of other occupations. Naturally the scale of this farming varied considerably. Thus Francis Pendleton, merchant, owned seven cows, swine worth £1 11s and malt and barley worth £4 13s 4d at his death in 1574. He also owned some twenty acres of land on the east side of Newton Lane. William Baguley, a clothier who seems to have died at the beginning of 1573, had a horse, five cows and a calf, a pig, hay worth £3 6s 8d and barley and oats worth £2 13s 4d. He held three fields by lease in Blackley and Broughton and occupied a house with a field and a barn, which was probably 'the greate barne' of the inventory. It held building and other timber, perhaps left over from the house he had 'latelye builded' in Deansgate. Three men who died in 1588 show a similar combination of farming and other occupations. Thomas Brownsword, clothier, had 'kyne and yonge cattell being in number 15' valued at £20, a pig, a horse, twenty bushels of barley valued at £10, eight and a half sieves of oats valued at £4 5s, some hay and a churn and cheese press. He held land and houses by leases valued at £660. James Bradshaw, saddler and dealer in Irish yarn, had '6 kyne and a stirke and 1 acker of ottes', together valued at £14 13s 4d. He, too, held property by lease. The last of the trio, Adam Oldham, was described as a yeoman in his inventory, but he was also a dyer with a fully equipped dyehouse. He owned some ten acres of land, once part of the Heathes, and may have leased land but unfortunately his will has not survived and there is no reference to leases in his inventory. The inventory records in detail his valuable cattle: a brown cow (£2 6s 8d), a black pied cow (£2 6s 8d), a black cow (£2 6s 8d), a pied cow with a white face (£1 18s), a black heifer (£1 12s), a black cow in calf (£2 13s 4d), a pied stirk (£1), a cow (£2 6s 8d) and a calf (10s). There were also two swine, a grey nag, 'parte of a baye nagg and his grasse', twelve cheeses and a churn. This combination is also found in inventories of the 1590s. Thus Francis Hough, a clothier who died in 1593, had three cows as well as a gelding and a mare; he had also beef, suet, butter, cheese and corn valued at £2 10s 4d. Similarly William

Sandforth, a linen draper who died in 1598, had '2 milke kine', a fat cow, a pig and a horse; he had also nine loads of hay (valued at £3), barley and oats unthreshed valued at £3 10s 8d, and '5 hapes' of French wheat valued at 12s.

Though all these men could be described as farmers, they combined farming with other occupations and their farm stock usually accounted for a very small part of their personal estates. Thus Baguley's animals, hay and grain were valued at £18 11s 8d out of a personal estate of £584 16s; Bradshaw's cattle and oats were valued at £14 13s 4d out of an estate of £460; Oldham's cattle and pigs were valued at £18 6s 8d out of his estate of £164 17s 4½d. Hough's two horses with their saddles and bridles and his three cows were together valued at £18 7s out of his personal estate of £241 13s 2d. This disparity can become very marked with those whose farming was on a very small scale. Thus Robert Birch, a linen draper who died in 1583, had two cows and a heifer valued at £4 10s out of a personal estate of £470 15s 2d. Thomas Hardman, a mercer who also died in 1583, had two cows, two pigs and four loads of hay valued at £6 12s out of an estate of £451 6s 9d. Such men, and others less wealthy, with their one or two pigs and one or two cows were probably engaged in small scale farming simply to supply their own households. It was the home farm in miniature, or the home farm in an urban setting.

Others like Oldham and Brownsword clearly operated on a bigger scale than that, and the same was true of John Wharmby, a butcher who died in 1598. Wharmby had a considerable stock of animals: a mare, three pigs, twenty-six cows and six calves and four 'feedinge beasts' and, a very rare item, six sheep and a lamb. There is no evidence of any arable cultivation, but there was a 'mylke howse', cheese boards and butter. The four 'feedinge beasts' were at Warrington and two of the cows were 'in Yorkshire at the temple', whatever that means. This dispersal may reflect the difficulty of feeding so much stock in Manchester itself; the same difficulty probably lay behind the leasing of land including two meadows at Blackley, two more meadows in Crumpsall, a close in Cheetham and 'Barlowe Crosse fieldes'. As a butcher Wharmby had three 'flesh bords' and a 'kyllinge howse'. He had also, more surprisingly, a 'fysh chamber', and his debtors included 'Saxon Mr Tatton's man for heyring', which may have been for herrings. Wharmby's farm stock was valued at £97 6s 8d out of a total personal estate of £223 1s 9d, which was a very high proportion. His inventory has too many etceteras to give a full picture of his possessions, though the valuation is complete, but it shows that Wharmby lived in some style with his 'silver touthpycke', his 'staffe with a raper in' (presumably a swordstick), his apparel valued at £9 7s and his pewter valued at £4 8s 3d. His debtors included 'Mr Dee, Warden'; this was John Dee, who owed £1 17s 4d.

Though Wharmby was a butcher and apparently a fishmonger as well as a farmer, it is probable that his farming was the most important of his activities. In a few other cases farming seems to have been the sole occupation. Thus John Cowopp, who died in 1581 and was given no status or occupation in his will or inventory, seems to have been simply a farmer. He owned a mare, a hog, a stirk, four cows and two heifers. There were also unspecified 'catell' valued at £7 16s and 'pullen' or poultry valued at 2s. Though Cowopp owned a little malt and wheat, there is really no evidence that he did any arable farming. In his will he declared that Jane his wife had consented 'that everie one of my children shall have one cowe also out of the wholle goods before any division or destribucion therof be made'. So Ralph, the youngest son, was to have a cow called Throstell with her calf, Peter was to have 'the redd cowe called Cherrie', Gillian the cow called Blackwall, and so on for all six children. One of the cows was at 'Worall' in Cheshire (perhaps Wardle near Nantwich) where Cowopp had a tenement or messuage, one was with William Barlow of Didsbury and two were with Lawrence Barlow also of Didsbury As the will was made on 21 November 1581, this suggests a dispersal of stock for winter feeding, though Cowopp had hay valued at £2. He also owed £1 12s for hay. His total personal estate came to £51 12s 6d.

Two other 'mere' farmers seem to show a greater concern with arable farming. Both were gentlemen and considerable property owners. One was Richard Hunt, who farmed the market tolls and left property in Manchester, Salford and elsewhere to his eldest son John. At his death in December 1587 Hunt owned four cows and a stirk valued at £7 13s 4d, and butter and cheese valued at £3 10s. These were much less valuable than his grain: barley and oats 'bothe wydowed [sic? winnowed] and unthresshen' at £25 and meal and malt at £10 6s 8d. There were also carts, wheels and a plough. The Irish yarn valued at £9 suggests that Hunt had a side-line in the linen trade. Altogether his personal property was valued at £137 3s 2d. The other man was Thomas Beck who owned property in Lanca-shire and Cheshire and left a lease of a house in Ardwick to provide a dowry of £100 for his daughter Eleanor. At his death in 1588 Beck owned two nags, a colt, five cows and eight young beasts. His barley and oats were valued at £11, and he had hay at Ardwick and hay and wheat at Monsall. Though Beck owned carts, he had apparently no plough or harrow so perhaps the grain had been bought or perhaps he was a tithe owner. His animals, hay and grain accounted for half his personal estate, £42 9s. 8d. out of £84 16s 4d. He seems to have lived rather modestly apart from his silver plate which was valued at £19 16s 8d. He dressed modestly too for his apparel was worth only £2 10s, a very ungentlemanly sum.

There were some men in Manchester whose sole occupation was farming, but this was probably commoner in the more rural parts of the parish. Thus Nicholas Percival, a husbandman of Kirkmans-hulme[17] who died in 1596, had two horses, a cow and a stirk; 'korne growing in the ground' valued at £7, 'haye gresse' valued at £2 and two hives. His implements included ploughs, harrows, a 'haye karte and the shode wheles with the axeletree and the forneture with it' (valued at 26s 8d), a 'koalle carte and one peare of kloge whelles' (valued at 7s) and 'one turffe carte' (valued at 4s). The total personal estate came to £29 15s 4d, but even here the two horses and the three specialised carts suggest a side-line as a carrier. Ralph Thorpe, a husbandman of Failsworth who died in 1598, had two horses, five cows, three calves and a stirk. His oats and barley were valued at £10, his meal and malt at 50s, his hay at £4 10s, his 'salte fleshe and sweete and swines grease' at £3, his 'wheate sowen' at 20s, and his 'implements of husbandry' at £5. The total personal estate was £53. These inventories show a greater emphasis on farming as the sole occupation and on arable farming than was common in Manchester itself.

In Manchester the emphasis was more on dairy farming, and even the grain which the inventories reveal may sometimes have been bought by the testator rather than grown by him. Arable farming would seem to require more implements of husbandry than normally appear in the inventories. In any case concentration on dairy farming would be an obvious specialisation in an urban area with a demand for milk, cheese and butter, whether the demand came from the producer's own household or from the market. The same would be true of concentration on the pig. The same should have been true of concentration on the fowl, of which there is no evidence at all apart from a very occasional reference to hen coops and apart from John Cowopp's 'pullen'. Presumably the tradition that barnyard fowls belonged to the wife rather than to the husband accounts for their absence from the inventories. Was the same true of the cats, also absent, or were they regarded as 'wild animals' and so valueless? Dogs were absent too, though they certainly existed, for the Court Leet issued orders that they should not be allowed abroad unless muzzled.[18] They would scarcely be regarded as the wife's property; perhaps they descended from father to son with the burgage and the daggers.

Clearly agriculture played a role in Manchester's economy. In the broad sense any urban community had to be fed and had in practice to draw some of its foodstuffs from the surrounding country-side. Little is known in detail about this provisioning of towns, but on occasion it could involve distant sources of supply. In July and August 1597, a year of bad harvests, John Dee was bringing 'Dansk rye' by carrier from Wakefield to Manchester. He got twenty-one horse loads in all, which had presumably been imported through Hull.[19] In the narrower sense the agriculture practised within the township seems to have been relatively unimportant. Manchester was not a village, except in the Defoeian sense, and its economy rested, not so much on agriculture, as on industry and trade.

NOTES

[1] P.R.O., D.L., 1 207/M1.

[2] W. G. Hoskins, *Provincial England*, pp. 72n. 3, pp. 81–2; J. Tait, ed., *Taxation in Salford Hundred 1524–1802*, pp. 1–6. Ch. S. n.s. lxxxiii. (1924).

[3] Tait, *op. cit.*, pp. 21–6.

[4] *Ibid.*, pp. 59–60.

[5] Harleian MSS., 594, f. 102 (British Library, London).

[6] Professor Hoskins appears to assume this (*Provincial England*, p. 87).

[7] *Registers*, pp. 146–77, 373–97.

[8] 'The Protestation of 1641–2 in Manchester', *The Palatine Note-book*, i (1881) pp. 80–4, 102–8, 122–4, 136–40, 167–71, 210–15. The one woman was Elizabeth Martenscroft, a recusant.

[9] A. D. Dyer, *The city of Worcester in the sixteenth century*, p. 26; T. Atkinson, *Elizabethan Winchester*, pp. 32–3.

[10] *C.L.R.*, ii, p. 7.

[11] *Ibid.*, i, p. 257. Barley was grown on the Acres in 1584 (H. T. Crofton, 'Tithe corn book for Manchester &c. 1584', *Trans. Lancs. and Cheshire Antiquarian Soc.*, xxii (1904), 170–9.)

[12] *C.L.R.*, i, p. 177.

[13] *Ibid.*, ii, p. 17.

[14] *Ibid.*, ii, pp. 92–3.

[15] *Ibid.*, i, p. 15, ii, p. 195.

[16] J. Tait, ed., *Lancashire Quarter Sessions records*, i, p. 44. Ch. S. n.s. lxxvii (1917).

[17] A detached part of Newton township in par. Manchester.

[18] *C.L.R.*, i, p. 241, ii, pp. 17, 37, 49–50.

[19] J. O. Halliwell, ed., *The private diary of Dr. John Dee*, p. 59. Camden Soc., xix (1842).

CHAPTER IV

THE TOWN ECONOMY: INDUSTRY

The industrial life of Elizabethan Manchester finds little expression in the records of the Court Leet, much less than is often found in the records of incorporated towns and their gilds. The Court Leet duly appointed searchers of leather and in 1591 began to appoint an officer to assist the deputy aulnager in 'the messuringe of clothe'.[1] Otherwise its interest in cloth was negligible. In 1569 the Court Leet ordered 'that ther shall not be eny rogg or cottene wet openly in the stretes but that the same be donne other in his or their houses or backesydes' under penalty of 3s 4d.[2] A quarter of a century later the widow of Edward Borrow was charged with annoying 'the neighbors and passingers by weetinge [wetting] her clothe with noysome or contagious matter as well by nighte as by daye'. She was ordered to desist under penalty of 3s 4d.[3] No one could deduce from such scanty references to the major industry that Manchester was a 'cloth town'. The manorial survey of 1581 and the rentals do not reveal much about Manchester's industry either. They show the existence of the School mills and of the quarry at Collyhurst. The latter, which Leland described as a 'goodly quarry . . . hard by the town'[4], was held by Richard Rothwell and Stephen Pendleton at a rent of £5 p.a. in 1599–1600. A curious entry in the survey of 1581 stated that William Radcliffe, gent., had been granted 'one poste of stone conteyninge by estimacion in lengthe 16 yardes and in bredthe 8 yardes in and upon Colyhurste'. A note in the margin added that this was 'oon the nexte syde the quarrye to the towne' and another note denied that any such grant had been made. The survey also records that Henry Adamson paid 6d p.a. for 'one milne to grynde knyves uppon Colyhurste', which in 1599 was described as 'a mylnested upon Colyhurst to turne a grindlestone'. Alice, the widow of George Bolton, also paid 6d p.a. for 'one place for a grindell stone to grynde sheares', which was also on Collyhurst common, but by 1589 it had become 'a little mylnsted decayed'. The quarry at Collyhurst could provide one form of building material, but the important daub (for wattle and daub) came from 'the dawbehole by the pinfolde' for which Roger Bexwick paid a rent of 6d p.a. He seems to have had no monopoly of the supply of daub; in 1589 the Court Leet ordered that no one should 'make any doabe in any cartewaye or footewaye within the precinct of Manchester wheareby any passinger may be letted or avoyded [troubled]'. In 1598 it was forbidden to take any daub or clay 'betwixte the pynffolde and the Sudehill'.[5] It is not known where the timber for building came from.

Tanning also got some mention in the survey and rentals. In 1581 Margaret, widow of Hugh Shacklock, paid 8d p.a. as rent for a certain parcel of ground 'whereon are certen barkepittes and lyme pittes lyenge betwixte the water of Irke and the Walkers crofte'. Her husband, who died in 1578,[6] had been a tanner, for in 1566 he and nine other men had been fined 'for barkein horshe heids [hides] and shepes lether'. A year later he was one of the constables.[7] If all the ten men were tanners, it implies a considerable industry. Margaret may have carried on with the tanning after her husband's death; she certainly continued to own the bark and lime pits as well as the house in which she lived. She seems to have prospered for in 1599 she bought from George Travis a barn and two closes in Marketstead Lane which were subject to the considerable chief rent of 3s 8d, and the following year was assessed for the subsidy at £5 in goods.[8] Rather surprisingly she remained a widow until her death in 1606, some five months after she had conveyed her Marketstead Lane property to her son-in-law William Stanley.[9]

Tanning was a complicated industrial process which could take up to two years and which needed to be financed by some circulating capital.[10] Thus William Hunt, a tanner who died in 1588, had bark valued at £10 and hides and clout leather valued at £58 3s 2d. All these were in 'the barkehouse', and a dicker of the cow hides was 'in the ouse', or in other words soaking. As usual the fixed capital as represented by the implements of the trade, the knives, shovels, troughs and 'beatinge maules', was insignificant in comparison with the circulating capital as represented by the raw materials and the finished leather. Hunt combined his tanning with a little farming, but he had only two cows which no doubt supplied the eleven cheeses and filled the five pots of butter and ate the nineteen loads of hay. His personal estate was valued at £146 12s 10d, and he certainly lived in some luxury with his pewter valued at £3 3s 10d and his plate at £9 5s 6d and his fourteen or so beds which, even allowing for servants, seems excessive for a man with a wife but no children except apparently two married daughters. Hunt was not as wealthy as the richest Lincolnshire and Chester tanners,[11] but his personal estate compares favourably with those of many tanners of the period. He was better off than Francis Wirrall, a Manchester tanner who died in 1598. Wirrall left a personal estate of £93 6s 3d of which £34 15s 2d was accounted for by hides and leather. These included a dicker of hides 'suffyciently tanned' (£5), 'tow dickers and 7 hydes in the seacounde sett' (£12 3s), two and a half dicker 'in the fyrste sett' (£10 16s 8d), '9 hydes in the owsses' (£3 13s 4d), calf leather and skins, horse hides and 'swyne skynnes'. There was also 'barke in the barkehowse and in the wood' valued at £1 16s and a leather press and a pair of shears valued at 2s 9d. Among Wirrall's debtors were Ralph Worsley 'of Mamchester tanner' and Robert Siddall, butcher, from whom he had received fifteen calfskins, perhaps in part payment of the debt. Wirrall was comfortably off and had married Elizabeth, the daughter of Edward Hanson a well-to-do mercer.[12] He had no monopoly of tanning in the 1590s when there were at least seven other tanners in Manchester, including Robert Wharmby, tanner, who was slain by George Wirrall, tanner, in 1590.[13]

Tanning was only one of the two main ways of making leather. The other was the 'dressing' of light skins with oil or alum.[14] This was the work of the whittawer of whom there were at least three in Manchester in the 1590s and another and different three in 1601.[15] The earlier trio included Adam Hope who died in 1591 leaving a personal estate of £135 0s 1d. About half this sum came from skins, leather and wool. The skins included 'one thouzande and certen odd Irishe skynnes with the wooll belonginge to the same skynnes' valued at £28. It is interesting to note that 300 more Irish skins, presumably without their wool, were valued at only £2 6s 8d. There were 400 English skins (valued at £4) and a few deer and lambskins and even one dogskin. The English and Irish leather was valued at £9 9s and the coarse and fine wool at £25 10s. For the dressing process there was alum valued at £2, but all the 'workelomes belonginge to the occupacion' were valued at only 13s 6d. Hope did a little farming, but he had only his saddle horse, a hog and two cows 'with grasse for the same the next summer'. His house had the distinction of containing a 'servauntes parlor', which held nothing but two beds and their bedding, and one of the larger private armouries which contained a sallet, skull with a cap, a sword, two daggers, a bow, half a sheaf of arrows and a blackbill. There is no evidence that Hope combined leather dressing with glove making, which was a general term applied to the making of all sorts of light leather goods. Manchester possessed one or two glovers,[16] and in 1601 Simon Mallon was exporting 'Manchester gloves' through Liverpool to Dublin.[17] It is possible that the leather industry was more important than the surviving evidence suggests, but Manchester was not really a 'leather town' in the sense that Leicester or Chester was.

Nor was Manchester a metal-working town, though there had been some such working there in Roman times.[18] Manchester had its blacksmiths like John Cowopp who paid a rent of 4d p.a. for his 'hovell anendste the smythie', kept a dangerous 'great mastiffe' which nearly 'overthrew' the foreman of the Leet Jury, maintained a 'mydinge in his backsyde' which was 'a noyance to the hedge of Rodger Bexwicke', and later kept pigs which annoyed Bexwick's widow.[19] Robert Janny, another blacksmith, also had a 'hovell anendst his smythie' which 'croched uppon the hye streete ... to the greate anoyance of pashingers with lodes'.[20] At a more respectable level there was a goldsmith, Robert Walshman, who seems to have led a blameless life which culminated in his appointment to the office of scavenger in 1596 and of an ale taster in 1597, the year before he died.[21] Smiths were to be found in many places that had no specialised metal industry. Apart from a reference to 'Manchester pins' in a mercer's inventory,[22] there is no evidence that Manchester had the sort of specialised metal working that was developing in other parts of Lancashire.[23] The pewter, for example, that inventories reveal, does not seem to have been made locally, but to have come from London and Wigan. Manchester's economy rested neither on leather nor on metals, but on the making and marketing of cloth.

The Lancashire textile industry had two distinct branches, the making of woollen cloth and the making of linen.[24] Both branches were to be found in Manchester where it is difficult to say which was the more important. Four types of woollen cloth were produced in the county, cottons, kerseys, rugs and friezes. All these were narrow cloths made from carded wool on looms which required only one weaver and not two, as was the case with broad cloths. In general they were woven by independent weavers, who owned their raw material and sold their cloth, usually undyed and undressed. There is no convincing evidence of a 'putting out' system in which capitalist clothiers distributed wool to spinners and yarn to weavers and paid the spinners and weavers at piece rates. In Manchester the organisation of industry seems to have conformed to this general pattern, but there is very little evidence on carding and spinning as specialised occupations. Carding was a male occupation which, in other parts of Lancashire, was done by men who combined it with spinning by the female members of the household and with farming.[25] Spinning was normally a part-time occupation for women and girls, and as such it leaves little trace. Very few of the inventories of men who died in Manchester record the possession of spinning wheels, but perhaps such wheels were regarded as the property of the wife or perhaps spinners were the wives of men who owned too little to merit an inventory. It is indeed possible that much of the yarn woven in Manchester had been carded and spun in the more rural parts of the parish.

The woollen weavers are almost as elusive as the spinners, though they certainly existed. It is usually impossible to tell, however, whether they lived and worked in Manchester or elsewhere in the parish. Thus Richard Walwork, a husbandman who died in 1592, combined weaving and farming, but he seems to have lived at Crumpsall within the parish but outside the township of Manchester.[26] Weavers emerge from their obscurity when they combined weaving with other processes. The most interesting example of this was John Nabbs who died in 1570. He called himself a clothmaker in his will, and his inventory shows that the description was apt. He owned cards, spinning wheels, a loom and 'a sherebord and handels' as well as 184 stones of wool and flocks valued at £36 and nineteen pieces of cloth valued at £25. His total personal property, which included two cows, came to £89 0s 6d. Thus Nabbs did all the processes from carding to shearing, no doubt helped by his six servants to each of whom he left a crown in his will. He also left two fullers 12d each. This integration of the processes under one roof was also found in the West Riding where John Pawson, a Leeds clothier who died in 1576, had a very similar establishment, though he did the dyeing as well.[27] It is doubtful whether it was common in Manchester where the clothier more often limited himself to one or two processes. Thus Francis Hough, a clothier who died in 1593, had 'two loomes with theire furniture' and 'sheremans sheres with handells'. His stock of 'wooll, flockes, yarne, trayne and measures' was valued at £81 18s 3d and his friezes and rugs at £10 2s 10d. It looks a straightforward case of a clothier embracing two processes, weaving and shearing, and perhaps, considering the size of his stock, doing some dealing in wool, but Hough had also some 'fernando barke' (brazil) and logwood and '2 fornaces, a greate leade and an olde leade'. The furnaces and leads were valued at £3 7s 7d, and there was fuel valued at nearly £3. All this suggests that Hough added dyeing to the weaving and shearing. Whatever he did, he was prosperous enough, for his personal estate was valued at £241 13s 2d, which included two horses, three cows and £9 9s 2d in silver and gold.

In Manchester as elsewhere the term clothier could cover a variety of functions, but there is little doubt that the Manchester clothier was essentially a man who bought cloth from the weavers and who often undertook the shearing of the cloth and sometimes also its dyeing, though much dyeing may have been done in the wool. This would lend support to the view that when weaving moved out into the countryside, cloth finishing remained urban. Even clothiers who owned a loom or two may have bought cloth as well as made it. When the clothier owned no loom and where there is no evidence of a putting out system, it is clear that the clothier must have bought his cloth. William Baguley, a clothier who died probably early in 1573, is a good example of this. Baguley had no wool, cards, spinning wheels or looms; he had four pairs of shearmen's shears and thirty packs of cottons of which fifteen packs had been sent to London and fifteen were at home. This cloth was valued at £262 10s. His function as a clothier was to buy cloth and shear it for the London market. This, combined with farming, had made him a man of substance. His goods, including £38 9s in gold and ready money, were valued at £422 17s 6d; he owed £12 7s 6d and was owed £174 6s, so that his total personal estate was £584 16s. It is not surprising that he lived in some style in a house with five rooms where the pewter was valued at £4 19s 2d, the plate at £8 18s 4d and his own apparel at £7 9s 4d.

Shearing was also one of the processes undertaken by Thomas Brownsword, a clothier who died in 1588, but his shapeless inventory is more difficult to interpret. Apart from being a farmer on a considerable scale, Brownsword was primarily a dealer in flax of which he had a stock valued at £18 10s. He had also a spinning wheel and thirty-four pounds of white yarn which may have been spun from the flax by the two women servants to whom he left 10s apiece in his will. More surprisingly he had a shearboard and two pairs of shears, though the only cloth in his possession which they could have sheared was a white cotton piece and four yards of frieze. This cloth and some 'cullard Myllian fustian' and four and a quarter yards of 'queenes burrato' have led to the view that Brownsword had a shop in which he sold cloth[28], but this seems unlikely. The cloth may have been for his own use, for his doublets were made of burrato and Milan fustian. In whatever way Brownsword made his living, he was a rich man for his personal estate was valued at £1109 5s 5d. Cloth shearing was not the path to that sort of affluence, and indeed independent shearmen resented the practice by which a clothier employed shearmen on his own premises. In 1595 the shearmen of Manchester and Salford, led by William Sorocold, petitioned the Privy Council against the practice and claimed for themselves the sole right to shear such cottons, rugs and friezes 'as are used to bee within the County Palantine of Lancaster'. This claim was largely accepted by the Privy Council which decreed that 'no trader useinge to buy clothe within the saied county to carry or cause to bee carryed out of the same' should shear such cloth 'within his owne howse or elswhere, eyther by himselve or any other by his procurement', but should have it sheared by such shearmen as be 'thought fitt and woorthie to have the doinge thereof'. This was a time of bad harvests and high grain prices which are reflected in the statement that 'yt ys thought there be diveres who, for the tyme, use to take into theire howses suche persons as they neyther give meate nor drinke unto, and but very small wages for the present tyme'.[29] The restriction of the order to traders who carried or caused to be carried cloth out of the county suggests that it was aimed at the clothiers who sent their cloth to the London market. Whoever the decree was aimed at, the activities of John Leese suggest that it was not very successful.

John Leese, who died in 1598, was described in his will as a cloth-worker. He had no woollen yarn or loom, but in his garden were 'twoe payre of tenters' valued at 26s 8d. Tenters were used to stretch cloth back into shape after it had been fulled. Their inclusion in Leese's inventory is puzzling, not so much because their use had been forbidden by statute the year before,[30] but because tentering seems normally to have been done by the fullers, and there is no evidence that Leese had any connection with fulling. In Lancashire fulling was not done by clothiers but by independent fullers who operated the fulling mills and were paid a fee which was sometimes 6d a cloth.[31] Whatever may be implied from Leese's ownership of tenters, there is less mystery about his workshop with its 'sixe payre broad sheares' (valued at 40s) and '56 dossen of handles at 3d the peece'[32], though it is very rare indeed to get a separate valuation of the wooden handles that fitted into the shears.[33] Leese left to John Barlow, shearman, four dozen 'of handle stockes and one paire of sheres'. Despite the Privy Council order of 1595, Leese was clearly shearing in his own house cloth which he had not made. It might be argued that he was not going to send the cloth out of the county, but that seems unlikely in view of the scale of his operations. In his will Leese made some small bequests and then left the residue of his personal estate to his daughter Ellen, but if Ellen died before reaching full age or before marriage or before she could lawfully make a will to dispose of the property, then the property was to go to the children of Henry Travis and of William Sorocold, shearman, presumably the same William who had acted as spokesman for the shearers in 1595. Leese not only sheared cloth but also dyed it, for which he had a dyehouse with '2 greate dyinge leades' valued at £5 and madder and brazil valued at £8 9s 4d. His two hundred and seventy-five pounds of white linen yarn valued at £27 10s 6d suggest that he may have dyed linen yarn as well as woollen cloth. He certainly had a shop in which he sold a range of woollen cloths; there were kerseys in a variety of colours, black, white, blue, silver, green, yellow and 'sad seawater greene', red frieze, red, white and blue gladen, white rugs, and French tawney kersey, which may really have been French, for at 4s a yard it was as expensive as stone grey broadcloth. The shop's equipment included 'a pendis borde' or pentice, which was fixed above the shop window to keep the rain off the stall below. Leese's activities as shearman, dyer and shopkeeper seem to have been lucrative for he left personal property valued at £272 9s which included £39 15s 4d in money and gold. He lived in a very well furnished house of nine rooms (excluding the dyehouse, workshop and shop); there was silver plate valued at £18 14s 3d, pewter at £5 5s 10d, standing beds with ceiled testers, painted cloths and much household linen. His own apparel (including a sword and two daggers) was valued at £5 5s 4d; his late wife's wardrobe was more elaborate still with its 'shepe collour gowne with velvet cape and layde with velvet lace' valued at £3 and its 'red scarlet petycote with velvet lace and sylke fringe' valued at 33s 4d.

Leese was apparently not only breaking the order of 1595 with his shearing, but in 1581 and 1583 he, along with Adam Oldham and Stephen Hulme, had been prosecuted for practising the art of dyeing without having been apprenticed to it.[34] As in the case of shearing, it was the independent craftsmen who objected to their craft being practised by clothiers and clothworkers. The result of the prosecution is not known, but clearly Leese was not stopped from dyeing, and nor was Adam Oldham. In July 1587 the Shuttleworths of Smithills near Bolton paid 12d to Adam Oldham of Manchester for dyeing 'towe pounde of yarne blewe'.[35] At his death in 1588 Oldham had a dyehouse containing 'one great leade fornace with the curbe' (valued at £4), 'one other greate leade with a curbe and a lidd' (£2 13s 4d), another 'leade sett in a keyre of wood' (£1 6s 8d), 'one great keire for a dye fatt' (£1 13s 4d), a quantity of galls and brazil, and 'fire wood and other tymber about the saide diehouse with kiddes' (£8). There was also a quantity of 'clothe that is owinge for dyinge' which included tammy, 'a pece of red yarne', four pounds woollen yarn and fifteen 'skyns of lether dyed greene'. The cloth seems to have cost 4d the yard for dyeing and the woollen yarn 9d a pound. Such figures suggest that dyeing was fairly expensive, but dyeing is one of the processes of the cloth industry about which little is known. Oldham was owed a total of £32 14s 8½d by some fifty debtors, but unfortunately the reasons for the debts were not given. His total personal property was valued at £164 17s 4½d, but it should be remembered that he was a farmer as well as a dyer. The two occupations enabled him to live in the considerable comfort of a well furnished house of three chambers, two parlours and a hall 'with seelinge and benches 24 yards'.

C

When wool had been carded and spun, the yarn woven, the cloth fulled, dressed and dyed, then the finished product had to be marketed. It was partly the nature of the processes and partly the nature of the market that determined the role of the Manchester clothier. Cloth woven by independent weavers was sold in the unfinished state to clothiers who saw to the dressing of the cloth and, except where it had been dyed in the wool, to its dyeing. It is possible that some of the cloth destined for foreign markets was left undyed, but there is no evidence of this. Most of the Manchester cottons that were exported went to France and not to those areas which received undressed and undyed cloth shipped by members of the Merchant Adventurers Company. Some cloth was sold locally, but much was sent by the Manchester clothiers to distant markets. Some went to Stourbridge Fair; in 1567 seven Manchester clothiers were taking their cloth there.[36] Some may have taken the long road to Southampton as it did earlier in the century.[37] A little found its way to Bristol down the Severn; in 1570 Miles Wilson and Roger Saule, clothiers of Manchester, sent forty northern kerseys and 120 Manchester cottons from Bewdley to Bristol. In 1592 George and Charles Travis, also clothiers of Manchester, sent both woollen and linen cloth from Gloucester to Bristol.[38] Nearer ports were to be found in Chester and Liverpool, with which Manchester men had connections through the import of Irish linen yarn. Both ports exported cloth, but it is impossible to tell how much of this originated in Manchester.[39] All these outlets for Manchester cloth were much less important than London, which was the main centre for the export of Manchester and northern cottons. Thus in 1594–5, 73,611 goads of Manchester and northern cottons were exported from London,[40] but as neither northern nor even Manchester cottons were necessarily made or marketed in Manchester, it is impossible to use such figures as an indication of the size of the Manchester to London trade. Although that trade cannot be precisely measured, there is no doubt of its importance.

The trade in woollen cloth, and especially in cottons, between Manchester and London was very similar to the trade in Welsh cottons between Shrewsbury and London.[41] The Shrewsbury Drapers who bought up Welsh cloth, sheared it and sent it to London were playing the same sort of role as the Manchester clothiers. This involved sending the cloth to Blackwell Hall in London; in 1561–2 it is known that at least five Manchester clothiers were selling cloth there.[42] The bigger clothiers sometimes operated as family partnerships, with one member of the family looking after the London end of the business. That seems to have been true of the Mosleys, probably the biggest of the clothiers, though little is known about their business. Nicholas Mosley lived in London where from the 1570s he was exporting Manchester cottons, sometimes assisted by his son Rowland.[43] Nicholas's brother Anthony seems to have managed the Manchester end of the business. It is some indication of the scale of his operations that, at his death in 1607, Anthony had cloth valued at £254 in his warehouse at home as well as cloth valued at £224 at the fullers. He left a personal estate of about £2000.[44] Not all clothiers operated on this scale, but Lawrence Robinson, a Salford clothier who died in 1587, owned cloth worth nearly £500 and a total personal estate of nearly £2000.[45] More typical perhaps were William Baguley and James Rillston. Baguley, it will be recalled, had cloth valued at £262 10s, half of which was in London.[46] Rillston, who died in 1578, was described in his will as a 'cotton-man'. He held much property on leases for years; there were two fields held from Sir Edmund Trafford, five houses of which three belonged to the Warden and Fellows of the Collegiate Church, and 'certaine backside houses, shoppes, chambers and warehowses beneath Peter Barlowes house in the Deansgate', which were presumably the business premises and which he left to Edward, the eldest of his nine children. The nature of Rillston's business can only be determined from the list of debts attached to his will, for no inventory has survived. He was a clothier who dealt in cottons which he had had fulled at a cost of 6d a cloth. His debts for fulling show that Thomas Gorelt had fulled 188 cottons and 'Fields the walker' had fulled fifty-five, which is some indication of the scale of Rillston's business. The cottons, or some of them, were sent to London where they were handled by Rillston's cousin, George Hunt, a citizen and haberdasher of London. In 1578 Hunt owed for eight packs of cottons at £11 11s a pack. The evidence suggests that Hunt was buying the cottons rather than acting as Rillston's agent, but it is not possible to be certain about the business relationship between the two men. The personal relationship was obviously close, for Hunt's children had stayed in Manchester with Rillston who was owed £10 for their table for a year and 18s 2d for their apparel, mending and other necessaries. Perhaps the children had gone north to avoid the plague in London. Their stay in Manchester had not inspired Rillston to leave them anything in his will, though he made their father one of the overseers of the will.[47]

The organisation of the linen industry in Manchester was similar to that of the woollen cloth industry. There were some differences, however, especially in the provision of yarn and in the disposal of the finished cloth. The transforming of flax into yarn was a more complex process than the carding and spinning of wool, for the fibre had to be extracted from the stem by soaking, drying and beating before it could be spun. After it had been spun, the yarn was bleached, sometimes by weavers, sometimes by specialised bleachers and sometimes by yarn dealers. Apart from some bleaching there is little evidence that these complicated processes were carried out in Manchester where much of the linen yarn seems to have been imported from Ireland. It came in through Liverpool and to a lesser extent through Chester, and was sometimes sold in Manchester by Irish merchants.[48] However the yarn was obtained, the weaving of it was largely in the hands of independent weavers, though these ranged from purely manual workers to those who combined weaving with dealing in yarn or cloth. Thus John Dickenson, a linen weaver who lived in Deansgate and died in 1590, had 'a lome and all thinges belonginge to it' valued at £1 and 'ould heald yarne and hempe' valued at 1s 4d. His personal property was valued at £15 7s 8d. Unfortunately the inventory does not specify the number of rooms, but their contents seem to have been shabby for some thirty items were described as 'old'. Even so, there were four coffers and an ark, brass pots and £2 in money. John Pycroft, a linen weaver who died in 1591, also had 'a loome and all thinges parteininge to the occupatione' and, according to his will, a 'lome house'. Pycroft's personal property was valued at £13 9s 5d. This was rather less than Dickenson's, but Pycroft seems to have lived in greater comfort. He had three butteries, a good deal of pewter and pots and pans, two chandeleers, six chairs and four stools, painted cloths and seven feet of glass. It is rather a reminder that the total valuation of an inventory may appear low without that implying squalid living conditions. But perhaps there was more to Pycroft than meets the eye; his will declares 'it is my will and my mynde that Alice my wife shall have the use and occupation of the coffer in the shoppe in the towne solonge as she will pay the shop rente'. It would be interesting to know what exactly that meant.

  John Dickenson and John Pycroft were probably typical of the small working weavers in Manchester, but another Pycroft is more difficult to place. This was William Pycroft, a linen weaver who died in 1588 and whose relationship to John Pycroft cannot be established. William owned a warpstock, reeds, shuttles and 'in the loumhouse 5 pairs of loumes'. He had yarn 'in the high chamber' valued at £4 7s and sacking valued at £3 6s. All this fitted into the picture of a linen weaver, but he also had woollen yarn worth 15s 8d and durance, a woollen cloth, worth £2 8s. This suggests that he combined linen and woollen weaving; this was unusual, but would have been possible with five looms, which is what '5 paire' means.[49] The looms in turn suggest an establishment that was bigger than was normal for a working weaver, who could not have operated them without assistance. It is perhaps significant that Pycroft called himself a linen webster in his will and was called a linen occupier in his inventory. Unlike Dickenson and John Pycroft, he combined weaving with some farming, for he had two cows and a stirk. His personal estate was valued at £57 15s 6d, of which £33 17s was for debts owing to him.

Above the level of the working weavers were men who combined weaving with other occupations such as dealing in yarn or shop-keeping. Thus William Sandforth, who died in 1598, was described as a linen draper in his will, but he did some farming and owned '3 payre of loowmes with furniture', 168 pounds of Irish yarn (valued at £19 12s), fourteen and a half pounds 'broken yarn and clewes' and two pieces of sackcloth. His supply of yarn hardly justifies the assumption that he was a yarn dealer, but his stock of linen (sheets, pillowcases, napkins etc.), though only valued at £4 19s, almost certainly represented the modest contents of his linen draper's shop. His personal property was valued at £77 10s 8d. On the other hand Robert Clough, a linen weaver who died in 1591, had 'loomes and reedes with their appertances' valued at £2, yarn valued at £60 19s 1d and cloth valued at only £3 0s 4d, which strongly suggests that he was dealing in yarn. His total personal property came to £100 4s 6d, including debts owing to him of £13 18s, of which unfortunately there are no details.

Some men operated in a more complex manner and on a larger scale than did Sandforth or Clough. Robert Birch, a linen draper who died in 1583, had '2 paire of lomes and a reale', 518 pounds flax valued at £9 9s 6d, yarn valued at £66 14s 1d and thirty-two broad pieces of linen, forty-six pieces of sackcloth and three bolster pieces valued at £96 2s. It is unlikely that Birch used so much yarn or produced so much cloth on his own looms. It is more likely that he sold flax to spinners and yarn to weavers, and bought much of his cloth. At his death he owed £117, all of it to members of his family (his mother, a daughter and two brothers); he was owed £285 10s 4d by some 130 debtors whose names alone were given. There is little doubt that some of these debts were for linen yarn or flax, and indeed Mr Lowe has traced half a dozen of the debtors and in each case the debtor 'was either a linen weaver or was connected in some way with the industry'.[50] Allowing for the debts he owed and was owed, Birch left a personal estate of £470 15s 2d. His inventory suggests that he lived rather modestly for one who was so well-to-do; even his nag was valued at only 26s 8d, but he had £96 13s 4d 'in ready money and gould', which may explain the lack of conspicuous consumption.

The big fortunes in linen were made, not by the manufacturers, but by the traders who dealt in flax, yarn and finished cloth. That was the case with Isabel Tipping whose husband Richard had been engaged in the linen trade until his death in 1592. Isabel inherited more than a third of her husband's personal property as well as an interest in his real property, and carried on the trade until her own death six years later.[51] She died a rich woman. Her goods included sackcloth at home valued at £263 and sackcloth in London valued at £128. Her stock of yarn, mostly white, was valued at £450. She had £471 17s 'in silver and gould'. Some of the entries of her inventory are illegible, but the value of the personal estate was at least £1500. Even this was surpassed by another linen dealer, Richard Nugent, who was described as 'of Manchester' though he lived in Salford. At his death in 1609 his personal estate was valued at £2344 and included canvas in London worth more than £200 and yarn at home worth about £127.[52]

There can have been few giants or giantesses like Richard Nugent and Isabel Tipping in the linen trade, but on a lesser scale some combined that trade with other occupations that had nothing to do with linen. James Bradshaw, who died in 1588, was described as a saddler in his will and in his inventory. The latter is unusual in merely summarising the contents of his rooms, but 'the shoppe wares' valued at £14 16s probably represent the saddlery. If so, they were worth much less than the Irish yarn, separately valued at £70. Clearly Bradshaw dealt in Irish linen, and his list of debtors shows that he sold some of it on credit. Thomas Shelmerdine of Ardwick and John Bradshaw of Gorseybank both owed for yarn. Bradshaw's total personal property was valued at £460, which included no less than £217 6s 11d in debts owing to him, £13 in money, £38 for three leases and £14 13s 4d for cattle and an acre of oats. Andrew Renshaw, who died in 1591, was given no occupation in his will or inventory, but the latter shows that he combined shoe-making with dealing in yarn. The shoemaking was represented by £4 for 'showes and bootes', 6s 4d for knives, 'worcke lowmes, bote treese and lastes', £1 for broken leather and 36s for whole hides. The yarn dealing was represented by £58 10s for three packs of yarn. Two and a half packs were at Blackley and Moston, perhaps for bleaching, and half a pack had been sold to John Shawcross for £10 payable 'at Bartholomew tyde next'. As Renshaw's personal estate came to £111 13s 2d, slightly more than half of it was represented by yarn. It may well have been the yarn rather than the boots and shoes and the 'grassing and cattell' (valued at £10 16s 4d) that sustained the modest comfort of the chamber, parlour and 'house' revealed by the inventory. Finally Robert Bridghouse, who was described as a joiner in both his will and his inventory, had 'yarne uppon the grasse' (i.e. being bleached) valued at £40 at the time of his death in 1593. This accounted for almost 40 per cent of his personal property which was valued at £102 11s 2d. It would be interesting to know whether it was the joinery or the yarn dealing that provided the comfort of a well furnished house with a 'house' or hall, three parlours, three chambers, kitchen, closet and 'yealehouse' where ale was brewed in quantities large enough to provide a stock valued at £1 3s.

Dealers in yarn seem to have been more important in the linen than in the woollen cloth industry. This arose from the nature and source of the linen yarn. Locally produced yarn had to be bleached, and this was often undertaken by the dealers who acted as middlemen between the spinners and weavers. The Irish yarn was presumably bleached before it was exported from Ireland, but this trade was very largely in the hands of Irish merchants for whom it was more convenient to sell by the pack than to sell in smaller quantities to weavers. Some Manchester merchants engaged in this trade, Richard Fox, for example, imported Irish linen yarn through both Liverpool and Chester between the 1560s and 1590s, but this simply meant that as a yarn dealer he was getting his supplies direct rather than through an Irish intermediary.[53] The importance of the yarn dealer is difficult to assess for his very presence may be concealed under some misleading occupational label. Outside the township but within the parish of Manchester, men who called themselves chapmen were engaged in the linen trade. Robert Brucke, a chapman of Rusholme who died in 1591, had yarn worth some £30 and pieces of sackcloth worth £17 6s 8d; he seems to have had no loom, though he did own some 'sacke reedes'. His debtors included George Travis who was described as a Manchester linen draper and may have been the Manchester clothier of that name. Another chapman, Edward Richardson of Ardwick, who also died in 1591, owned 'loomes and reades and their furnyture', two and a half packs of linen yarn 'lyinge at whytinge in the crofte' (valued at £42 1s 6d) and a further 135 pounds of white yarn. His cloth included ten 'sackcloth peeces'. He sold both yarn and cloth on credit, for John Whitworth, the younger, owed him £5 8s for six pieces of sackcloth at 18s the piece and 'uxor Christopher Kynler' owed £2 2s for white yarn. Insofar as these men were chapmen, it was in the general sense of chapmen as dealers; they were certainly not 'petty' chapmen. They both did some farming, and Brucke, whose personal estate came to £94 5s 2d, was a bee-keeper. Richardson's personal estate was valued at £161 12s 1d, which included £21 in 'readye money'.

Though the Manchester linen industry is in some ways better documented than the woollen industry, it is still difficult to be sure about the market for the linen cloth. Some linen was sent to London, usually by the big dealers,[54] but it is unlikely that London was as important a market for linen as it was for cottons. It is still more unlikely that the linen sent to London was destined for export. London imported continental linen on a large scale throughout this period. Lancashire linen cloth found a market in a wide range of provincial towns in central and eastern England,[55] and it is reasonable to assume that Manchester linen formed part of that trade. There is some evidence too of linen cloth going down the Severn valley. In 1592 two Manchester clothiers shipped some from Gloucester to Bristol[56] and a little later Edward Ellor was operating in the same area. Ellor's name first appeared in October 1585 when he was due to be sworn to the office of market looker for white meat and against his name was written, not *juratus*, but 'Bristoll', which Earwaker took, probably rightly, to mean that Ellor was then in Bristol.[57] Eight years later Ellor bought a burgage, consisting of a house and garden in Hanging Ditch, from Thomas Galley.[58] At his death in 1596 he held other property by leases valued at £93 7s 10d. His inventory shows that he was doing some farming; he had only one cow, but he had also 'a haye carte, a mucke cart and plowes and harrowes', which were unusual possessions for someone to whom farming was a side-line. For Ellor was some sort of a clothier though he was never described as such. His possessions included 'one warpinge stock and wales', two looms, sackcloth and yarn (together valued at £14), and some canvas, featherbed bolstering and 'red cloth'. All this would suggest a clothier engaged in the linen trade, but the list of debts 'owinge to the testator' shows that he also dealt in woollen cloth. Neither the domicile of the debtors nor the reason for the debts is always given, but the debts suggest that Ellor travelled a sort of western circuit extending from Kendal in the north to Salisbury and Sherborne in the south. Ellor was owed money by men in Kendal, Wigan, Heptonstall, Worcester, Gloucester, Bristol, Sherborne and Salisbury. At Worcester the landlord of The Sign of the Keys had 'in his custodye of mine which I left with him 8 peces of frize and a cottonne'. At Bristol Ellor had a chamber in an inn where he had left a coffer; he had also left eight and a half pieces of sackcloth with John Harrison of Bristol. It is not surprising that he should have owned two horses, saddles, packcloths, cords and 'woonetalls', which seem to have been ropes or cords used to fasten the pack on a packsaddle. It is more surprising that his stock should have included two and a half dozen scythes and six dozen 'sworde skalles'. It was probably Ellor's trading rather than his farming that accounted for his personal estate of £323 10s, nearly half of which was in debts owed to him.

Finally, apart from the long-distance trade in linen cloth, there was a local market in Manchester and its hinterland. Probate inventories bear witness to the widespread use of domestic linen in the form of sheets, pillowcases, napkins and so on. Such goods were sold by linen drapers like William Sandforth. Linen cloth by the yard or piece was sold by linen drapers and by mercers, though it is not possible to be sure that 'hollands' and canvas sold by mercers had not in fact been imported. Big country households like the Shuttleworths got some of their linen made by direct labour, but that is less likely to have happened in the towns.

The combination of the woollen and linen cloth industries stamped Manchester as very much a cloth town. These industries were the main, though not the only, road to riches. So long as cloth production remained a domestic industry it provided two different avenues to wealth. A clothier might prosper by operating a putting out system under which he put out wool to be spun and yarn to be woven in the workers' own homes, and then marketed the finished product. Such a system was common among the clothiers of Wiltshire, but there is no evidence that it operated in either the woollen or linen cloth industries in Manchester. There the other avenue was open, an avenue that was commercial rather than industrial, though it would be wrong to draw too fine a distinction between the two. Those who took that road might prosper through dealing in linen yarn and linen cloth or through finishing and marketing woollen cloth. Activities of this sort needed contact with a market, often a distant market, and with sources of supply which were usually nearer at hand. They made, or helped to make, a town into a regional centre where the urban production of cloth was supplemented by a rural industry which sought an outlet for its products in the town. The operations of clothiers and merchants suggest that Manchester was such a centre.

NOTES

[1] *C.L.R.*, ii, pp. 56, 63.

[2] *Ibid.*, i, p. 129. Rugs and cottons were woollen cloths.

[3] *Ibid.*, ii, p. 90.

[4] *V. C. H. Lancs.*, iv, p. 175.

[5] *C.L.R.*, ii, pp. 30, 145.

[6] *Registers*, p. 263.

[7] *C.L.R.*, i, pp. 263, 268.

[8] *Ibid.*, ii, p. 147; J. Tait, ed., *Taxation in Salford Hundred*, p. 72.

[9] *Registers*, p. 372; *C.L.R.*, ii, p. 216.

[10] L. A. Clarkson, 'The organization of the English leather industry in the late sixteenth and seventeenth centuries', *Econ. Hist. Rev.* 2nd series, xiii (1960), pp. 245–56.

[11] *Ibid.*, p. 254; D. M. Woodward, 'The Chester leather industry, 1558–1625', *Trans. Historic Soc. of Lancs. and Cheshire*, 119 (1967), p. 109.

[12] *C.L.R.*, i, 245n.1; *Registers*, p. 434.

[13] J. Tait, ed., *Lancashire Quarter Sessions records*, i, pp. 5, 112, 121; *Registers*, p. 274.

[14] Clarkson, *op. cit.*, p. 246.

[15] J. Tait, ed., *Lancashire Quarter Sessions records*, i, pp. 5, 112, 121; L.R.O. Inventory of Edward Ellor (1596).

[16] J. Tait, ed., *Lancashire Quarter Sessions records*, i, pp. 113, 246.

[17] Lowe, p. 17.

[18] G. D. B. Jones, *Roman Manchester*, pp. 143–57.

[19] *C.L.R.*, ii, pp. 50, 108, 164.

[20] *Ibid.*, ii, p. 60.

[21] *Ibid.*, ii, p. 113, 127; *Registers*, p. 322.

[22] L.R.O. Inventory of John Shaw (1581).

[23] G. H. Tupling, 'The early metal trades and the beginnings of engineering in Lancashire', *Trans. Lancs. and Cheshire Antiquarian Society*, lxi (1949), pp. 1–34.

[24] The best account is in Lowe.

[25] Lowe, p. 26.

[26] *Ibid.*, p. 27; *Registers*, p. 292.

[27] H. Heaton, *The Yorkshire woollen and worsted industries*, pp. 97–8.

[28] Lowe, p. 49.

[29] R. H. Tawney and E. Power, eds., *Tudor economic documents*, i, pp. 223–6; Lowe, p. 39.

[30] 39 Eliz. c. 20.

[31] Lowe, pp. 36–8.

[32] The value of the handles was 14*s*, which shows that the 'peece' was a dozen.

[33] For a nineteenth-century picture of shearing showing the wooden handles see W. H. Chaloner and A. E. Musson, *Industry and technology*, plate 186.

[34] Lowe, p. 36.

[35] J. Harland, ed., *The house and farm accounts of the Shuttleworths*, i, p. 39. Ch. S. xxxv (1856).

[36] Lowe, pp. 60, 91.

[37] B. C. Jones, 'Westmorland pack-horse men in Southampton, *Trans. Cumberland and Westmorland Antiquarian and Archaeological Society*, n.s. lix (1960), pp. 65–84.

[38] P.R.O. Exch. K.R. Port Books, 1128/14, 1243/5.

[39] D. M. Woodward, *The trade of Elizabethan Chester*, pp. 13, 15, 42; Lowe, pp. 75–8.

[40] Lowe, p. 79. The goad was one and a half yards.

[41] T. C. Mendenhall, *The Shrewsbury Drapers and the Welsh cloth trade in the XVI and XVII centuries*, Chs. II and III.

[42] Lowe, p. 60.

[43] *Ibid.*, pp. 71–2.

[44] J. P. Earwaker, ed., *Lancashire and Cheshire wills and inventories*, pp. 18–20. Ch. S., n.s. xxviii (1893).

[45] Lowe, p. 41.

[46] *Supra*, p. 53.

[47] Lowe, pp. 37, 40, 62.

[48] D. M. Woodward, *The trade of Elizabethan Chester*, pp. 7–9; Lowe, pp. 48–9.

[49] Lowe, pp. 101–2.

[50] *Ibid.*, pp. 54, 103–5.

[51] There is a contemporary copy of Richard's will in M.C.L. L1/28/8/1. His inventory has not survived.

[52] Lowe, p. 55; *C.L.R.* ii. 241, n.1.

[53] *Ibid.*, pp. 15–16.

[54] *Ibid.*, pp. 54–5.

[55] *Ibid.*, p. 58.
[56] *Supra* p. 56.
[57] *C.L.R.* i, p. 251.
[58] *Ibid.*, ii, p. 77.

CHAPTER V

THE TOWN ECONOMY: TRADE

The trade of an unincorporated town can never be fully assessed and described. For such a town there are no lists of freemen and no gild records to show, however inaccurately, the size of the different groups engaged in trade. For Manchester the absence of occupational descriptions in other sources merely makes the analysis of the town's traders more difficult and more incomplete. Yet it is possible to get some idea of the town's trade and of the men engaged in it. All retail trade in market towns was basically of two kinds; there was the periodic trade of the market and fair, to which should perhaps be added the periodic trade of the pedlar, and there was the permanent trade of the shopkeeper. Little is known about the activity of pedlars in Manchester, though Henry 'the cutler' whose goods were apparently distrained in May 1600 was presumably a pedlar. His stock of knives and their sheaths was carried in 'a large square boxe . . . with a locke uppon yt'.[1] Rather more is known about the market and the shopkeepers.

Manchester had an annual fair and a weekly market. Nothing is known about the trade of the fair, which was held on 20–22 September on the Acres Field, and the activities of the market are largely known from the attempts of the Court Leet to control them. The market was held on a Saturday, though in 1593 there is a curious reference to 'the two markett dayes in any weeke to wytte Saturdaye and Mundaye'.[2] There was obviously an attempt to forestall the Saturday market for in 1603 the Court Leet noted the inconveniencies and dangers that arose from some who kept a market in the open street every Friday for the sale of incle points, gartering, thread, buttons and other small wares. This was forbidden as prejudicial to the traders themselves and to the Saturday market. The prohibition was renewed in 1613 and then lifted the following year when it was said that the trading took place on Friday evening.[3] The time and the nature of the goods rather suggest that pedlars were involved and that they came to town on the Friday evening and did a bit of trading before market day.

The Court Leet was concerned with space as well as with time; it tried to confine market trading to the market place and some streets adjoining. Thus coopers, occupiers of wood ware and sellers of apples had their place about the conduit 'in the olde market place'; sellers of fish had their boards in the street called the Smithy Door, where the boards were to be set 'over the chanel', but they were not to stand 'anendes the dorre or wyndowes' of Ralph Sorocold's cellar so as to stop the light into it. Sorocold was a vintner.[4] Similarly those who sold bread in the market had to 'bringe theire breade unto the Smithie Doare to be soulde',[5] but the sellers of turnips, besoms and straw hats had to stand 'no higher in the streete then nowe the dwellinge howse of Edward Cuncliffe'.[6] References to the old market place imply that there was also a new one. It is possible that expanding trade was putting pressure on the areas allocated for stalls, for market traders seem to have been spreading out into the streets. In April 1596 it was reported that various foreigners had set their stalls 'affore dyverse shoppes in the towne to the greate hurte of the inhabitantes', and so they were ordered to 'place them in the oulde Market place'. The offenders included John Baxter of Rochdale and Ralph Gorton and Henry Shakeshafte, both of Warrington, which shows that the market could attract traders from eleven to eighteen miles away.[7]

The Court Leet was concerned not only with where stalls were placed, but also with the wholesomeness of the foodstuffs sold from them or from shops. To that end it appointed annually a number of officers including market lookers for corn, fish and flesh, and white meat, 'officers for holesome breade', aletasters and 'officers for fruytes'.[8] There is little evidence of their activities except that in 1566 Thomas Siddall was fined 8d 'for sellinge unlawfull motton'.[9] Thomas was probably the son of Richard Siddall, a yeoman of Withington who died in 1558 leaving a shop in Market Street to his elder son Edward and lands in Moston to his younger son Thomas.[10] It was necessary to ensure, not only that food was wholesome, but also that it was available in the market. Many Acts of Parliament had tried to deal with this problem by forbidding forestalling, which was really intercepting supplies before they reached the market, and regrating, which was buying in order to sell again in the same or in a nearby market.[11] Such offences were dealt with by Quarter Sessions, but the Court Leet made its own orders about them and punished those who disobeyed. Thus in 1563 it amerced three women and two men for 'for-staling the market' and in 1566 six men for the same offence.[12] Regrating in various forms was forbidden by the Court Leet. In 1585 no stranger not inhabiting within the town was to buy apples or other fruit before nine a.m. and was not 'to retayle any beinge boughte of the same daye', and no 'inhabitor within the towne' was to buy apples or other fruit and 'sell them by whole sall of the same day' or 'by any color' buy any for any stranger. The penalty was forfeiture of the fruit, two-thirds going to the lord of the manor and one-third to the informer.[13] In 1586 no butcher or other person was to buy flesh, fish or other victual within the town 'by grosse' and sell the same by retail the same day on penalty of 10s. Later this restriction was applied to any butter, cheese or other white meat.[14]

Forestalling was discouraged by insisting that goods should be bought and sold in the open market. In 1591 it was decreed that no one should buy any fruit except on the market day 'and in the oppen markett'; inhabitants of the town were not to buy before nine a.m. and strangers not before ten a.m. Similarly no one was to buy any corn or grain within the town 'but in the open markett', and was not to 'sell the same corne or grayne so boughte in the towne at any tyme hereafter'.[15] Much of this was an attempt to check the growing practice of private trade, which threatened to undermine the older ideal of public trade in the market.[16] A decree of the Court Leet in 1595 must be seen in that light. It stated that no one 'shall sett any corne, in any house, uppon the Marketday but shall bringe the sayde corne into the open markett . . . and shall nether open any sacke, nor make any pryce of the sayd corne and grayne, untill the market bell be runge'. Those who brought grain to the market and were left with any unsold, were not to set any of the corn or grain left unsold 'in any howse, shoppe or warehouse, within the same towne, but shall carye the sayde corne and grayne so leffte unsolde, forthe of the sayde towne of Manchester' under pain of 20s.[17]

The regulations suggest the obvious fact that the weekly market was the occasion for buying agricultural produce, much of which had been brought in from the surrounding countryside. The besoms and straw hats were probably country products too, and the buttons and small wares were perhaps intended to catch the countrywoman's eye, but these were in the nature of frills. The real business of the market was the buying and selling of provisions. There is no method of measuring this trade, but in the case of one group of traders, the butchers, it is possible to get some idea of their numbers.

When Nicholas Mosley charged rents for butchers' stalls in 1599 they were recorded in detail in the rental of 1599–1600, which distinguished between native butchers who paid $\frac{1}{2}d$ a week per stall and the foreign butchers who paid 1d. In both cases a butcher sometimes held two stalls. In the ten weeks ending at Midsummer 1599, twenty-three native butchers paid rent for thirty-three stalls and six-teen foreign butchers paid rent for seventeen stalls. In the following six months to Christmas 1599 there was some decline in numbers to twenty natives (twenty-nine stalls) and to thirteen foreigners (four-teen stalls). Finally in the period from Christmas 1599 to 25 March 1600 the native butchers maintained their numbers (twenty-one with thirty stalls) while the foreign butchers declined to eight with one stall each. These fluctuations do not lend any support to the old-fashioned view of wholesale autumn slaughtering of cattle. The figures raise the interesting and largely unanswerable questions of who exactly were these butchers and why were there so many of them. Nothing is known about the foreign butchers except that one of them, Robert Potter, was from Stockport. Little is known about the natives either. Robert Barlow, who paid rent for two stalls, was clearly the Robert Barlow, junior, who had been ordered to remove his stall or flesh board in 1597.[18] He may have been the son of Robert Barlow, a butcher who in 1592–3 owned half a burgage in Millgate containing two tenements in the tenure of himself and Henry Wharmby. The Wharmbys were a family of butchers two of whom, the widows of John and Henry Wharmby, held four stalls in 1599. They may have been related through their late husbands to Robert Wharmby, a butcher who died in 1592. Robert left his real and personal property to his wife Joan having 'heretofore preferred all my children in marryage, and that with better portions then they coulde have nowe by my deathe' and having left Joan 'to discharge greate somes of money'. In fact he owed £13 4s, including 4s for a calf, and was owed £2 4s 8d, including 20s by Robert Hulme, gent., 'for fleshe'. His goods (excluding debts) were valued at only £23 8s 7d and they include nothing that suggests a butcher's shop. It is tempt-ing to assume that John and Henry had been his sons and that he had 'preferred' them by handing over four stalls which had then passed to their widows. If that were so, John had prospered, for he was the well-to-do butcher and farmer who died in 1598.[19]

Other stallholders of 1599 can be identified as butchers and presumably they had shops as well as stalls. Edward Dyson, a but-cher who died in 1598, had 'twoe standinge fleshebordes in the market' valued at £4, but he had also 'waies, ropes and other shop geare', though they were valued at only 2s 6d. Dyson apparently died childless for, apart from some small bequests, he left all his personal property to his wife Ellen, who does not seem to have carried on her late husband's business. The personal property was valued at £34, and the inventory shows a comfortably furnished house with two chambers and two parlours, all of them containing beds.

The nature of the stallholders of 1599 is less interesting than their numbers. How, in the summer of 1599, did a place the size of Manchester provide the customers for thirty-nine butchers trading from fifty stalls? If the customers were confined to the inhabitants of the township, this might give an average of about a dozen households per butcher, which would not make much sense. In fact the market must have drawn its customers, as it did its suppliers, from a much wider area than Manchester itself. Mosley's opponents, who claimed that 'the whole countrey rounde abowte doe weekely repayre for there provision of victualls' to the flesh shambles, may well have been right.[20] Even so, the number of butchers and their stalls still seems remarkable in a period when so much stress has been laid on declining standards of living.

The difference between market trading and shopkeeping was not simply that the former was periodic and the latter continuous, but that in general they dealt with different sorts of goods though there was, of course, some overlapping. Basically markets dealt in native foodstuffs, and shops sold manufactured goods and imported foodstuffs. As a shopping centre Manchester possessed a number of shops which ranged from the specialised to the more general store. At this period the most specialised shops were usually those of the craftsman retailer who sold the goods he had produced. James Bradshaw, the saddler who also dealt in linen yarn, had a shop in which he presumably sold his saddlery, and Andrew Renshaw, a shoemaker and dealer in yarn, had a stock of boots and shoes valued at £4.[21] Both these men did some farming, and so too did Ottiwell Hodgkinson, a shoemaker who died in 1588. He had two cows, a calf, a mare and hay, together valued at £8 4s. For shoemaking there were one and a half dickers of leather (valued at £7 13s 4d) and the tools of his trade (boot trees, lasts, knives, shaving irons etc.), valued at 13s 4d. His stock of shoes was meagre, only six pairs valued at 8s, but Roger Bexwick owed him 7s 4d for a pair of boots and three pairs of shoes and was in turn owed 3s 4d 'for 20 stone of haye'. Rather surprisingly a William Gost owed 9s for a Bible. Hodgkinson had a 'certaine of yorne' valued at £1 15s 4d, but that seems rather a small stock for ranking him as a yarn dealer. His personal estate came to £87 13s, one-third of which he left, by a nuncupative will, to his seven children. He seems to have lived in as much comfort as such a family would permit. There was a well furnished house of three chambers, a hall, a parlour and a buttery; there was pewter valued at £2 6s 8d, a stock of provisions (butter, cheese, beef and flitches of bacon), valued at £2 1s 8d, and even a Bible and other books valued at 13s 4d.

The craftsmen retailers were not confined to the leather crafts.

They included goldsmiths like Robert Walshman who died in 1598. Walshman was a working goldsmith; apparently childless, he left 3s 4d and 'my iron tooles and the harthe' to Martin, son of 'my olde dame Edwarde Carvers wyffe' to whom he also left 3s 4d. His stock of silverware, some 100 ounces in all, was valued at £23 11s 10d and included salts, plates, bowls, a tankard and a beaker. In addition there were silver filings and old silver valued at £3 13s, broken gold valued at £3 15s and 'oulde silver sente to London by John Hardye which he is to paye at his cummynge home £11 odde money I saye'. John Hardy was the carrier who had taken the old silver to London. The probate valuations show how much of the cost of silverware was represented by the raw material; old silver was valued at 4s an ounce, the silverware at 4s 8d and 5s the ounce. Walshman's inventory also shows his activity as a moneylender or pawnbroker, for it includes a list of 'pawnes whereon money is lente'. They were a curious collection. Robert Buckley had pawned 'an Arras coveringe' for £2, John Assheton, gent., a brass pot for 7s and a gold ring for 2s, Adam Hulme of Warrington four spoons, a salt and a goblet for £6, Mr William Radcliffe of the Conduit four spoons for £1, Adam Hulles a hat for 1s, and an unspecified depositor a sword and a dagger for 7s. One borrower was forgiven his debt, for in his will Walshman ordered his executrix (his wife Alice) to deliver to James Bradshaw 'the gowne which he hathe layde to pawne without receyvinge any parte of the money which the saide James oweth me'. Other debts owed to Walshman were recorded in his 'debte booke', and given in the inventory. Most of them seem to have been straightforward loans of money, though John Warrington had been lent a gold ring price 12s, and some unspecified borrowers had apparently been lent malt, rye, barley and 'a cowe to gyve mylke'. These loans came to £20 3s. The personal estate was valued at £128 15s 10d, which included £34 15s in cash. Walshman had a fairly impressive wardrobe valued at about £6; he employed two maidservants, to whom he left 6s 8d and 2s respectively, but his house, whose rooms were not specified, was modestly furnished. It contained a reasonable stock of pots, pans and pewter, and the inevitable featherbeds, but the total household goods were valued at only a little over £11. Some men who were less well off than Walshman, lived in houses better furnished than his. It is not known whether Walshman was the only goldsmith in Manchester in the 1590s. An earlier goldsmith, Robert Marler who died in 1582, seems to have left no son to succeed him in the business.

The craftsman retailer with his specialised and sometimes small stock of goods is usually easy to describe and classify, but it is sometimes difficult to tell whether the draper falls into this category. Was

William Sandforth's small stock of linen made on his own looms and how much of Robert Birch's cloth had he himself made?[22] It is impossible to say, but the draper seems to have been the most specialised of the shopkeepers dealing in cloth. He was specialised in the sense, not that he confined himself to one sort of cloth, but that he confined himself to cloth. William Awyn, who died in 1590, was a draper of this type. At his death Awyn had in stock only cloth and only about four kinds of it, though in a variety of colours. The most important kind was kersey in a range of colours which included white, black, grey, blue, green and 'sheepe couler'. There was some frieze in black, white, grey and red, sixty-seven yards of cottons in black, white and yellow, and four yards of 'blacke gladen'. The entire stock was valued at £17 16s 10d, which was rather more than half the total valuation of goods of £31 6s 10d. Much cloth had been sold on credit. Awyn was owed £17 7s 3d, most of it for cloth; he owed £8 16s, of which £2 9s was owed to Thomas Holme 'Kendallman'. Thus his personal estate was valued at £39 18s 1d. There is no evidence that he possessed any real property, but his will, which might have revealed some, has not survived. As he had a quite valuable cow, it is reasonable to assume that he had some pasturage for her, but that may have been leased. His own domestic circumstances were modest, but there were at least two parlours, a chamber and a 'house' or hall as well as the shop and a cellar.

The Manchester haberdasher may also have dealt in a very limited range of goods, but the evidence for this is scanty. The most notable and the only documented Manchester haberdasher was George Clarke, who can hardly have been typical. In 1598 Clarke, already described as a haberdasher, was apparently employed by Lawrence Perrin, haberdasher, to whom he was bound in a surety of £100 to pay for any goods he had 'credited and trusted forthe ... without the lycence and consente of the sayde Lawrence Perryn'. Two years later Clarke was formally bound as 'a covenanted or hyred servante' to Perrin for four years in return for meat, drink, lodging, washing (apparel excepted) and £5 p.a. Later still Clarke set up as a haberdasher, leasing a shop in the street called the Smithy Door; perhaps he was helped by his marriage in 1609 to Alice, daughter of Ralph Gee and sister-in-law of Charles Worsley, gent., of Platt in Rusholme. Clarke certainly prospered. In 1636 he conveyed property worth £100 p.a. in trust for the poor of Manchester. He died the following year still in business as a haberdasher. His inventory shows that he sold only hats, hat bands and hat facings of velvet and that his stock in trade was worth less than £20. It was a misleadingly modest stock, for in fact Clarke left a personal estate of £2982 16s 1d, which included £745 2s 4d in silver and gold and

£2067 9s in debts owing to him and in money 'laid out'. Half this personal property went to his wife Alice who died in January 1638. Her personal property was valued at £1458 11s 3d, which included £8 11s 8d for hats in the shop, but it is difficult to believe that wealth on this scale had been accumulated solely from selling hats.[23]

To pass from the Manchester draper or haberdasher to the Manchester mercer was to enter a different sort of shop, where the choice of goods was wider and the range of prices greater. In general mercers no longer sold only mercery; they usually combined mercery with grocery wares and often with stationery as well, but in declining order of importance for mercery remained their chief line. This can be illustrated by the stocks held by three Manchester mercers at their deaths in the 1580s. John Shaw, mercer, who died in 1581, had his mercery wares in hampers, the contents of each being valued separately by the appraisers. They included a variety of cloths: Bustian, buffin, canvas, camlet, calico, holland, 'levin taffytie',[24] mockado and sackcloth. There was silk by the ounce and silk lace, points and fringe; statute lace and thread laces, incle and leather points and brass, thread and glass buttons; Coventry blue thread and French garters. The local, or the Chester, leather industry may have been represented by the gloves (tufted, wrought or fine) and by the five dozen purses. The 3500 Manchester pins should have come from a local industry too, but they were less important than other pins elaborately classified by numbers from three to seven, the higher the number the more valuable the pins. A bare and partial recital hardly does justice to Shaw's stock of mercery wares, which was quite impressive. It was certainly more impressive and more valuable than his stock of groceries. This was meagre, consisting of a little pepper, cloves, ginger and bays (probably bay leaves or berries) and rather more currants, raisins, prunes, candles and soap and '2 dossen of refuse licorys'. As usual with groceries, most of the things had been imported. The stationery 'department' was more meagre still. It comprised some 'pen and incke hornes', three quires of writing paper, and the inexplicable 'four papers of the Kings'. Even if the three dozen 'of halfe peny ware', curiously valued at 1s, and the six dozen 'bow stringes' could be classified as stationery, it would not amount to much.

Shaw's total stock of shop goods was valued at £87 12s 1d compared with £46 7s for his household goods, his five swine, his horse and his lease of a house in Millgate. According to his will Shaw owed £28 19s 2d and was owed £8 3s 2d, some of it apparently for groceries. Thus his total personal estate was valued at £113 3s 1d. Apart from leaving 'a dublet, a jirkyn and a paire of hose' to his father, Roger Shaw, Shaw left his property to his wife Joan and his seven children, some or all of whom seem in fact to have been step children.

The other two mercers, Thomas Hardman and Edward Hanson, operated on a larger scale than Shaw for they each had two shops. Hardman, who died towards the end of 1583, had a shop in Manchester where he sold much mercery, less groceries and very little that could be called stationery. His inventory shows a good stock of cloth, chiefly taffeta, mockado, canvas, durance, holland and various sorts of continental fustian. Some of the cloth was very costly: velvet valued at 21s a yard and taffeta and satin at 12s. Silk was costly too, with 'Bolonya silkes' at 18s a pound, 'silk lacis' at 25s a pound and 'collored stichinge' at 27s a pound. Even these were outdone by the Venice gold (gold thread) at 5s 4d an ounce. There was a bewildering range of lace and laces, some 'knite hose', gloves and the usual French garters and pins. The grocery wares seem largely concealed under the heading 'grosre in one chest £9 17s', but there was also soap, currants and galls. The stationery had shrunk to some reams of paper unless the 'primuars' valued at 7s were school primers. The contents of the shop were valued at £293 13s 3d. Hardman had also a warehouse which contained 'salterie and grosere', logwood, paper, gunpowder and a vast stock of hats, some described as hats and some as felts. There were just over 300 hats, which suggests that Hardman may have been a wholesaler as well as a retailer, and indeed two of his debtors were hatters. The stock in the warehouse was valued at £73 7s 6d. Finally there was a shop in Warrington with the same sorts of cloth (including 'Norwiche chamlet'), lace, buttons and other mercery. It too had some groceries (including ten pounds of white sugar) and paper. Its contents were valued at £223 7s 11d. Hardman's stock of goods in his Manchester shop, his warehouse and his Warrington shop were valued at £590 8s 8d, to which should be added £12 4s 8d for 'grosserie in the howce and at London'. Thus his stock came to over £600 which was a very high figure for a provincial shopkeeper. His remaining goods, including three horses, two cows, two pigs and £25 10s for leases, came to £148 5s, making a grand total of £750 18s 4d.

It is an impressive total, but unfortunately there were the debts. Hardman owed £608 12s 3d to fourteen creditors. The reason for these debts is not stated, but the biggest of them, for £200, was owed to Ralph Sorocold, presumably the merchant of that name who died in 1593. In his will Sorocold referred to his goods in England which implied that he had assets abroad, so perhaps he had been supplying Hardman with imported wares. On the other hand Hardman was owed £309 0s 8d (ignoring the desperate debts of £90 14s 11½d). The long list of debtors gives hardly any clue to the reason for these debts, though William Napton and Thomas Sewell of London owed £54 16s 8d for five packs of cottons, and Richard Awyn owed for some cloth and a pair of hose. If the desperate debts are ignored as irrecoverable, then Hardman's personal estate was worth £451 6s 9d. Apart from bequests amounting to £6, he left his estate to his wife Joan and their five children. His rather chaotic inventory does not give any clear impression of his house, but it was well furnished and contained ample linen, eighty-eight pieces of pewter and fifty ounces of plate.

The last member of the trio of mercers, Edward Hanson, died in July 1584. His inventory is much decayed, so that some entries are missing and some are illegible. It shows a shop in Manchester with the usual mercery wares of cloth, lace, thread, pins, hose and buttons. This stock of mercery was smaller and less varied than Hardman's, but Hanson's stock of groceries may have been larger than Hardman's and was certainly given in a more detailed form. It presents a better picture of what an Elizabethan could buy from a provincial grocer. Spices were represented by ginger, pepper, mace, cloves, aniseed and nutmeg; sweetening by sugar, 'browne candie' and treacle; dried fruits by currants; medicine or drugs by liquorice, brimstone, wormseed, arsenic, verdigris, argol (for making cream of tartar) and fenugreek; the cloth industry by alum and the dyestuffs, galls, madder, logwood and 'fernando' (brazil). Finally there was soap (some of it Castile), wax, potash and onion seeds. Most of these things were imported and some, like pepper, mace and cloves, were expensive. Hanson can scarcely be said to have had a stationery department in his shop, but he did stock some paper, three books, unfortunately not described, and a 'recignis . . . of the eagle and child'.[25] Hanson also had a shop in Bolton which had a stock of mercery wares, some groceries and some books (valued at 1s 6d). Because of the state of the inventory, the total value of his personal property cannot be determined, but it was at least £391, which included £154 in money and £101 8s 6d in 'obligacions and billes'. The latter apparently included £64 10s for six packs of cottons which had been sold to William Napton, William Woodcock and Thomas Sewell, citizens and grocers of London.[26] Thus both Hardman and Hanson seem to have combined their retailing with selling cottons for the London market and selling them largely to the same men.

Inventories give a good picture of the sort of goods a shopkeeper stocked, but they give little idea of the number of shopkeepers in the town. Between 1585 and 1600 there were at least eight mercers and five drapers in Manchester for whom no inventories survive. The surviving inventories show that Manchester mercers kept a good stock of mercery, a much smaller stock of groceries and a still smaller supply of stationery. This combination of goods made their shops much less specialised than those of the craftsman retailers or the drapers and haberdashers, but it did not quite make them into general stores. The main missing element was ironmongery or hardware. There is no trace in Manchester of an ironmonger so described, but labels are deceptive in this period as the case of John Billing shows. Billing, who died in 1588, was described in his will as a glazier, and indeed he was a glazier. In his workshop was 'his vice to drawe leade and other workelomes' valued at £1 and five cases of glass valued at £6, and Mr Richard Hunt and 'my Lord of Derbie' owed him for glass. The widespread use of window glass, which inventories reveal, should have provided adequate work for a glazier, but Billing had another shop in which he sold a curious mixture of things. These included trenchers, 'earthen potts', paper, logwood, alum, yarn, incle, garters and points, but his main stock was in hardware. This included 330 pounds of 'newe brasse panns of baterie' at £5 8s a hundredweight, 202 pounds of kettles at £4 13s a hundredweight, sixty-five pounds of 'ketles bannded with iron', 237 pounds of new brass pots, thirty-four pounds of frying pans, 122 pounds of 'newe pewter dishes, platters and voyders' at 7d a pound, sixty-five pounds of pewter cans, bowls, pots and porringers at 9d a pound, and thirteen pounds of 'quartes, pintes and one chamber pot' at 6d a pound. There was also brass and iron wire, two dozen chafing dishes, thirty-four candlesticks and a good amount of scrap metal in old pewter, old brass and old iron. Billing also had a shop in Rochdale where he stocked the same sort of metal goods but in much smaller quantities. His stock there included an unusual item, '9 spones of copper' valued at 1s.

As if that this were not enough for one man, Billing had '7 wevynge loomes', valued at only 1s each, which suggests that they were for weaving incle, for he had 'yncle in London' valued at £16. He had also a cow, a horse and some hay. He certainly seems to have prospered among it all, for his personal property was valued at £325 9s 11d. This included £105 3s 2½d for debts owing to him. The nature of these is rarely apparent, but ten of the debtors were Wigan men which suggests some link with the Wigan pewter industry.[27] His debtors included Lord Derby, Sir Edmund Trafford and Sir John Radcliffe, so he had his share of the carriage trade in debts. Billing lived in some style with an exceptional quantity of household linen, twenty-eight ounces of plate, and apparel 'for his owne bodie' valued at £8 7s. It is doubtful whether this style could be maintained by his widow and his eight children (and one unborn) to whom his goods were left.

The stocks held by Manchester shopkeepers, and especially the mercers, imply a demand for manufactured goods and imported foodstuffs that ranged from the necessaries of life to expensive luxuries. Some of that demand came from within Manchester as the apparel, linen, pewter and plate of the inventories show, but it is doubtful whether a place the size of Manchester could itself generate sufficient demand to absorb the amount and range of goods available in its shops. It is more probable that both the market stalls and the shops drew their customers from a wider area than the township itself. Yet the nature and extent of a town's economic hinterland are difficult to establish, and they are especially difficult in the case of Manchester, where there were no out-burgesses to provide evidence of a market area as they were at Preston,[28] and no lists of apprentices which might show country boys coming in to learn a trade as they do for Bristol and some of the London livery companies. Indeed the latter show an occasional Manchester boy going up to London to be apprenticed like Samuel Proudlove, son of George Proudlove of Manchester, yeoman, who was apprenticed to William Cockayne, Skinner and Merchant Adventurer of London, for ten years in 1589. Ten years later, Samuel, now a Skinner and Merchant Adventurer, was himself taking an apprentice, but not from Manchester.[29] Nor can much be learned by approaching this problem from the angle of the country customer himself, for that depends on the survival of household accounts which reveal his shopping habits. Here the only relevant accounts are those of the Shuttleworths when they were living at Smithills near Bolton.

The Shuttleworths bought goods at a great many places, including London, but their purchases in Manchester were small. Towards the end of 1582 they bought some spices there for 6s 10d, and in January 1584 4d was 'spent in Manchester when one was sent thither to bespeake for a light saddell'. The saddle with bridle, cropper, and stirrup leathers with iron, costing 16s in all, was collected the following month. Later in the year the position was reversed when William Birchall was sent to Manchester to sell onions, of which he sold twenty-six ropes at 1d a rope. His expenses were 3d. Servants normally received from 2d to 4d on their trips to Manchester, but the family spent more lavishly. In May 1588 7s 3d was spent in Manchester when the display of the light horse and demilances was 'shouede before the lyffetenannce there', and in August, Thomas Shuttleworth spent 4s 8d for a day and a night there. The following year £4 14s 9d was paid for a quarter pack of Irish yarn 'and a pounde more', and in 1590 £5 8s was paid for two steers, which was an unusual purchase, for the Shuttleworths normally bought their cattle almost anywhere but Manchester. It may be one sign that a town was a regional centre when it had a doctor who was worth consulting. In 1592 when Sir Richard Shuttleworth was unwell, 6s 8d was paid to Thomas Cogan, physician and High Master of the Grammar School, 'for his advicesse for fisike' and a further 6s 8d for the physic itself.[30] Desultory purchases in Manchester continued; some silk and lace in 1593, halters for horses, a little wine and twelve 'kyne feet' and twenty-eight 'calffe feete' in 1594, and more wine and ropes in 1596.[31] Even allowing for the fact that the printed Shuttleworth accounts are very incomplete, they do not suggest that Manchester was the Shuttleworths' favourite shopping centre.

If little can be learned about Manchester as a regional centre from the shopping habits of the Shuttleworths, rather more can be learned from the debts owed to the shopkeepers. Unfortunately these debts are often recorded without the domicile of the debtor or the reason for the debt. Where the domicile is given it is often impossible to tell whether the debt represented goods bought on credit or money lent. However, both forms of debt involve some economic contact or relationship between creditor and debtor, and it is the geographical spread of such contracts or relationships that helps to delineate an economic hinterland. The most useful list of debts for this purpose is that of the draper William Awyn. He was owed money for cloth from customers in many places within the parish, including Moss Side, Trafford, Gorton, Ordsall, Chorlton, Broughton, Stretford, Salford and Rusholme. Outside the parish he had debtors at Carrington and Mottram in Cheshire, and at Clifton and Pendleton in Lancashire. Other lists of debts show a similar, though sometimes wider, distribution. Thus the mercer, Thomas Hardman, had debtors within the parish and at Rochdale, Blackburn, Lancaster, Rossendale, Bolton, Burnley and Preston in Lancashire, at Ripon, Holmfirth, Skipton and Ossett in Yorkshire, and at Knutsford and Congleton in Cheshire. John Billing's debtors extended as far north as Preston, and included a number in Cheshire at Altrincham, Handforth, Stockport, Sale, Baguley and Cholmondeley. Borrowers in north Cheshire towns also appear among James Bradshaw's debtors. Similarly John Birch, an innholder who died in about 1591, had debtors in Sale, Peover and Bowdon.

No doubt debts usually represented goods bought on credit or money borrowed, but they could also represent a service provided on credit, as the case of Isabel Barlow shows. Isabel was the widow of Robert Barlow, a smith who was probably the householder of that name who died in July 1587.[32] Robert seems to have left his widow comfortably provided for, and he also left her his 'booke' of the debts owing to him. Isabel died in October 1594 owning household goods, a cow and a calf and the lease of a field together valued at £31 13s 8d. She was owed £60 14s 1d of which at least £22 was owed for 'showing' or 'shoing', in other words for shoeing horses or oxen. The men who owed for shoeing were spread out over the parish of Manchester and extended beyond it, to places like Altrincham, Carrington, Sale and Baguley in Cheshire and Flixton, Ashton on Mersey and Barton in Lancashire. The size of some of the debts suggests that men had their horses shod regularly in Manchester. James Wood of Withington owed 22s 4d and Oliver Barlow of Sale 37s 5d. Such sums must have represented a lot of shoeing, for the Shuttleworths seem to have paid 7d to have a horse or an ox shod.[33] It would be interesting to know whether other craftsmen gave such extended credit as Barlow or his widow seem to have done.

The evidence of debts suggests that Manchester retailers and merchants found a market for their goods and their money not only in the township but also in the sixty square miles of the parish. It is more difficult to say how far beyond the parish boundary such contacts extended, but they clearly reached across the Mersey into north Cheshire and northwards, eastwards and westwards into the parishes bordering the parish of Manchester. This gave Manchester a market area comparable with Preston's which had an inner zone extending from seven to twelve miles and a more irregular outer zone that could extend to twenty miles.[34] Such an area would help to explain the large number of butchers' stalls in Manchester's market and the stocks held by the shopkeepers. Manchester's role as a regional centre was combined with her role as a cloth town which involved her in the long distance trade in cloth. It was this combination that largely accounted for the wealth of the place.

NOTES

[1] *C.L.R.*, ii, p. 170.
[2] *Ibid.*, ii, p. 78.
[3] *Ibid.*, ii, pp. 189, 278, 295.
[4] *Ibid.*, i, pp. 121, 128.
[5] *Ibid.*, ii, p. 145.
[6] *Ibid.*, i, p. 201.
[7] *Ibid.*, ii, pp. 107, 122.
[8] *Ibid.*, ii, pp. 149–52.
[9] *Ibid.*, i, p. 263.
[10] *Ibid.*, i, p. 42; J. Booker, ed., *A history of the ancient chapel of Birch*, pp. 124–7, Ch.S. xlvii (1859).
[11] 5/6 Edw. VI, c. 14.
[12] *C.L.R.*, i, pp. 263–4.
[13] *Ibid.*, i, p. 254.
[14] *Ibid.*, i, p. 259, ii, p. 130.
[15] *Ibid.*, ii, p. 57.
[16] J. Thirsk, ed., *The agrarian history of England*, iv, pp. 506–63.

[17] *C.L.R.*, ii, p. 101.

[18] *Ibid.*, ii, p. 123.

[19] *Supra* pp. 44–5.

[20] *Supra* p. 15.

[21] *Supra* p. 60.

[22] *Supra* p. 59.

[23] M.C.L. MS. M 35/5/1/2–6, 12–15, MS. M35/1/16/1; *C.L.R.*, iii, pp. 301–14. Clarke's charity still exists (G. B. Hindle, *Provision for the relief of the poor in Manchester 1754–1826*, pp. 134–5, Ch.S. 3rd. ser. xxii. 1975).

[24] Levant taffeta.

[25] Perhaps meaning a copy of a badge; the eagle and child was the crest of the Stanleys.

[26] *C.L.R.*, i, p. 245 n.l. where the information is taken from Hanson's will which is no longer extant.

[27] They included William Bankes of Wigan who may have been the pewterer of that name (R. J. A. Shelley, 'Wigan and Liverpool pewterers', *Trans. Historic Soc. of Lancs. and Cheshire*, xcvii (1946), p. 22.

[28] H. B. Rodgers, 'The market area of Preston in the sixteenth and seventeenth centuries', *Geographical Studies*, iii (1956), pp. 46–55.

[29] *Miscellanea genealogica et heraldica*, ed. J. J. Howard, 3rd ser., i, pp. 78, 247.

[30] For Cogan see 'Thomas Cogan, the students' physician', *The Palatine Notebook*, iii (1883), pp. 77–84, 131–6, 149–51.

[31] J. Harland, ed., *The house and farm accounts of the Shuttleworths* i, pp. 5, 13, 20–2, 45–6, 55, 58, 72–3, 81, 89, 100–1, 105–6. Ch.S. xxxv (1856).

[32] *Registers*, p. 258.

[33] J. Harland, ed., *op. cit.*, i, pp. 76, 139, 149.

[34] H. B. Rodgers, *op. cit.*, pp. 50–5.

CHAPTER VI

WEALTH AND FAMILY

Elizabethan towns showed great unevenness in the distribution of wealth among their citizens, but it is not clear that urban wealth was always closely equated with status. The conventional grading of society into nobles, knights, esquires, gentlemen, yeoman, husbandmen and labourers was more appropriate to the countryside than to the towns, which had their own distinctions between natives and foreigners and between those who were freemen and those who were not. Manchester distinguished between natives and foreigners, as the market regulations show, but as an unincorporated town it had no freemen. This did not mean that, within the manorial structure, no distinctions were drawn. The Court Leet certainly made distinctions, though it is difficult to tell what exactly they meant. On 1 October 1561 the Court Leet imposed graduated fines on those who failed to attend the Court; knights were to pay 2s, 'the squires' 12d, gentlemen 8d and 'the others' 6d. This was the conventional grading, and it seems to have been found inappropriate. In 1569 'thos which owe apparance at this courte and have not appered' were to show reasonable cause why they were absent or 'be amercied for this tyme the fre houlders in 12d, the burgeses in 6d, thinhabitantes 2d'. This was reaffirmed the following year, but in 1573 'forren freeholders' were to pay 12d. It is doubtful whether foreign freeholders attended the court, and this distinction seems to have been dropped for in 1577 freeholders were to be fined 2s and burgesses 6d, and there was no mention of the 'inhabitants'. It is possible that the 'inhabitants' emerged under a new name in 1595 when the fine on burgesses was raised to 12d and 'everye burges tenante' was to pay 6d for non-attendance.[1] The distinction between the burgess and the 'burges tenante' was logical enough, but it is not clear why the latter owed attendance at court. Indeed the Court Leet itself seems to have believed that a 'tenant for yeres' was under no obligation to do suit and service.[2] Nothing more is heard of the burgess tenant as a separate category, for in 1601 the Court Leet reverted to a classification which combined the categories of 1561 and 1569. The fines for non-attendance were then fixed at 3s 4d for an esquire, 2s for a gentleman, 1s for a burgess and 4d for 'everye inhabitante'.[3] It is impossible to tell what these distinctions meant in terms of wealth or, in some cases, in terms of social status. In an urban setting they may have meant very little, except in providing further proof of the contemporary practice of seeing society in hierarchical terms. Great inequality existed, but this may be seen more closely in the distribution of wealth than in the rather arbitrary distribution of social grades.

Manchester conformed to the general pattern of Elizabethan towns by displaying great inequality in the distribution of wealth among its inhabitants. The crude statistics of probate inventories show that personal property varied from £1 13s, to over £1500. The former was the exceptional case of Arthur Kershaw, the yeoman who seems to have been swindled out of his property; the latter was the case of that wealthy widow, Isabel Tipping, who carried on her late husband's business as a dealer in linen yarn and cloth. The more usual lower limit for inventories was £10 to £15, and there are very few below that level. There is no doubt that poor people existed, but neither the Court Leet, whose records survive, nor the church-wardens, whose records are lost, throw much light on them. The Court Leet followed the common practice of trying to prevent beggars, or potential beggars, from settling in the town. In 1578 it decreed that no inhabitants within the town should take into their houses any inmates unless the said inmates were able to get their living without begging. The order was repeated in 1582 with emphasis on 'hoares or notorious offenders' who were got with child in other hamlets or parishes and came into Manchester to 'lye in childbed'. Two years later control was extended to single women who baked and brewed and used other trades to the great hurt of poor inhabitants with wives and children, and who abused 'them selves with yonge men'. No single woman was to be 'at ther owne hands or kepe anny housse or chamber within this towne' or sell ale or bread to the 'hurte of the poore inhabitants and howseholders of this towne'. Later complaints show that these 'good orders' had not been 'putt in execution'.[4]

Both the indigenous poor and the attempts to relieve their poverty remain elusive. That the former existed and the latter were made are clear. In 1599–1600 the manorial accounts included 40s 'bestowed uppon the poore in Manchester at Christmas 1599', and the agreement over Collyhurst common in 1617 provided that the lord of the manor should pay £10 p.a. for the use of the poor of Manchester. Men and women left bequests to the poor in their wills.[5] Perhaps the most significant of such bequests was that of Humfrey Haughton, a clothier who died in 1598 and left 20s to ten poor shearmen of Manchester. Bequests to the poor were not very frequent, which may have indicated a lack of charity rather than a lack of the poor. It is in fact quite impossible to tell how serious a problem poverty was or how many of the population were wage earners faced with a rising cost of living. The Elizabethan lay subsidy returns, with their limited and arbitrary lists of taxpayers, are no help here. Even earlier subsidy returns may be subject to misleading conclusions when it is assumed that the under-valuation of wealth applied only to those above the exemption limit and not to those below it. Fashionable estimates that one third or one half of the urban population consisted of the poor or of those at subsistence level may be correct, but they cannot be applied to Elizabethan Manchester because there is no way of testing their validity.

The obscurity of the poor in Manchester is not surprising; the numbers and wealth of the well-to-do are more unexpected. These are revealed by probate inventories or, where no inventory is available, sometimes by wills. Wills are not very satisfactory as indicators of total wealth. They often do not give details of real property. This might not matter so much when most of the property was personal, but they do not give full details of that either. In Manchester a testator was rarely free to dispose of his personal property as he might wish. Manchester lay within the Northern Province where the custom or law prevailed that a married man with children must leave one third of his personal estate to his wife and one third to his children. Only the remaining third, 'the dead man's part', was he free to dispose of as he wished for the good of his soul. The widower with children had to leave half his personal estate to his children; the married man without children had to leave half to his wife.[6] Thus a married man with children could not make bequests from his third of the personal estate which exceeded the value of the third left to his wife or the third left to his children. This in effect meant that if he made bequests from his part totalling £20, then his total personal estate should have been at least £60. Thus in the absence of an inventory, wills may give some indication of the minimum value of a personal estate. One or two examples will show how wills may be used in this way. Robert Marler, a goldsmith who died in 1582, left a third of his personal estate to his wife, a third to his daughter, and from his own third made bequests totalling at least £50, which implied that his total personal estate must have been at least £150. John Glover, a yeoman whose will is dated 27 September 1571, made bequests of £21 from his third, implying a total personal estate of at least £63.

Wills alone can reveal considerable personal estates, but they do not show whether in fact the assets would cover the bequests. Testators might be optimistic. Probate inventories are a much more satisfactory indicator of wealth, but their shortcomings need greater emphasis than they usually receive. Inventories do not include any freehold property. This omission might not be so very important in an urban area where much property was held by leasehold. Unfortunately, if Manchester inventories are any guide, they do not always include the value of leases, which could be considerable. In theory the value of leases should have been included in inventories because it was part of the personal property. In practice that value was sometimes included and sometimes omitted. The reason for this remains obscure. It is possible that leases were omitted when they were leases for life or lives, on the strict legal grounds that such leases were real, and not personal property. It is almost certain, however, that all the omissions of leases from inventories cannot be explained on these grounds. Just as the value of leases may be omitted from inventories, so too may debts. There are cases where the debts owed by and owing to the testator were recorded in the will but not in the inventory. If, in such cases, the valuation of the personal estate is taken simply from the inventory it can be very misleading. Thus the inventory of the clothier, William Baguley, makes no mention of debts; his will however records that he owed £12 7s 6d, and was owed £174 6s. If these debts are taken into account, the inventory valuation of £422 17s 6d is raised to £584 16s. Clearly debts which are recorded in the will but not in the inventory must be brought into the reckoning, otherwise the inventory valuation may be grossly misleading. There is a danger in doing this if there was a considerable gap in time between the will and the inventory, but that was very rare indeed. In a sense any debts, whether in the will or the inventory, may be misleading because it is not known whether in fact they were recoverable, but nothing can be done about that except perhaps to ignore those debts described as 'desperate'. In only three Manchester inventories were parts of the debts so described, and these have been ignored; in all other cases debts, whether in the will or the inventory, have been included in the valuation of the personal property. It is doubtful whether this has always been done when inventories have been used.

There are fifty-seven usable Manchester inventories for Elizabeth's reign.[7] They show that the median value of personal property was £101. This is a high figure. Professor Hoskins has given details of forty-five inventories for Leicester between 1557 and 1612, and there the median value of personal property was just over £28. Leicester, with a population of perhaps 3000, was a bigger town than Manchester and one with a flourishing leather industry.[8] At Banbury the forty-one inventories dating from 1573 to 1589 show a median value of only £6 7s 2d, but their editor points out that the wealthier testators preferred to have probate granted by the Prerogative Court of Canterbury and so their inventories are not included.[9] A comparison between Manchester and Worcester is more instructive. They were both regional centres and cloth towns, though Worcester, with perhaps 4250 people in 1563, was probably more than twice the size of Manchester. Dr Dyer has shown that the eighty-eight inventories for Worcester in the 1580s yield an average value of £44·3; the tweny-one Manchester inventories for that decade yield an average value of £207. For the 1590s the figures are, Worcester ninety-three inventories and an average value of £51, Manchester twenty-nine inventories and an average value of £156.[10] Too much should not be made of these figures because of the disparity in the number of inventories; it is very probable that as the number of surviving inventories increases, the average value of the personal estate declines. Even so, the contrast between the two towns is very marked.

In Manchester the twenty-eight men and women with personal property above the median value included two gentlemen, Richard Hunt and John Marler, four widows, Margaret Hurlestone, Alice Pendleton, Joan Edge and Isabel Tipping, though Isabel should be counted as a clothier rather than a widow, two yeomen, Adam Oldham who was also a dyer and Roger Bexwick, who was probably also an innkeeper, and John Glover, the singing man. The leather industry was represented by William Hunt, tanner, Adam Hope, whittawer, and James Bradshaw, saddler, who was also a dealer in yarn. The group of well-to-do shopkeepers was represented by Robert Walshman, goldsmith, John Wharmby, butcher, John Billing, glazier and shopkeeper, Robert Birch, linen draper and dealer in flax and yarn, and three mercers, John Shaw, Edward Hanson and Thomas Hardman, of whom the last two were also engaged in the cloth trade with London. A well-to-do craftsman, Robert Bridghouse, joiner, was also a yarn dealer. The eight remaining testators were all clothiers or in some way engaged in the production or sale of cloth or yarn. Indeed at least half of those with estates above the median had some connection with the cloth trade. Joan Newall, the widow whose personal property constituted the median value, kept an inn.

Those with personal estates below the median included one gentleman, Thomas Beck, whose wealth probably lay in real property, six widows or spinsters, and a minister, John Buckley. There were also two butchers, a tanner, a shoemaker, a baker, a tailor and two drapers, one of whom, William Sandforth, also dealt in yarn. Of the remainder, half-a-dozen were either clothiers or linen weavers. Thus in this section, which is slightly more weighted by the women, just over a quarter was engaged in the production or sale of cloth or yarn.

In the 1570s, 1580s and 1590s there was clearly a group of fairly wealthy clothiers, yarn dealers and shopkeepers in Manchester which in an incorporated town might well have formed a ruling oligarchy. It is by no means certain that they did so in Manchester or indeed could have done so in a place ruled manorially through a court leet. The Court Leet was presided over by the lord's steward, who from 1582 to 1601 was Richard Swinglehurst, gent. He chose the jury which varied from twelve to twenty-three in number, but was usually fifteen to eighteen. Their names recur with monotonous regularity and belong to the leading local families. The jury in turn elected the boroughreeve and the other officers of the town. In 1578 when the steward tried to get the re-election of John Gee for a third consecutive term as boroughreeve, the jury rejected him in favour of Robert Langley. They no doubt regarded Gee, who was deputy receiver of the manor, as too much of a lord's man, but they were also asserting their right to elect. No future boroughreeve held office for two consecutive years until the nineteenth century.[11] The boroughreeves were also drawn from the leading local families; between 1580 and 1600 they included two Mosleys, Anthony and Oswald, merchants like Ralph Sorocold and Henry Pendleton, clothiers like Humfrey Haughton, linen dealers like George Tipping and Richard Nugent, and gentlemen like Thomas Beck.[12] There were many more offices men could hold. On 5 October 1598 the Court Leet Jury appointed 106 officers including the boroughreeve, six market lookers for corn, eleven market lookers for white meat, thirteen 'bylawmen' to enforce the by-laws, sixteen scavengers and thirteen officers for mastiff dogs that go in the streets unmuzzled and not sufficiently muzzled. Seven men each held two offices and so ninety-nine men in all were appointed. Again the well known names occur: Mosley, Nugent, Tipping, Birch, Sorocold, Bexwick and so on.[13] Any man of substance can hardly have avoided taking part in this elaborate charade. Perhaps that is too harsh a term, but it is difficult to see why a place the size of Manchester should need to fill more than a hundred offices each year; or why, to put it another way, perhaps one out of every twenty inhabitants should have been an official, even if unpaid; or why, to put it yet another way, one out of every four or five households should have been called upon to supply an official. Even the unworthy motive of creating offices in order to fine people for refusing to fill them does not seem to apply. It would appear that the number of officers was only equalled by their inefficiency.

The opposition to John Gee's appointment in 1578 and the greater opposition to the enclosure of Collyhurst common in 1602 show that the authority of the lord of the manor could be challenged, if not always successfully. Such incidents were rare, however, and there is no evidence of a wealthy oligarchy making a sustained effort to gain control of the government of the town. No doubt the leading families exercised considerable authority within the Court Leet, but their role, as that of the Court itself, was largely administrative. The Mosleys might be more grasping than earlier absentee lords, but they were local and were connected with the leading families not only by their cloth trade but also through their marriages. Moreover patronage may be the cement of politics, but there was little of that available to the leading families; the paid manorial offices were firmly in the gift of the lord of the manor. There was not even any corporation property to be administered or manipulated, nor any gild property either. Indeed apart from religion and business, the range of activities open to leading burgesses was very limited. There were no charters to be fought for or local members of parliament to be chosen and then briefed on the town's needs. There were national regulations to be enforced on the tanning of leather, the measuring of cloth and the wearing of caps on Sundays, but there were no gild monopolies to be defended or controlled. The relative absence of any really meaningful civic duties combined with the presence of a degree of economic freedom may help to account for the size and wealth of the local patriciate.

Manchester's leading burgesses may not have formed a ruling class or even a pressure group, but they had some cohesion through kinship and marriage. This is a difficult and indeed a tedious matter to establish, partly because there were a number of families of the same name who also favoured the same Christian names. Thus Anthony Mosley married Alice, the daughter of a merchant, Richard Webster, who was not the clothier of that name who died in 1589, for Alice's mother was a widow at her death in 1587. Anthony's daughter Ellen married Walter, the son and heir of Richard Nugent, with a dowry of £300,[14] and his nephew Rowland Mosley married Anne the daughter of Humfrey Haughton, a rich clothier. Finally Anthony's brother Oswald married Cicely, the daughter of Richard and Isabel Tipping, who were both very rich cloth and yarn merchants. In this way some of the richest families in the town were linked together through marriage. Others were linked more distantly to this golden circle. Isabel Tipping left 'a spurr ryall' to her 'cousin' Thomas Brownsword whose father was Isabel's brother as well as being brother-in-law to Robert Birch, the well-to-do linen draper who died in 1583. Similarly the butcher, John Wharmby, was

D

Richard Nugent's brother-in-law, and when Richard's son Walter died in 1614 without issue most of the Nugent wealth went to a William Wharmby.[15] In the outer circle, but by no means the outer darkness, the merchant family of the Pendletons was related to the Becks, the Brownswords, the Marlers and the Birches. In a small town such connections are a commonplace, but they suggest that even the rich did not feel compelled to choose their marriage partners from outside their locality or their class.

These groupings were based more on wealth than on any clearly defined status, for the urban middle class never fitted very well into the Elizabethen dream of a hierarchical society. The urban gentleman existed, but very few of Manchester's leading burgesses were consistently described as gentlemen. In April 1593 all the Court Leet jurors were described as gentlemen, but that was an aberration on the part of the clerk, Charles Leigh, and by the October meeting they had been cut down to size except for the foreman, Robert Langley, who was a gentleman.[16] Whatever their status might be, some of the burgesses were wealthier than many a rural gentleman.

Urban wealth has not been studied as intensively as rural wealth, and the sort of questions that should be asked about it are not easy to answer. Those questions are basically how did a townsman acquire his wealth, how did he deploy it during his lifetime and how did he dispose of it at death.

Manchester men of any substance acquired some of their wealth by inheritance, but there was some difference between the inheritance of real and of personal property. Property held of the manor normally went to the eldest son, but leasehold property was often more widely distributed at death. Indeed leasehold property should have been included in the personal estate, one third of which went to the testator's children. Whether this distribution of the personal property gave a man much of a start in life depended on the value of the property and the size of the family. John Shaw, mercer, left a third of his personal estate of £113 3s 1d to his children, but there were eight of them; James Bradshaw, saddler, left a third of his personal estate of £460 to his two sons. No doubt excessive *morcellement* was checked by nature; in the large families some of the children would die young and their portions would pass to the survivors. The evidence is not conclusive but it suggests that inheritance was less important as a source of wealth in Manchester than it was in more rural areas. The exception to this was the wealthy widows.

It is tempting to project the image of the self-made Manchester man back from the nineteenth to the sixteenth century, but there is hardly enough evidence to sustain such a projection. Wills and inventories give a static picture of a man's wealth at the end of his life; the actual process of accumulation cannot be determined in the absence of other personal or business records. It seems clear, however, that most accumulation came from the cloth trade, either through the finishing and marketing of woollen cloth or through trading in flax, linen yarn and linen cloth. The bigger fortunes came in this way, and even men like James Bradshaw, who called himself a saddler, and John Billing, who called himself a glazier, were also dealers in yarn. Similarly the wealthy mercers, Edward Hanson and Thomas Hardman, were engaged in the London cloth trade. The cloth trade was not the only path to a competence; that could be achieved in shopkeeping, the leather industry or in combining farming with butchering, but the real prizes came from cloth.

Those who prospered beyond the point where they required all their resources for their own business could find a use, and presumably a profitable use, for their capital in money lending. After 1571 interest up to 10 per cent was legal, and the legal maximum seems to have been the market rate. Money lending in various forms was common, but it is difficult to assess largely because the sources rarely reveal the nature of debts. Some debts were incurred simply by buying goods on credit from shopkeepers, clothiers and yarn dealers. Others were a form of pawnbroking as when the goldsmith, Robert Walshman, held a variety of pawns or pledges upon which money had been lent. This was not confined to goldsmiths. When the wealthy draper, George Pendleton, died in 1585 his debt books passed to his widow Alice who died three years later. Her inventory shows similar pledges: Henry Knowles of Yorkshire was to pay £1 16s 8d on a gold ring, Richard Thorpe's wife had 'layd' a gown for £2, 'wyddow Billington' had 'layd' a silver salt for £3 and John Blomeley six silver spoons for £1. All this was petty borrowing compared with Geoffrey Hale's debt of £100, Thomas Goodyear's of £100 and Adam Holland's of £60. Some money had been lent on mortgage for the appraisers recorded 'one morgage of certen lands and tenements in Manchester lyenge in Dennesgate and one shoppe in the holdinge of Nicholas Hartles [Hartley] lyenge in Smythye Dore pawned by old Mrs Fox and Richard Fox her sonne for the somme of fyftye pounds and now forfeyted as doth appere by the covenants'. It was one way to acquire urban property.

Borrowing could work both ways. Robert Birch, the linen draper who died in 1583, was owed £285 10s 4d, much of it in small amounts, probably for yarn, but he himself owed £117, all of it to members of his family. Had his mother, his daughter and his two brothers been supplying him with working capital? Selling on credit, unless accompanied by buying on credit, would need a good deal of working capital, and there is no evidence that Birch bought his yarn on credit. Similarly the mercer, Thomas Hardman, both owed and was owed large sums of money, but the nature of these debts remains unclear. Another mercer, Edward Hanson, on the other hand, seems to have left no debts but was owed £101 8s 6d on obligations and bills. Thomas Brownsword, the clothier who died in 1588, had no debts either, and he was owed £293 4s 1d. Though it is often impossible to disentangle credit sales from the giving and receiving of loans, there is no doubt that 'lent money' was an important form of investment. There is no evidence, however, that money lending had developed as a separate and specialised occupation. Even the rich had not abandoned their trade in goods for trade in money. They successfully combined the two.

The way a man deployed his money during his lifetime may show not only his business acumen but also his social aspirations. The richer Mancunians preferred to keep their assets in fairly liquid forms, in goods, loans, leases and even cash. Sometimes they held surprisingly large amounts of cash at their death. Isabel Tipping had £471 17s, Alice Pendleton £206 'in money found in the house', Edward Hanson £154 and Robert Birch £96 13s 4d. The merchant Francis Pendleton held one fifth of his personal estate 'in gould and money'. Apart from some of the Mosleys, there is little evidence that men used the profits of trade to acquire landed estates and to turn themselves into country gentlemen. It is true that George Pendleton, draper, gave his daughter Cicely a dowry of £200 on her marriage to a minor Cheshire gentleman, but equally Anthony Mosley gave his daughter Ellen a dowry of £300 on her marriage to the son of a rich mercer and linen dealer. When Isabel Tipping bestowed some of her wealth on her married daughters it went to Anne, the wife of Thomas Rillston of London, presumably a branch of the Manchester Rillstons, to Cicely, wife of Oswald Mosley, and to Dorothy, the wife of John Fox, yeoman of Pilkington near Bury. If men were not very interested in social climbing, they were interested in seeing that there was no social descent. Sons who reached manhood and daughters who got married during their father's lifetime were 'advanced' or 'preferred'. Thus Robert Wharmby had preferred all his daughters in marriage during his lifetime, and Andrew Renshaw had given two of his five daughters 'a certayne rounde summe', but the two youngest daughters had not received 'any thing of theire owne'. None of these girls was married; the married daughter had received 'but a slender portion of my goods heretofore in name and for her filiall portion'. There is little information about these gifts *inter vivos*, partly because there may have been no reason why they should be recorded and partly because so many children were minors when their father died. They had to wait for the will.

It is much easier to see how men disposed of their property at death than it is to tell how they acquired it. That is especially true of personal property, for a will may simply refer to arrangements already made for the distribution of real property. In showing how men disposed of their property, wills give some idea of what men thought about family and social obligations. They may even give some idea of men's religious views as expressed in the commendation of the soul 'into the hands of allmightie God my onelie maker and redeemer trustinge onelie by the death and bloodsheddinge of Jesus Chryste to be one of the electe children of salvacione and by none other meritt whatsoever', as John Cowopp's will expressed it. It has, however, been apointed out that such expressions may represent the beliefs of the writer of the will rather than of the testator himself.[17] Cowopp's will was written by John Glover, perhaps the 'singing man' of that name, who also wrote William Baguley's will, which expresses similar sentiments though not quite in identical words. Most Manchester wills of this period are copies, and so it is not possible to group them by handwriting and thus establish that a group of wills was written by one man who used a similar form of words in each. Certainly the form of words used in commending the soul was often so similar as to suggest that it originated with the writer rather than with the testator.

Whatever meaning is to be read into the religious formulas, the rest of the will certainly expressed the testator's instructions for the disposal of worldly goods. In Manchester, as elsewhere, the testator's first purpose was to provide for his wife and children. In this he had to follow the principle of partible inheritance of personal property as laid down by the 'custom', and wills show that conformity to the custom was almost universal. Indeed men stated, as did Thomas Hardman, that their goods were to be divided 'according unto the lawe and custome of the cuntrey'. When John Cowopp wished to leave a cow to each of his children, he got his wife's consent to this, expressed in the will, because cattle were part of the personal estate of which she had a right to one third. Thus widows automatically received one third of the personal property and they received it absolutely, or as the wills sometimes put it, 'forever'. A widow did not forfeit her part if she re-married, and she was free to leave it, or what was left of it, at her death. In a sense she received an automatic jointure. Over this the testator had no choice, but he was free to decide whether or not to supplement his wife's part from his own third of the personal property. This was commonly done, usually by the testator leaving the residue of his part to his wife and children, or sometimes to his wife and younger children. Thus Ottiwell Hodgkinson by his will of 30 December 1587 left the residue of his part to his wife Isabel and the three youngest of his seven children. If there were no children the wife was entitled to half the personal estate and even in these cases she was often left the residue of the other half. The goldsmith Robert Walshman, who was childless, left half his personal property and the residue of his own half to his wife Alice. This meant in effect that Alice inherited all but about £10 of an estate valued at £128 15s 10d.

Even when wives were provided for on this scale, there was still the problem of where, as widows, they should live. When a man occupied his own house and left it to his eldest son who was a minor, which was not uncommon, then presumably the widow and family continued to live there, but that might only postpone the problem until the son reached his majority. The widow needed security of tenure during her widowhood, and that could be provided by the will. William Hunt, whose children were apparently all married, left the lease of his house to his wife for life with reversion to a son-in-law. Similarly John Davie left the house where he lived to his wife Margaret so long as she 'kepethe her in honeste name and lyvethe soole and unmaryed'. Such provision was easy where there were no children or the children had married. The childless Robert Bridghouse left his house to his wife Anne, and Robert Marler, whose only child was a married daughter, left his house to his wife Margaret during her widowhood. It is probable that most of this property that widows occupied during widowhood was held by lease. It is in fact difficult to find a widow living in Manchester who had not a home of her own, which would support the view that households were nuclear rather than extended. It is easier to find spinsters who must have been living with their relatives or been lodgers. Margaret Bexwick, a spinster who died in 1599, owned her clothes, some wool and rather surprisingly a loom, but no furniture apart from a coffer. She may have lived with her uncle Hugh Birch for she left his two children 5s each and the residue of her property to him 'desyringe hym to consider Elizabeth Hall widowe for her paynes taken with me in the tyme of my sycknes'.

A widow was assured of a basic one third or, if there were no children, one half of the personal estate, and in many cases this was supplemented by a share of the testator's own part. Whether this resulted in affluence or penury depended very much on the size of the estate; when that was large, the widow was very well provided for. Thus George Pendleton, a draper who died in 1586, included in his personal estate the £200 he had paid on his daughter Cicely's marriage to John Croxton. He then left a third of this estate to his wife Alice, who was also given a life interest in all his real property and leases and an equal share with Cicely in the residue of his own third. Alice died in 1591 with plate, household stuff and apparel valued at £88 15s 6d, debts owing to her of £295 4s 4d and money in the house together with 'one gold rynge whiche she had on her finger when she dyed' valued at £206 12s. As Alice owed only £4 5s 9d, including 4s 6d for tithe hay and £1 12s 'to the cundite in Manchester', her total estate came to £586 6s 1d. It is hardly surprising that she lived in style in a house with a kitchen, hall, parlour and at least four chambers with their 'standinge celed' beds, their 'paynted hengings' and their say curtains with fringe. Her 'apparrell for her bodye' was valued at £20, her 107 ounces of plate at £24 9s 7d and her pewter, more than 180 pounds of it, at nearly £5. It was all rather grand. The only discordant note was the solitary cow, which was 'sicke' and valued at only 6s.

Not all widows had been as fortunate in their choice of their man as Alice Pendleton. At the other end of the scale was Grace Whitworth, a widow who died in 1591. Her personal property was valued at £2 12s 6d, and many items of it, the featherbed, the pillows, the blankets, the gowns and petticoats, were described as 'old'. Her most valuable single possession was '1 brasse pott which ys laid to pledge'; this she left to Adam Parrene 'so that he come and paye so much as the said pott ys pledged for'. Grace left most of her goods to her daughter Elizabeth and the child in her womb; if the daughter and child died the goods were to go to Adam Parrene. There was no mention of a son-in-law. Grace owned 'a payre of sheeres', which suggests that she may have been a shearman's widow. Goods worth only £2 12s 6d suggest some degree of poverty, but it is very difficult to say where the poverty line began. Elizabeth Orred, a widow who died in 1588, had goods valued at only £6 8s 3d, but they included seventeen pieces of pewter, thirty-three pounds pot metal, four chairs and five stools, 'a silver pynne and a payre of hooks', a pair of camlet sleeves, 'a kerchefe of callicoe' and a fair amount of clothes. Here the impression is not one of poverty but of reasonable comfort. Neither of these inventories suggests that these widows had any occupation; there are no spinning wheels or pigs or even hens, and shearing was not a woman's job.

Some widows clearly had occupations, which were probably those of their late husbands. Thus Isabel Tipping continued her husband's business as a dealer in linen yarn and cloth until her death or, as the Victorian editor of her will, the Rev. G. J. Piccope, put it, 'from the inventory it appears that the testatrix was in trade'.[18] So indeed she was, and it had made her perhaps the richest woman in Manchester. Alice Pendleton, on the other hand, did not continue her husband's business as a draper, but she still lived on the premises; one of her chambers was 'over the shopp' and there was a warehouse which contained no cloth but only 'olde bordes and other things' valued at 2s.

Innkeeping was another possible occupation for a widow. Thus Margaret Bowker, a widow who died in 1591, seems to have kept an inn. She had a cellar, buttery and brewhouse with 'one fornas or lead', a house or hall with 'one cupboard and one shelf and the pewter theron', and at least two parlours and three chambers with beds in them. Moreover she was owed 3s 4d by Mr Robert Hawge 'for table of his son', 15s by Mr Brearton of Ashley, 21s 8d by Thomas Percival and 10s by 'Syr' Robert Barber, a minister, all 'for the lyck [like]', though it is not clear whether they owed these sums for the tabling of themselves or of their sons. Barber was an executor of Margaret's will and a witness to it. Margaret's personal property, which included three swine, was valued at £19 1s 3d. There is no doubt that Joan Newall, a widow who died in 1593, kept an inn. She had a buttery, a little buttery which contained the 'pewter that is dayly occupied', a kitchen with 'a fornace and courbe', a bolting house, a 'howse' or hall with chairs, stools, a form and pewter on the shelves, three chambers and two parlours. She also had 'in malt and ale 33s and in money taken for ale 17s.' Joan must have been twice widowed for she left to her eldest son, George Dodge, 'my fornace and corbe as it standeth and also all my brewing keares, ston troughs, stownds, eshins and all such other treene ware fit and convenient for brewing together with all my drinking pots, mugs and glasses (one pot covered with silver only excepted)' and 'my cupbord in the littell buttrye with all the pewter accustomed to stand thereon, the 2 littell tables in the house and also all the stowles, chears, formes and shelves in the house, buttries and taverne'. Joan Newall clearly kept a superior establishement to Margaret Bowker's. It was well furnished and even the 'apparell for her bodie' was valued at £12 2s 8d. Her total personal property was valued at £101 18s 4d, excluding unspecified but desperate debts of £30, which may have represented one of the occupational hazards of innkeeping. It seems reasonable to assume that Joan's relative affluence owed something to the successive 'parts' which as a widow she must have received from her two husbands.

In some respects it was easier for a monogamous testator to provide for his wife than for his children, who were usually more numerous. Such children were entitled to a third of the personal property even if they were married or adults. Thus Roger Bexwick left a third of his personal property to his sons, Hugh and Miles, and to his daughter Margaret. The sons were both of age and the daughter was married to Simon Mallon. A married daughter might, however, be required to 'cast in' her marriage portion if she wished to obtain her share of the children's third. Thus John Pycroft, a linen weaver, left the child's part to his son Edward, but if his daughter Ellen, the wife of Thomas Percival, would 'cast in to be devided all suche parte and filliall portion as heartofore she had of me', then she could share the children's third with Edward. The same principle could be applied to sons who had been 'advanced' at the time of their marriage. Thus Richard Tipping left a third of his personal estate to his children, but his eldest son John was only to share in that third if he put in the money which his father had given him 'the day of his marriage'.[19] Stepchildren could also share in the children's third if they 'cast in' any personal property left to them by their late father. John Birch, innholder, left the second one third of his personal property equally among his own children and his wife's children by her first husband provided the latter cast in 'suche portions of goodes, as was leffte to theym by the deathe or laste will of theire late father Henry Wirrall to be devyded with the seconde parte of my goodes, amongste theym and my owne children'.

There were, however, cases where all the children were not included as beneficiaries of the children's third. Thus Richard Hunt, gent., who was a widower, left half his personal estate to his seven younger children, though his eldest son John was only twelve, but John had been provided for out of the real property. The same seems to have been true of Thomas Beck's eldest son Randal, who was not a beneficiary of the children's third. Similarly the merchant Ralph Sorocold left the children's third to his ten younger children and one unborn; the eldest son Thomas had been endowed with land. Children might be endowed not only with real property and leases but also with a share of the testator's own third of the personal property. That was commonly done by leaving the residue of that third, after funeral expenses and specific legacies had been paid, to the wife and to all or some of the children. Here again there was some emphasis on the younger children.

It was natural that Manchester fathers should show this concern for their children and especially for the younger ones, for many men died leaving sons and daughters who were minors. This raised the problem of who should have control or, as the wills put it, 'the tuition, rule and government', of the minors. Again it was natural that this should normally go to the mother, but there were exceptions. The linen draper, William Sandforth, gave the control of his son John and of a child unborn, not to his wife Jane, but to his brother Robert. As Jane was with child, this may have been a precaution in case she died in childbirth. Similarly John Nabbs, the cloth-maker, left the bringing up of his only child, a son, to James Chorlton and Ralph Radley, and not to his wife. Sometimes the mother was given the bringing up of only the younger children or of only the girls. James Bradshaw gave the 'rule' of his younger son to his wife Ellen and of the elder to his brother-in-law Adam Smith. James Radcliffe, an innkeeper who died in 1593, had five children of whom the eldest, Alice, was married. Of the four younger children, Cicely was assigned to her mother, James to a 'loving friend' Nicholas Baguley, Edmund to his uncle Edward Radcliffe, and Robert to another loving friend, James Wood. The reason for assigning children in this way may simply have been the belief that their guardians could give the boys a better start in life than their mother could. When the testator was a widower some arrangement had obviously to be made for the bringing up of the younger children. Thus John Leese, widower and cloth worker, left most of his personal property to his daughter Ellen and appointed William Birch as her guardian until she married or reached her majority. Birch was to have the 'disposinge and puttinge forthe of the filiall portion and child's part of goods of the said Ellene', though £10 of 'the said filiall portion' was to be occupied by James Audley, draper.

This stipulation is a reminder that there was a financial side to guardianship. Those who were given the tuition, rule and government of children were usually given the use of the children's portions. It was a form of wardship. No doubt the portions were used for the children's maintenance and upbringing, but they could also be loaned out. Robert Birch, the linen draper, left a third of his personal estate to his two daughters, Catherine and Cicely, who were put under the governance of their mother Isabel, but Birch's two brothers, John and James, were to have the use of the girls' goods during their minority, paying £6 13s 4d p.a. to their mother towards the 'finding' of the girls. As the girls had inherited about £245 from their own part and from other legacies, the two brothers would seem to have made a good bargain. A child's portion could of course be lent without any authority for this in the will. In 1593 Francis Hough, clothier, left his personal property valued at £241 13s 2d to his five children and made his 'loving friends' Richard Nugent and John Wharmby his executors. When John Wharmby died in 1598 the debts he owed included £90 1s 9d for 'the children's porcions of Francis Hough'; he also owed £20 to his own children for the legacy left to them by his father-in-law Edmund Nugent. In this way a child's portion could provide a source of working capital for a relative or friend of the family.

The custom of inheritance dictated the shape of a man's will if he had a wife or children; only the bachelor and the spinster, the childless widower and the widow were free to dispose of their personal property without restriction. Bachelor testators were rare in Manchester, and indeed it is not always possible to be certain that the deceased was a bachelor. Thomas Holme, a tailor who died in 1588, seems to have been one. His personal property consisted of £23 0s 8d in money owed to him and £4 for the 'shapenne apparell for his bodie'. He apparently lived with his master, Thomas Charles to whom he left 20s, as well as 10s to his godson, Charles's son, 12d to each of the rest of his master's children and 12d to each of the servants in his master's house. Charles's wife was left 8s 'for her paynes takinge with me'. Other bequests went to Holme's sisters, a brother, an uncle and to the poor. Thus Holme combined thought for his kin with appreciation of his adopted home. John Glover, 'one of the singinge men of the Colledge of Manchester', seems also to have been a bachelor, but he had a comfortable home of his own complete with pictures, including 'the great picture', books, 'a siteron' and a close stool. He held much property by leases which were valued at £104. These he left to his brothers Robert and Edward, subject to the payment of £13 6s 8d to his sister Anne. Nothing went to brother William who had wrongfully detained a 'midding steed' left to Glover by his father. The two favoured brothers also got John's apparel which included 'my dublett of ash cooler with the silver buttons uppon the same and one payre of breeches quilted and stiched with red silke'. He seems indeed to have been a bit of a dandy with his three gold rings and '2 perles and 2 stones'; even his yew bow had 'a redd handle'.[20] Finally John Buckley, 'preacher of the worde of God', who died in 1593, seems to have been a bachelor. From his personal property valued at £35 19s 5d he left money to the poor, books to his friends and small legacies to his godchildren and relations. Perhaps it was the influence of the 'custom' that led him to divide the residue of his property into three parts, which he left to two sisters and to a nephew and his wife.

Spinster testators were as rare as bachelors, and their wills show the same pattern of bequests. Thus Ellen Radley, a spinster who died in 1592, made small bequests of her clothes, household goods and money to her sisters, a brother and goddaughters. Joan Barlow, who died the following year, left small sums to an uncle, two aunts and three cousins, and £10 to another cousin, Julian Cowopp, the daughter of John Cowopp. The residue of the goods went to Joan's mother, Isabel, the widow of Robert Barlow, who died in 1594.

The childless widower was rarer in Manchester than the bachelor or the spinster, and it is doubtful whether the will of a single one has survived. Richard Webster, the clothier who died in 1589, is a possible candidate, but if he is the 'Richard s. of Richard Webster' whose burial was recorded on 28 October 1589[21], the entry would imply that he was a bachelor. Whatever his marital status Webster was a well-to-do man who scattered legacies of £5 on his brother-in-law John Newton, £20 on each of Newton's three sons, £6 13s 4d on an uncle and £40 on a married sister. He even left 40s to be bestowed on his friends 'at a drinkinge after my buriall', which may suggest bachelorhood and was certainly a rare bequest in Manchester, which was rather godly in these matters.[22] Webster's bequests, which totalled at least £152, are rather reminiscent of those made by the wealthier widows, though they might have children and grandchildren to leave their money to. Thus Alice Pendleton left her daughter Cicely and her husband John Croxton £150 and their children £100. Alice was the daughter of Henry Gee, and she left legacies to a great brood of six Gee brothers and to six of their children. Isabel Tipping, who had more to leave than had Alice Pendleton, had also more children to leave it to, and so concentrated her bequests largely on her children and grandchildren, who received named bequests of £1200 in all. After bequests to servants, friends and the poor, the residue went to her youngest son Samuel. Considering Isabel's great wealth, this concentration on the immediate family seems excessive. Had she really no personal friends to whom she wished to leave more than 'a spurr ryall' or 10s 'and my best hat'?

Wills clearly show a great concern for the immediate family whatever the marital status of the testators. That family also included the domestic servants; at least that was the view of their masters and mistresses, whatever the servants themselves thought about it. It was natural therefore that testators should make bequests to their servants, but in Manchester only about a quarter of them did so. The proportion seems low, but it would be rash to draw any conclusions from it about the actual distribution and employment of servants. It is unlikely that gentlemen like Thomas Beck and Richard Hunt or a rich mercer like Thomas Hardman employed no domestic servants even if they made no bequests to them. Apart from Thomas Holme, the tailor who left 12d to each of his master's servants, which may have meant his fellow workmen, bequests to servants were made by the well-to-do. They varied greatly in amount. The lowest was 2s which Robert Walshman left to a maidservant Anne, but he also left 6s 8d to another servant, Elizabeth Johnson; the difference may have reflected length of service or a below stairs hierarchy. John Birch, innholder, left his two servants 3s 4d each, which was the amount Joan Newall left to 'that servant woman that shall dwell with me at the day of my death'. A more common bequest was 10s. The yeoman, John Glover, left his two maidservants 10s each in gold, and Humfrey Haughton, the clothier, left the same amount to every servant in his house at the time of his death. Another clothier, Thomas Brownsword, also left his two women servants 10s each and another servant, William Brownsword, £4. William, who was presumably a relative, was more likely to have been employed in his master's business than as a domestic servant. The same was probably true of Robert Marshall's servant Joseph to whom he left 10s and to whom he owed £30 to be paid at the end of his four years' service. Marshall also left 10s to a woman servant, Isabel Hartley; perhaps she was related to Nicholas Hartley, for Marshall left his wife Elizabeth 'a black gowne of the best cloth shee can buy at Nicholas Hartley his shoppe'. There were some bequests of over 10s. Alice Pendleton left to each of her two maid-servants Margaret and Dorothy 20s and a gown and a petticoat, and Robert Marler left £2 to each of his servants. Isabell Tipping left one servant, Alice Gee, £5 and another, Margaret Newton, 10s. Alice Gee had served the Tippings for some years as she had been left 40s and a gown by Isabel's husband in 1592.[23]

It is difficult to compare these bequests with servants' wages, partly because there is little local evidence on such wages and partly because the money wage was supplemented by free board and lodging. In the 1580s the Shuttleworths were paying women servants from 12s to 30s a year, but the 30s was almost certainly paid to a house-keeper. If that is excluded, the range was 12s to 18s.[24] In additional of course there would be board and lodging and might be perquisites. In the light of this, some of the bequests do not look very generous, especially in relation to the size of the estates. That a testator could be generous is shown by the unusual case of Margaret Hurlestone, a widow whose late husband, Randal Hurlestone, esq., had presided over the Court Leet as Steward from 1573 to 1582. When Mrs Hurle-stone died in 1589 she left 'to misteris Grante my red peticote', to a niece 'a sylver bole guilte', 'to my servante George Worsley a testor of a bed of sea [say] and valance thereto', and 'fortie gownes of frize, that ys to saie 20 to poare men and 20 to poare women to goe before mee to the churche.' All the rest of her 'goods, leases and tacks' she left 'unto Ellyn Longelande nowe my servante'. Her personal property was valued at £123 7s 3d, of which £93 7s 3d was for the contents of her house and £30 for 'a lease of the privie tithes of the Colliage of the blesed Marye, of Manchester, for 3 scoare and 18 yeares yet to come'. Margaret had lived in greater style even than Alice Pendleton. Her clothes alone were valued at just over £40, and included such items as '1 gowne of riche taffeta laid with 3 laces of billament' and 'a dammask gowne with 2 yards of velvet', each at £6 13s 4d. There was a bed in the great chamber 'with a tester of dammaske and fringed with silke and curtens of sarsnet and a kyveringe of ares [arras]'. The quality of the household linen is shown by the '2 dammaske table clothes and 2 diaper table clothes' valued at £4. What Ellen Long-land did with all this finery is not recorded, nor is it known what Margaret's relatives thought of her will.

Where the custom of inheritance applied, bequests to servants came out of the testator's own third of the personal property. That third was originally intended to be used for the benefit of a man's soul through bequests to the church and for good works. By Elizabeth's reign that concept was wearing thin, especially as regards the church. That was certainly so in Manchester. The majority of men and women in Manchester who made wills expressed a wish to be buried in the parish church, though they may not all have meant that literally. Indeed Margaret Bexwick, Elizabeth Orred and Grace Whitworth each expressed the wish to be buried in the churchyard. Others, however, often specified the actual place in the church where they wished to be buried. Two of the Becks, two of the Pendletons and Humfrey Haughton wished this to be in the Jesus Chapel, 'neere to the place where my wyves be burryed' as Haughton put it, or 'where my children do lie' according to George Pendleton. Others were equally specific. George Barlow wished to be 'nere to the place where I have beyne accustomed to kneele', Isabel Barlow and James Bradshaw, 'nere to the fontestone', John Glover, yeoman, 'betwene the quere and the chapter house yf they will suffer it', Robert Marshall and Francis Wirrall 'in the southsyde yle', to which Marshall added sadly 'amongest my litle children', and Ralph Sorocold 'near unto the place where I use to sytt in the tyme of dyvine service'. This wish to be buried in the parish church was not matched by a desire to support that church with bequests. Alice Pendleton left £2 for repairing the Jesus Chapel, where the Pendletons were buried, and Humfrey Haughton left 10s, also for repairing the Jesus Chapel, and 20s for repairing the parish church, adding 'I meane the parish parte'. That was all; the secularisation of bequests was almost complete.

Manchester men showed the same reluctance to make bequests to their Grammar School as they did to their parish church. No registers of the Grammar School survive for this period, but it is reasonable to assume that some testators had attended the school, which might have encouraged them to make bequests to it or might, of course, have deterred them from doing so. The school had a distinguished High Master in Thomas Cogan, who married Ellen, daughter of Sir Edmund Trafford and widow of Thomas Willott.[25] Cogan's stepdaughter, Mary Willott, was Isabel Tipping's daughter-in-law. Isabel even left Cogan and his wife 10s each. These local connections of the High Master did not draw bequests to the school. Only Richard Webster, the clothier, made such a bequest in the form of £10 to the first two poor scholars from the Grammar School who went to the University. This lack of interest in education is rather surprising. Did it imply a lack of education in the testators themselves? One test of that is the ownership of books.

About a quarter of the testators owned books at their death, and

two of them had substantial libraries. John Buckley, the minister, left
little but some money and his books. The latter included thirty-six
schoolbooks, sixty 'bookes of divinitie of smale volumes', seventy 'litle
bookes that lye loose in the presse unsorted' and twelve more 'schoole-
bookes in another boxe in the presse'. The real heart of the library,
however, was the volumes listed individually in the inventory. These
consisted of about eighty-five titles, and included Bibles, commen-
taries and sermons; there was St Augustine, Peter Martyr, Henry
Bullinger, Erasmus, Calvin and Thomas Cartwright among others.
Some of these were left to Buckley's friends in his will; Robert Barber,
minister of the College, who had 'tabled' with widow Bowker, got 'my
large Geneva Byble in Englishe'. The other library belonged to John
Glover, the singing man. It was valued at £5 13s in the inventory
which gave no details of the books, but Glover left 'all my books
towching chirurgery and phisicke' to Philip Gosnell, all the books of
precedents in ecclesiastical and civil cases and the books on civil law
to Thomas Richardson, Dean of Manchester, and some volumes of
Cicero to a cousin, William Glover. Glover may have inherited some
of his books from his father, another John, who called himself yeoman
and was Clerk of the Court Leet.[26] By his will of 27 September 1571
John Glover, senior, gave the custody of his books to his wife, 'and
those children of myne that are desyrous to practis the same to have
free accesse to them'. In the end his wife was to 'bestowe them upon
which of my children she shall fynde wurthie of the same', which
seems a sensible arrangement.

Other men owned some books even if they did not amount to a
library, but unfortunately inventories do not always specify what the
books were. John Marler, gent., had 'bookes' valued at 40s, John
Wharmby, butcher, had 'one Acts of the monuments, 1 Byble,
Mr Smithes Sermons, book of Resolution, with the rest of his bookes'
valued at £1 5s, and Adam Oldham had 'a Byble with other bookes'
valued at £1 3s 4d. Ottiwell Hodgkinson also had a Bible and other
books, but valued at 13s 4d. Most of the books were religious, headed
by the Bible. John Davie and Robert Birch each had a Bible valued
at 12s, Thomas Brownsword had 'a Bible and a saltar' at 8s, William
Baguley 'a Byble and a Chronicle' at 10s, Adam Hope 'one Byble,
one salter and a prayer booke' at 10s, and John Leese 'a salter and a
booke of heven [heathen?] philosophie' at 4s. Isabel Tipping was the
only woman to possess books, and they were valued together with a
table and a carpet. Apart from John Glover, yeoman, for whom there
is no inventory, John Buckley and Ottiwell Hodgkinson, all the
possessors of books had personal property worth more than £100.
This was hardly surprising, for books were expensive. A Bible worth
12s represented at least a fortnight's wages of a skilled craftsman. The

modern equivalent, based on wages, would be for a skilled worker to pay over £100 for his Bible. About the end of the sixteenth century the Manchester burgess who had the money and the inclination could have bought his books from John Brown, a stationer who died in 1612. Unfortunately Brown's inventory does not describe his stock of books, but it shows that he also sold maps, pictures, spectacle cases, parchment and ink horns.[27]

If more men and women had possessed books could they have read them? It is impossible to say, for there is no general way of telling whether or not people could read. If literacy is defined as the ability to write one's name then there is some evidence on that, but it applies only to men. Women very rarely witnessed wills and they never seem to have acted as appraisers for inventories. The copies of their own wills rarely bear their signatures or marks; the two that do, those of Isabel Barlow and Margaret Hurlestone, both bear their marks, but this may mean, not that they could not sign their names, but that they were too ill to do so. Some idea of male literacy can be got from the witnesses to wills and from the appraisers of inventories, but they constitute a very crude sample for two reasons. Firstly, many inventories are not signed by the appraisers at all and in the case of some wills it is impossible to tell from the copy whether they were signed or 'marked'. Secondly, the sample includes some double counting. It is clear that some men witnessed or appraised more than once, but it would be very difficult to be sure that two or more witnesses or appraisers of the same name were one and the same man. No attempt has been made to disentangle them in this way. For what they are worth, which is not much, the figures show that of forty-nine witnesses to wills twenty-five signed and twenty-four made their marks; of sixty-four appraisers only twenty-one signed and forty-three made their marks. This difference between the witnesses and appraisers was natural enough. The witnesses were friends and relations and sometimes included clergymen and the writer of the will.[28] The appraisers must often have been craftsmen with a knowledge of the value of the goods. In 1573 John Davie's goods were appraised by a clothier, a smith, a glover and a tailor, and in 1588 Adam Oldham's by a linen weaver, a whittawer and two tanners. Margaret Bowker's four appraisers of 1591 were all described as 'artificers'. Though too much should not be made of these literacy figures, they do suggest that education might have benefited from more legacies.

When it came to making their wills Manchester men and women showed rather more interest in the poor and in public works than they did in their church or in education. About a dozen testators, or one fifth of the total, left something to the poor. This was usually in the form of a straightforward gift of money, ranging in amount from

30s to £20. The tailor, Thomas Holme, left 30s 'to the poare people', which was about 5½ per cent of his personal property and probably the highest proportion in any will. Thomas Hardman, the mercer, left 40s to the poor of the town of Manchester and John Buckley 20s to the poor and needy of Rochdale, 13s 4d to the poor of Manchester and 6s 8d to the poor of Salford. The Pendletons gave in cash and kind. George Pendleton left £3 6s 8d to be distributed to the poor on the day of his funeral and twelve black frieze gowns to twelve poor men who were doubtless expected to attend the funeral. His widow, Alice, left £3 to the poor and frieze gowns to six poor men and six poor women and frieze coats to twelve poor children. It would be interesting to know whether bequests to the poor were inspired by hard times, but it is impossible to tell whether there was any link between the bad harvest of 1586 and Elizabeth Webster's bequest of £6 13s 4d to the poor by her will of February 1587. The bad harvests and high food prices of 1594–7 may be reflected in the bequests of 1598 when Isabel Tipping left £20 to poor folks and Robert Walshman, the goldsmith, left £2 in cash and £1 in bread to the poor householders of Manchester and Salford. In the same year Humfrey Haughton, the clothier, made a number of bequests to the poor: 50s to the poor of Manchester, 50s to the poor of Salford, 20s to the poor of Stockport and Norbury in Cheshire, 20s to ten poor shearmen of Manchester, 'a gowne of Manchester rugg or Ratchdall fryce' to twelve poor men and twelve poor women, and a coat of the like stuff to six poor children 'that cann saye the Lordes prayer'. None of these bequests established any permanent provision for the poor. The nearest approach to that was Richard Webster's bequest to the poor of Manchester of £5 down and £2 p.a. for seven years. There was no endowment of almshouses and no creation of charitable trusts. The black gowns and the doles of money were traditional ways of bringing material comfort to the poor and spiritual solace to the deceased, but they were beginning to have an old-fashioned air.

Finally half-a-dozen men left money for public works. Humfrey Haughton left 10s 'towardes the repayringe of the payment betweene Manchester and Stopport' and 20s towards 'the repayre of the Cundytt in Manchester', forgiving the overseers of the conduit 'all such money as I have heretofore layd downe for the amending of the same', and George Pendleton left 40s for the conduit. The conduit, which stood in Marketstead Lane, was fed from a spring and constituted the public water supply. This 'speciall ornament of the towne' was kept in repair by the Court Leet which appointed overseers 'to gather and collecte the charitie of well disposed persons' for that purpose. When charity failed, the overseers could levy a rate to meet the cost of repairs.[29] Alice Pendleton's debt of £1 12s 'to the cundite' was presumably for failing to pay such a levy. Men seem to have had more interest in bridges than in the conduit, but given the importance of land carriage to the cloth trade that is not surprising. Robert Marshall, who was a chapman, left 20s for 'the repayringe of the arches of Salford Bridg' provided they were repaired before the following Michaelmas. Salford Bridge, on which the 'dungeon' or lock-up stood, spanned the River Irwell and so was the direct link between Manchester and Salford, but it was less popular as a subject for bequests than Crosford Bridge which spanned the Mersey in Stretford. Richard Webster left £3 6s 8s for the maintenance of the highway towards Crosford Bridge, and Humfrey Haughton left £3 'towardes the mayntenance of Crosford Bridge . . . to be bestowed by my executor uppon the said Bridge and uppon the abuttments and repayring of the banckes for the better defence of the same'. In his will of 1578 Thomas Hardman left £2 for the building of Crosford Bridge 'at such tyme as it is builded', which suggests that the bridge was being built or re-built at that time. The importance of the bridge seems to have been that it carried the road into Cheshire and so to the south.

The gifts and bequests made to charity in Lancashire in this period have been analysed by Professor Jordan, who emphasises 'the absorbing interest of Lancastrians' in fostering education, their continued though declining, interest in the needs of the church, and their relative lack of interest in the poor and in public works.[30] This analysis finds little reflection in the wills of Manchester men and women who died in Elizabeth's reign. Their bequests show little interest either in education or in the church, to each of which they left less money than they did to the poor or to public works. This did not imply generosity to the poor and a passion for civic betterment. Charitable bequests as a whole were meagre. Out of personal estates valued at £8987[31] some £37 6s 8d was given in cash to charity[32] It is, of course, possible that these men and women had given to charity during their lifetimes and that this has left no trace. If the purpose of the 'dead man's part' of the personal property was to provide the testator with the means to make charitable bequests, then most testators believed that charity began at home. It was natural that this should have been so. Of those who made wills that have survived, there were forty-two men who either had been married or were married at the time of their deaths. Thirty-five of these had wives and thirty-eight had children who survived them. Of the thirty-eight with children at least twenty-four, and probably more, had children some or all of whom were minors. It was natural, therefore, that a man, and very often a dying man, should seek to make as adequate a provision for his wife and children as his resources allowed. Hence the concentration of bequests on the wife and children from the testator's own third of the personal estate, which was over and above what was dictated by the custom of inheritance. Such bequests, especially for the children, were less a spring board for social advance than a safety net against social descent.

NOTES

[1] *C.L.R.*, i, pp. 70, 129–31, 160, 190; ii, p. 97.

[2] *Ibid.*, i, p. 129.

[3] *Ibid.*, ii, p. 170.

[4] *Ibid.*, i, pp. 197, 227, 241, ii, pp. 51, 178.

[5] *Infra.* pp. 102–3.

[6] G. G. Alexander, 'The custom of the Province of York', *Thoresby Society*, xxviii (1928), pp. 417–30.

[7] Appendix 2.

[8] W. G. Hoskins, *Provincial England*, pp. 88, 111–14.

[9] M. A. Havinden, ed., *Household and farm inventories in Oxfordshire 1550–1590*, p. 2 and *passim*.

[10] A. D. Dyer, *The city of Worcester in the sixteenth century*, pp. 26, 159.

[11] A. Redford and I. S. Russell, *The history of local government in Manchester*, i, pp. 47–8.

[12] *C.L.R.*, i, p. 269; ii, pp. 337–8.

[13] *Ibid.*, ii, pp. 137–40.

[14] J. P. Earwaker, ed., *Lancashire and Cheshire wills and inventories*, Ch.S. n.s. xxviii (1893), pp. 15–18.

[15] *C.L.R.*, ii, p. 290 n.2.

[16] *Ibid.*, ii, pp. 67, 73.

[17] M. Spufford, *Contrasting communities. English villagers in the sixteenth and seventeenth centuries*, pp. 320–44.

[18] G. J. Piccope, ed., *Lancashire and Cheshire wills and inventories*, ii, p. 151 Ch.S. li (1860).

[19] M.C.L. L1/28/8/1.

[20] G. J. Piccope, ed., *op. cit.*, iii, pp. 65–9 Ch.S. liv (1861).

[21] *Registers*, p. 273.

[22] For his charitable bequests see *infra.* p. 103.

[23] M.C.L. L1/28/8/1.

[24] J. Harland, ed., *The house and farm accounts of the Shuttleworths*, i, pp. 22, 31, 37, 40, 46, 50. Ch.S. xxv (1856).

[25] *C.L.R.*, i, p. 190 n.1; ii, p. 48 n.2.

[26] *Ibid.*, i, p. 139 n.1, p. 170 n.3.

[27] J. P. Earwaker, 'Notes on the early booksellers and stationers of Manchester prior to the year 1700', *Trans. Lancs. and Cheshire Antiquarian Soc.* vi (1888), pp. 1–26.

[28] The minister, Robert Barber, witnessed a number of women's wills; John Glover witnessed and wrote the wills of William Baguley and John Cowopp.

[29] *C.L.R.*, i, p. 15 n.3, pp. 160–1, 224.

[30] W. K. Jordan, *The social institutions of Lancashire 1480–1660*, p. 7 Ch.S. 3rd ser. xi (1962).

[31] This includes all estates where both a will and an inventory survive.

[32] Not including bequests to servants.

CHAPTER VII

HOUSE AND HOME

The physical setting in which Manchester families enjoyed their wealth or endured their poverty cannot be fully re-created. For many such families domestic life centred on the burgage or on part of a burgage, but the burgage combined well defined legal rights and manorial obligations with a very ill-defined physical structure. That structure clearly included the dwelling house, and the dwelling house itself might include a shop for retail trade or a workshop. Alice Pendleton's house contained a chamber over the shop and so too did John Leese's. Other specialised accommodation may have been separate from the house itself; this was probably true of the slaughter house and the milk house of John Wharmby, a butcher, and of the dyehouses of Adam Oldham and John Leese. It may also have been true of the warehouses and the brewhouses. It would be fanciful to compare the burgage with a Roman villa in an urban setting, but a burgage could certainly comprise domestic, industrial and agricultural premises and yet leave room for gardens and even orchards. Gardens were common, and even when a burgage, or half a burgage, comprised two or three tenements each might have its garden. Such gardens might provide room for the pigs and the poultry, but more serious farming required a larger area. It is not clear whether men who kept cattle held land contiguous to their burgages, though in many parts of Manchester that would have been possible. There was, for example, much farm land on both sides of the 'ribbon development' of burgages along Deansgate and Marketstead Lane. No doubt the burgages formed the headquarters for such farming as there was. This is suggested by the barns that occur on some of the burgages and by the middens and dung hills which the Court Leet sought to control. Middens and dung hills were forever 'noisome'. If they were kept next to a boundary pale or hedge, they were noisome to the neighbour; if they were kept 'to the streetewarde', they were noisome to passers-by. Despite repeated orders from the Court Leet against them, the nuisances remained.[1] Perhaps they were tolerable partly because the

Elizabethans were used to muck and smells and partly because there was sufficient open space in Manchester to mitigate their offensiveness.

Successive rebuilding of the city centre has obliterated the burgage as a unit and its buildings. Today the first Elizabethans would only recognise the Cathedral and Chethams Hospital, and they would not have known them either as a cathedral or as a school and library. Much of the Elizabethan street plan has miraculously survived, but property development may well make its future precarious. Pictures also survive of some of the buildings that once lined the streets and that may have dated back to the sixteenth century, but it is impossible to tell what changes had been made to such buildings in the intervening centuries.[2] Pictures showing the exterior of houses are no real substitute for the houses themselves; they reveal little or nothing of the internal lay-out of the rooms or of the use to which such rooms were put. After all families do not live in the street or garden looking at their houses; they live inside them. In the absence of the houses themselves, the only source that reveals their interiors is the probate inventory, which may record the individual rooms and their contents. That is not, unfortunately, always the case with Manchester probate inventories. Some of these inventories record the contents of the house without specifying the rooms in which they were kept. In some cases, especially with poorer testators, this might imply that there was only one room. Grace Whitworth, a widow whose meagre possessions were valued at £2 12s 6d and were not ascribed to any rooms, may well have lived in a one-roomed house. On the other hand Francis Pendleton, a 'merchantman' who died in 1574 with a personal estate of £218 8s 10d, clearly did not live in a one-roomed house even if his inventory specified no rooms at all. It would be very wrong to assume that the absence of reference to rooms implied a one-roomed house. In some other inventories the contents of the house were not valued systematically, room by room, but certain rooms were mentioned casually. Thus Thomas Beck, gentleman, had a bed 'in the lytle chamber', a press 'in a chamber' and 'implements in a buttrie', and John Cowopp, yeoman, had 'a standinge bedd in the parler on the backsyde'. It would be unsafe to draw conclusions about the number of rooms from such casual references.

Out of more than fifty Manchester inventories only twenty specify the rooms in sufficient detail to give a reasonably accurate description of the house as a whole. The house occupied by Roger Bexwick had the largest number of rooms; it had thirteen rooms, but it was almost certainly an inn rather than a private house. The same seems true of Margaret Bowker's house of ten rooms and Joan Newall's of nine rooms. The remaining seventeen houses varied in size from ten rooms to four if shops, workshops, warehouses and cellars are omitted. There was one house of ten rooms, one house of nine rooms, five houses of eight rooms, two houses of seven and one of six rooms, two houses of five rooms and five houses of four rooms. The largest of these houses was occupied by Robert Bridghouse, who called himself a joiner. The house with nine rooms was occupied by John Leese, a well-to-do clothmaker. Two men connected with the cloth trade, Adam Oldham, yeoman and dyer, and Edward Ellor, occupied two of the eight-roomed houses, as did Robert Wharmby, an affluent butcher. The other two houses in this group provided the domestic setting for those wealthy widows, Alice Pendleton and Isabel Tipping. Another widow, Isabel Barlow, whose husband had been a blacksmith, and Richard Hunt, gentleman, occupied the seven-roomed houses, and Ottiwell Hodgkinson, a shoemaker, had the house of six rooms. A wealthy clothier and a butcher with a personal estate of £34 each occupied a house of five rooms. Finally those who occupied the houses with least rooms included a draper, a baker and a whittawer with personal estates ranging from £15 18s 1d to £135 0s 1d. The number of rooms in a house was plainly not always a safe guide to the personal wealth of the occupant. Nor of course is this sample of inventories a safe guide to Manchester's housing as a whole. It is too small a sample and it is biased in favour of the wealthier occupants; twelve of the seventeen occupants had personal property above the median value of estates. No one should assume that the smallest houses in Manchester had four rooms. Nevertheless the inventories as a whole can be used to give a picture of the domestic setting in which at least a part of Manchester's population lived and worked.

The main room in most houses, especially the larger ones, was the hall or 'house' as it was often called. This was a survival from the medieval house in which the hall had been the centre of domestic life. The hall seems usually to have been on the ground floor, but it was not carried through to the roof; there were chambers or parlours above it. There are cases where the hall must have been on the first floor; the butcher, John Wharmby, had a back parlour beneath the 'house' and Adam Oldham had no fewer than two parlours and a chamber beneath his hall. This implies that Oldham's hall was large, and the inventory of its contents confirms this. There were twenty-four yards of 'seelinge and benches'; 'seelinge' was either panelling or wainscoting and presumably the benches ran along the wall beneath it. There was also a 'celed [panelled] cupborde', a 'foldinge table', a 'short framed borde', three chairs and two forms, three brass candlesticks and three brass flower pots, sixty-seven pounds of pewter, two brass pots weighing twenty-six pounds, and '25 lb brasse pann mettle'. The hall was glazed with eighteen feet of glass valued at 7d a ft. It was all rather splendid and might be described as bourgeois baronial. The hall was really a combined sitting room and dining room, though in Oldham's case it is just possible that the cooking was done in the hall. Unfortunately damage to the inventory at this point makes it impossible to be certain of this. Robert Bridghouse's hall had 'a fyre grate and a tostinge iron', but the contents of his kitchen show that the cooking was done there and not in the hall. In a negative way the hall could be defined as the one room, apart from the service rooms, which did not normally contain a bed.

The halls in the bigger houses were very similar in their furnishings. Thus John Leese's hall had a long table and two forms and 'celinge and benchinge at the backe of the table', which suggests something like a high table, though there is no evidence that this was placed on a dais as in medieval halls. There were four chairs and eleven cushions, a round table and three chests, five brass candlesticks and one of pewter, and a great deal more pewter of which thirty-six pounds of the finer quality was upon 'one standinge cupborde'. Finally there were two handy chamber pots. Similarly Robert Bridghouse's 'howse' had its 'seelinge and glasse', its 'framed table' and form, its six 'buffett stooles', its 'two throwne cheres' and 'one wycar chere', its dozen cushions, and its candlesticks, pewter, glasses and painted cloths. In the smaller houses, or at least the houses with fewer rooms, the hall served the same function though it might be less elaborately furnished. Thus John Davie, who dealt in cloth and linen yarn and had only four rooms, possessed a hall which, apart from the usual 'seelinge' and benches, contained only a board table, an old counter, a cupboard, six chairs and six cushions, and 'a sallett with a peyre of splents'. The same sort of furniture figured in the hall of another four-roomed house which was occupied by Andrew Renshaw, a shoemaker and dealer in linen yarn.

In its primitive form the medieval hall had been used for sleeping as well as for eating, drinking and social life in general. By the sixteenth century the halls in Manchester houses had retained their place as the centre of domestic life, but they were no longer used as bedrooms. The bedrooms were elsewhere, though they were not described as bedrooms or even as bed chambers. They were called parlours or simply chambers, and were to be found on any floor of the house. Edward Dyson, for example, had a nether chamber and a chamber above and a lower parlour and a parlour above, all of which contained beds. It was very rare indeed for a chamber or parlour not to contain a bed or beds. Among John Leese's four chambers there was one without a bed; it held two tubs of feathers, a corn sack, a basket, wooden vessels and turves. It was clearly a store room, and its location above the parlour, which was itself above the hall, suggests that it was a cockloft, though that would be an odd place to keep turves. Similarly Alice Pendleton had a parlour which contained no bed; it held 'a standing table with 5 buffet stoles', a little table, 'a standing celed cupborde', three chairs, 'dyvers paynted papers' and a close stool. Despite the rather incongruous close stool, this suggests a parlour in the modern sense of a sitting room. For a widow living alone (apart from servants), a sitting room might be cosier than the hall, which in this case contained a whetstone. As chambers and parlours normally contained beds, it is difficult to see what the distinction between them really was. Thus Adam Hope had a 'servauntes parlor' which contained nothing but beds and bedding, and John Wharmby had a 'servants chamber' which contained '2 bedsteeds with their furniture and one truckle bed and other implements'. The inventories suggest that there was no clear distinction between the parlour and the chamber, but that there was some distinction between parlours and chambers which were used solely as bedrooms and those which were used partly as bedrooms and partly as sitting or withdrawing rooms. Of Robert Bridghouse's three parlours and a chamber, one parlour and the chamber seem to have been simply bedrooms, for in neither of them was there anywhere to sit down except on the beds. In 'the parlor to the streete', however, there was a chest, a framed table and 'one forme with a seeled settle', and in 'the parler uppon the backsyde', 'one framed borde and seatts there unto belonginge', which suggests that, despite the beds, the rooms could be used as sitting rooms.

It is possible that the main parlour or chamber was put to this combined use as a bedroom and sitting room. Adam Oldham's main chamber, which was panelled or wainscoted and glazed, contained 'a standinge seled bed with seled tester', fringe and say hangings, and 'a truckell bedd'; in other words a panelled four poster with a panelled tester or canopy and curtains at the sides and a truckle or wheel bed which could be pushed under the standing bed during the day and which was often used for servants or children. In addition the chamber contained fifteen cushions, a framed table and a 'litle rounde table', two little desks, two chests, a form, two chairs, 'a seled cupborde' and a close stool. It also contained Oldham's 'byble with other bookes', and his clothes and the clothes of his late wife who had predeceased him by only three weeks.[3] Again this suggests a room that was used for more than sleeping. It was, of course, the main chamber of a well-to-do man, and it was matched by similar rooms in which the rich widows slept. Margaret Hurlestone's 'great parler' had, among other things, a bed with damask tester and silk curtains valued at £4 10s, '3 curtens of saye grenne and red for windowes', and ten cushions of which six were 'of tapestre' and two were 'of olde vestments', presumably popish. Similarly Alice Pendleton's chamber 'where shee dyd lye' had its 'standing celed bed with celed bench', its 'paynted hengings' and 'curtens of steyned worke', and its table and two chairs. It had also an 'inner chamber' with a bed and a cradle. Was this occupied by one of the maids, Margaret or Dorothy, or had it been the nursery for Alice's daughter Cicely?

Most parlours and chambers were less ornate than the master bedroom of the well-to-do. Edward Dyson, the butcher with a personal estate of £34, was more typical. His two chambers and two parlours contained beds, including 'a standinge celed bed' and 'a standinge bedd with cloth tester', arks and coffers, and 'a celed presse' in one parlour and a 'celed copborde' in the other. Similarly Adam Hope, a wealthier man than Dyson, had only a bed, 'two hengings' and an old chest in his chamber, and two beds, a cupboard, a chest, and two coffers in his parlour. Apart from their beds, Andrew Renshaw's chamber and parlour seem to have contained nothing but three arks, one of them old, three coffers, 'bordes' and a cradle, although his personal estate was valued at £111 13s 2d. In general, however, Elizabethan rooms were sparsely furnished in comparison with those of today and still more in comparison with those of Victorian and Edwardian times.

Just as parlours and chambers had developed from the nucleus of the hall so too had a range of service rooms, of which the kitchen and the buttery were the most common. There is little detailed information on kitchens and butteries in the inventories, and most of it relates to the larger houses. In such houses the kitchen was usually the place where the cooking was done. Thus Alice Pendleton's kitchen contained 'one great standing iron for the fire', an iron barr, '3 racenteles', a frying pan and a chafing dish; it probably also contained the sixty-five and a half pounds of brass pans and the iron pans and complicated ironware for the fire which weighed ninety-one pounds, though all these were valued separately with the pewter and the plate. John Wharmby's kitchen, too, had its fire irons and its 'pott brasse and pane brasse with irone, and treene warre',[4] and some bacon. Neither kitchens nor butteries were confined to the large houses. One of John Davie's four rooms was a kitchen, and John Pycroft, a linen weaver, had no fewer than three butteries described as the foremost, nearer and farthest buttery. They held some of his treen ware as well as sieves, boards and arks. In general butteries seem to have contained treen ware, pots and pans, and sometimes food. John Wharmby's buttery contained beef, and one of John Leese's butteries had butter, a salting tub, five beer barrels, 'twoe breade graters', which were slatted crates suspended from the ceiling for bread storage, as well as pots and pans, trenchers and 'a rose styll', presumably for making rose water. In his other buttery, described as 'the lytle butterye in the kytchen', Leese had a 'brass fornace', which suggests that the buttery may have been used for brewing, for a furnace was normally a brewing lead or cauldron with its own heater. The specialised brewhouse existed, but its seems to have been rather rare outside the inns. Robert Bridghouse had a brewhouse or 'yealehouse', but unfortunately its contents were valued along with those of the kitchen. However they obviously included the 'furnes', the 'three greate keares' which were brewing vats, the malt and the ale. The 'ale brewed' was valued at £1 2s. The equipment for brewing on this scale was quite expensive; Bridghouse's furnace was valued at £1 10s and his 'keares' at 13s 4d.

Brewing may have been done in the cellars or taverns as they were often called. These were fairly common, but their contents suggest that they were store rooms for boards and miscellaneous household goods or 'one bord and other small implements' as Francis Wirrall's inventory put it. In any case the brew-it-yourself householder may have been less common than is often supposed. The belief that nearly everyone brewed his own ale in this period is difficult to reconcile with the large numbers of alehouses. On 26 March 1573 'the moste parte of the Jurie' of the Court Leet thought thirty 'alehowses and inns to be sufficient in Manchester'.[5] If this quota was achieved there might well have been one inn or alehouse for every fifteen families. On the other hand only about 42 per cent of the inventories record utensils that could have been used for brewing, and these were found largely among the goods of the more prosperous testators. The less prosperous presumably relied on the off-licence facilities of the inns and alehouses for their domestic supplies. Of wine there is very little trace.

When Elizabethan moralists described the changes of their time, they stressed, as did Phillip Stubbes, the growing extravagance in dress[6] or, as with William Harrison, the increased use, even by 'merchantmen', of 'tapestrie, Turkis worke, pewter, brasse, fine linen, and thereto costlie cupbords of plate' as well as of feather beds and pillows once 'thought meet onelie for women in childbed'. Harrison thought that such changes had not gone very far 'in some parts of Bedfordshire, and elsewhere further off from southerne parts'. That may have been true, but the 'amendment of lodging', as Harrison called it, was certainly found among the 'merchantmen' of Manchester, just as some extravagance of dress was found among their wives or widows.[7]

The 'amendment of lodging' was most marked in the provision of bedding, household linen, pots and pans, and pewter and plate, which was what Harrison had claimed. Bedding varied in quantity and quality but the ideal equipment for a standing bed is perhaps revealed by an entry in the inventory of Robert Birch, a well-to-do linen draper: 'a feather bed, a mattrisse, 2 blanchetes and a caddowe [a woollen coverlet], a paire of sheetes, a bolster and a pillowe lyinge on the standinge bed 40*s*'. Not all beds, standing or otherwise, lived up to this standard, but many did, and there is no doubt about the widespread use of the feather bed. Thirty-four inventories record feather beds, and this is almost certainly an underestimate for a few inventories do not record individual items. Nor was the feather bed confined to the master bedroom. Roger Bexwick had ten feather beds, but that may simply mean that he kept a comfortable inn. Among the private householders William Hunt and John Leese each had seven feather beds and Francis Wirrall had six. The distribution did not coincide entirely with wealth. It is interesting that John Nabbs, a clothmaker who died in 1570, had no feather bed although his personal estate was valued at £89 0*s* 6*d*. Perhaps he was old fashioned, for later in the century people much poorer than he had their feather beds. George Barlow, a baker who died in 1584 with an estate of £15 18*s* 1*d* had two such beds, and even that very poor widow, Grace Whitworth, had an 'old' feather bed. On the other hand John Pycroft, a linen weaver, had only 'a chaffe bedd', and it is hard to believe that he retained this simply because he was old fashioned. Feather beds were hardly ever valued separately in the inventories, but John Cowopp had 'one new fetherbed and an olde fetherbed' valued at £2 10*s*. This was a very high valuation, perhaps because one of the beds was new. George Barlow's two feather beds together with two bolsters were valued at £1 6*s* 8*d*, and Edward Hanson had a feather bed with a bolster and two pillows valued at £1 4*s*. It is impossible to generalise from these and similar valuations except to say that feather beds show a wide range of value and that in some cases they were fairly expensive items.

The household linen included sheets and pillowcases for the beds as well as table or board cloths, table napkins and towels. It was sometimes called 'napery ware', though this term might be limited to the table linen. The wealthier households had large quantities of linen which suggest some degree of gracious living as well as an ample supply of laundry maids or washerwomen. Thus Margaret Hurlestone's linen was valued at just over £26 and included thirty-four pairs of sheets, eighteen pairs of pillowcases, twenty-eight table cloths, fifty-three towels and 112 napkins. This was exceptional, but William Hunt, tanner, had thirty-four pairs of sheets, ten board cloths, fifteen pillowcases, nineteen napkins, twelve towels and a sieve cloth valued at £9 11*s*. 4*d*, and Francis Pendleton, merchantman, had unspecified 'napery ware' valued at £10 9*s*. Most people could not afford stocks of linen on this lavish scale, but given the absence of cotton as an alternative fabric and given the presence of a local linen industry, it is hardly surprising that the use of linen was widespread. At least 87 per cent of the inventories include some household linen, and in some eighteen cases this was valued at £3 or more. There was obviously some correlation between the amount of household linen and the wealth of the householder, but it is difficult to tell how far down the social or financial scale the use of linen had penetrated. The baker, George Barlow, had six pairs of sheets (valued at 12s 8d), but he seems to have had no pillowcases or towels. John Pycroft, the linen weaver, had sheets, pillowcases, a towel and a table napkin valued at £1 4s 4d out of personal property valued at £13 9s 5d. Though one of the sheets was described as new, the linen seems to have been for his own use and not for sale, though he may have woven it himself. Ellen Radley, a spinster with an estate of £10 12s 3d, had 'a paire or 2 of old shettes', a towel and '4 old table napkins'. Even Grace Whitworth had '3 old sheets' among her possessions which had a total value of £2 12s 6d. This was a far cry from Margaret Hurlestone whose linen was worth ten times Grace's total possessions, but it does suggest that you had to be very poor indeed to own no household linen at all.

Much of the household linen was required for the beds, in the form of sheets and pillowcases, and for the table or 'board', in the form of table cloths and table napkins. A little was used for cooking, in the form of sieve cloths, but cooking also needed a whole range of implements and utensils. Some of these were of iron, as the spits, the brandreths, cobirons, gridirons and so on, but many of the utensils were of brass[8], which was more expensive than iron. William Harrison noted the increased use of brass in the home, and the Manchester inventories seem to support his view. Brass was used for a variety of articles including candlesticks, flower pots and mortars and pestles. Adam Oldham, for example, had three brass candlesticks, and three brass flower pots, and Alice Pendleton had ten brass candlesticks and a mortar weighing sixteen and a half pounds. William Sandforth, a linen draper, even had '1 brasse lion', which was valued along with his brass candlesticks, ladle and mortar and pestle. Most of the brass, however, was in the form of pots and pans, which were usually valued simply by weight and described as 'pan metal' and 'pot metal'. The pan metal was given a higher value than the pot metal, but the reason for this is not clear. Perhaps the pan metal was tougher and more resistant to heat on the grounds that pans were put directly onto the fire whereas pots were hung over the fire. Pan metal was valued at from 5d to 12d a pound and pot metal at from 4d to 5d a pound. On the very rare occasions when ironware was valued by weight it was at 1½d to 2d a pound. There is no convincing evidence that these valuations reflected changes in the general price level.

The wealthier Manchester households were usually well supplied with brassware. Richard Hunt, gentleman, had 'brasse with two morters and candelstyckes' valued at £5, compared with his 'iron ware as spytes, goberts and 2 drippinge pannes' valued at £1. John Leese's 165 pounds pot metal and eighty-nine pounds pan metal were valued at £4 13s 9d, and in addition he had brass candlesticks, three morters (of which two weighed thirty-eight pounds) and a brass furnace. The weight of individual pots and pans was often high, which meant that the actual number of utensils was smaller than the total weight of the brass might imply. Thus Alice Pendleton had 'one brasse pan' weighing thirty-seven pounds, two other brass pans together weighing twenty-eight and a half pounds, and '7 brasse pots in weight 94 lb.'. Robert Walshman, the goldsmith, had four brass pots weighing thirty-nine pounds and 'one lytle brasse pott weighte 10 lb.'. These were lighter on average than John Davie's seven brass pots, which weighed 106 pounds, and much lighter than Thomas Brownsword's twenty-nine pounder. Perhaps the size of the pots and pans was some indication of the size of the family to be cooked for. The use of brassware was certainly widespread for at least 79 per cent of the inventories reveal it. They include John Pycroft, the linen weaver, with his '2 great pannes wayinge 24 lb. at 6d a pounde' and his 'pott mettall 5 pottes 54 lb. at 4d a pounde', and Grace Whitworth with her '2 old brasse potts' and her '1 brasse pott' which was 'laid to pledge' for 10s 8d.

Brass pots and pans were used in the actual cooking of food, but the serving of food and drink was more likely to involve the use of treen ware or pewter or even silver. Treen ware was the traditional wooden ware of the kitchen and table. It included platters, dishes, bowls and spoons, and was perhaps the product of a forest industry about which little is known. It survives today in the wooden spoons, the breadboards and the wooden fruit or salad bowls. According to the evidence of William Harrison's oldest inhabitants, one of the things 'marvellouslie altred in England' was 'the exchange of vessell, as of treene platters into pewter, and woodden spoones into silver or tin'.[9] Treen ware may have been considered rather old fashioned by Harrison's day, but it was still widely used. It was apparently very cheap. It may have been the cheapest type of domestic utensil, but it is difficult to compare it with earthenware of which there is little evidence. Its cheapness may be reflected in the fact that inventories do not record treen ware in detail; they simply value it as treen ware. The valuations range from 1s for William Hunt's treen ware to £1 5s for John Cowopp's. Though most householders in Manchester had some treen ware, its value was small in relation to household goods as a whole. There, as elsewhere, treen ware was being replaced by pewter.

The finest pewter was made of tin with small amounts of copper, bismuth or antimony as hardening agents, but most pewter was an alloy of tin and lead.[10] It had a variety of domestic uses including candlesticks and chamber pots, but its main use was for dishes, plates, basins, cans, drinking pots, spoons and salts. It was used therefore in the preparation and serving of food and drink, but not in the actual cooking for which its low melting point made it unsuitable. The use of pewter was widespread in Manchester as elsewhere, but unfortunately the Manchester inventories usually give the total value of pewter without any indication of quantity or they value it by weight. Thus Richard Hunt, gentleman, had 'peuoter with potts of peuotter' valued at £5, which was, rather suspiciously, exactly the same as the value given to his brassware and 14s less than the value of his linen. These three items, pewter, brass and linen, accounted for about 30 per cent of the value of his household goods.[11] Similarly John Wharmby's pewter was valued at £4 8s 3d, which was slightly less than the value of his linen. Valuation by weight was rather more common and rather more informative. Pewter was valued by weight at anything from 4d to 8d a pound. The differences in valuation no doubt reflected differences in quality which in turn may have reflected the difference between London and more local pewter. In 1573 John Davie had eighty-four pounds of 'pewter London metall' valued at 6d a pound and thirty-six pounds 'in pewter vessells Wigan metall' at 4d a pound. Ten years later Robert Birch's London pewter was valued at 8d a pound and his Wigan at 6d a pound. The wealthier Manchester households had a large 'poundage' of pewter. William Baguley, the clothier, had 170 pounds, William Hunt, tanner, 166 pounds, Thomas Brownsword, another clothier, 140 pounds, and John Leese, clothworker, at least 125 pounds. The wealthy widows inevitably appear once again; Alice Pendleton had 183½ pounds of pewter and Isabel Tipping 134½ pounds. The figures are perhaps more impressive when the actual number of pieces was given. Thus Thomas Hardman, a mercer, had 105 pieces of pewter and John Shaw, another mercer, had fifty-three pieces. This ownership of pewter was not confined to the well-to-do. At least 84 per cent of the inventories show the possession of pewter. Elizabeth Orred, a widow with an estate of £6 8s 3d, had seventeen pieces of pewter valued at 17s. John Pycroft, the linen weaver, had forty-two pounds of pewter as well as '4 pewter kannes, 2 saltes and a little pewter pott'; altogether his pewter was valued at £1 3s 5d or some 13 per cent of the value of his household goods. Even Grace Whitworth had a pewter dish.

It would be wrong to think of pewter as simply the poor man's silver, for it was owned and used by all ranks of society except perhaps the very poorest. Silver plate was a different matter. It was very expensive. Whereas pewter was valued at 4d to 8d the pound, silver plate was valued at 4s to 5s 2d the ounce. The cost of plate, and perhaps also its beauty, made it an ideal form of conspicuous consumption, but it could also be a form of investment, easily realisable or easily pledgeable. The difficulty was to afford it in the first place, but a surprising number of Manchester burgesses or their widows owned some plate. Ignoring John Wharmby's silver tooth pick and Elizabeth Orred's silver pin and pair of hooks as hardly constituting plate, there were at least thirty-two inventories that record the possession of plate. It is not surprising that twenty-five of these also record personal estates above the median value. The commonest articles were, of course, silver spoons, as they probably still are. In about eleven cases spoons were the only silver people owned. Robert Wharmby, the impecunious butcher Wharmby, had six silver spoons valued at £1 out of a personal estate of £12 9s 3d, but this was exceptional. Indeed the ownership of plate seems to have been a very personal thing that sometimes bore little relation to the value of the estate. Robert Birch, the linen draper with an estate of £470 15s 2d, had only two silver spoons valued at 8s, and Edward Ellor, with an estate of £323 10s, had only 'one stone pott armed with silver' valued at £1. On the other hand William Hunt, a tanner with an estate of £146 12s 10d, had forty-three and a half ounces of plate valued at £9 5s 6d. The bigger displays included goblets, salts, bowls, and pots as well as spoons. Thus John Leese's seventy-five and a quarter ounces of plate valued at £18 14s 3d, comprised seventeen spoons, a bowl, a salt and a 'French boule duble gilte'; Alice Pendleton had 107 ounces of plate valued at £27 14s 11d and comprising two salts, three goblets, a pot, two dozen apostle spoons and two other spoons. These she had inherited as Isabel Tipping had doubtless inherited her forty-four silver spoons and other plate valued at about £20, some of which she left to her married daughters and a daughter-in-law. Indeed inheritance may partly explain both the ownership of plate and the somewhat eccentric distribution of that ownership.

With few exceptions the prosperous burgesses who owned plate also owned arms, though the connection between the two may simply be that such ownership reflected a certain level of wealth. Men were under a statutory obligation to own arms and armour according to their income from land or the value of their personal property.[12] This national legislation was supplemented by local decree. The Court Leet laid it down that every burgess was to find an able man 'in harnes' to wait upon the Steward on the Fair Day, and that 'every person beinge appointed to watche shall bringe with him a jacke, a sallet and a bill at the least'.[13] Not every burgess had this equipment, but two dozen inventories show the possession of some arms or armour. The common weapons were the sword, the dagger, the bill, and bows and arrows. Firearms were represented by calivers and a solitary dag or pistol, and armour by sallets (headpieces) and the occasional coverlet, jack and 'coat of plate'. The possession of these things varied greatly. Robert Birch and Edward Hanson, who were both prosperous, had only a caliver each, and Thomas Brownsword, who was even more prosperous, had only 'a forest byll' valued at 1s 8d, which was well below his statutory quota of arms. On the other hand Adam Oldham had, scattered about his house, a dagger and girdle, a sword, a bow, a sallet, a black bill and an old plated coat, and John Wharmby had a dag, a caliver, a head piece, a flask and touch box, and a yew bow with '18 bearinge arrowes and 9 pryckinge arrowes'. The actual use men made of these weapons is not revealed in the static picture presented by the inventories. The Court Leet, reflecting the national devotion to the obsolescent, was concerned with the provision of butts for the archers, and the records of Quarter Sessions show that the sword, the dagger and even the partisan or long-handled spear could come in handy for assaults on private, if not public, enemies.[14]

The more prosperous Manchester merchants, clothiers, shop-keepers and their widows had considerable material comforts in their well-furnished houses and considerable finery in their well-stocked wardrobes. Some of them owned books, but very few had any pictures apart from the painted cloths which were framed and hung on the walls of quite humble homes. Inventories record only two or three mirrors, which suggests that the Elizabethans must have known better what their neighbours looked like than what they themselves looked like. They record nothing associated with children except the occasional cradle, and yet wills show that some houses must have been alive with children even at the time of their father's death. The custom of treating children as miniature adults may account for the absence of domestic equipment specifically for them, but it should not be forgotten that the houses were family houses. Even the Court Leet recognised the existence of children if only by solemnly allowing those of twelve and under to play 'gede gadye or catts pallet' in the streets.[15]

Though inventories are the best source for showing the physical setting of domestic life in Elizabethan Manchester, they are misleading in the sense that they do not really reveal the more primitive aspects of that life whether it was lived by the rich or by the poor. They provide some evidence on this. They show, for example, that the windows in some houses were wholly or partly glazed because the glass in such windows was regarded, not as a fixture, but as moveable

and therefore part of the personal estate. It was for this same reason
that panelling or wainscoting was valued in the inventories; as Isabel
Tipping's inventory put it, 'in seelinge, glasse and other moveables'.
In her will of 18 April 1592 Joan Newall declared that 'all the glasse
lattice and al such other furniture as now standeth in every window
throwout my whole house together with all and every lock and keye
belongine to every door in and about my sayd whole house shall stand
remayne and continew forever as herelowmes of right belonging unto
the same house'. As a result her inventory contains no valuation of the
glass. Other inventories value the glass in fourteen houses or about
30 per cent of the houses they cover. It is impossible to tell how many
windows in these houses were glazed. Robert Clough had 'glasse in
windowes' valued at 9s, and John Billing, the glazier, had 'glasse in the
wyndoes' valued at 10s. Such valuations may have represented considerable glazing, for Thomas Hardman, the mercer, had thirty feet
of glass valued at 15s or 6d a foot. In other cases the valuation was
lower; Thomas Brownsword and John Pycroft had glass valued at
4d a foot. It would be unwise to draw too firm conclusions from this
evidence. The inventories show that some houses were at least partly
glazed and suggest that many were not glazed at all. This may be true,
but it is not certain that inventories always valued window glass when
it occurred any more than they always valued leases.

Though unglazed windows could be covered by shutters or window
sheets, the absence of glass must have affected the heating of rooms.
Domestic heating is difficult to assess especially in a place like Manchester where the Elizabethan chimneys and fire places have dis-
appeared along with the houses. Inventories show that the Manchester householder had a considerable range of domestic fuels. Thus
John Cowopp had 'all fuel as kidds [faggots], gorse, woode, turves and
coles' valued at £9 6s 8d, which was slightly more than a sixth of his
personal property. The fuel was valued on 3 January 1582, but it was
a large stock of winter fuel even for a prosperous farmer and arouses
the suspicion that Cowopp may have been dealing in fuel. In other
cases the fuel may have been industrial as well as domestic. William
Hunt's twelve loads of wood (valued at £1 4s), twelve loads of coal
(also valued at £1 4s) and twelve loads of turves (valued at 10s) may
have included some industrial fuel for Hunt was a tanner. George
Barlow's 'gorse kiddes and wood kiddes and other wood fewell' and
his 'turves and coles', together valued at £3 7s, equal to a fifth of his
personal estate, must have included fuel for his oven, for Barlow was
a baker. Others held considerable stocks of what seems to have been
purely domestic fuel; William Baguley's was valued at £3 and so too
was Edward Dyson's supply of wood, turves, coals and kidds. Francis
Hough's store of wood, coal, turves, 'cannell' and kidds was valued

E

along with his dung at £2 19s 11½d, a curiously precise figure reminiscent of a bargain price. Coal was an ambiguous term in this period for
it often meant charcoal. Charcoal was used in the chafer, a small braz-
ier on which the chafing dish was placed to keep food warm, and
perhaps also in John Leese's warming pan, but the coal of the
inventories seems to have been mineral coal. Cannel was certainly
mineral; it was a bituminous coal that burns with a bright flame. It
seems to have been more expensive than ordinary coal; Robert
Walshman's load of cannel was valued at 3s 4d compared with 2s 6d
a load for his coal and about 10d a load for his turves or peat. Many
people had stocks of fuel, about three dozen of the inventories record
them, but the inventories suggest that fireplaces were confined to a
limited number of rooms, more especially the halls and kitchens.
There is nothing surprising in this, for the idea that the whole house
should be heated is either very Roman or very modern. Manchester
is almost built on coal and half surrounded by peat; its Elizabethan
inhabitants may have lived in houses not noticeably colder than those
of forty years ago.

It was not so much in their heating as in their water supply and
sanitation that Elizabethan houses displayed their primitiveness, and
it was a primitiveness that affected all ranks of urban society. Manchester had its public water supply in the Conduit, a pipe-line which
brought water from springs in or near what is now Spring Gardens.
The water was tapped at the Conduit head in Marketstead Lane.
This system had been established by private benevolence early in the
sixteenth century and was maintained by bequests and by levies on
the inhabitants. It was in constant need of repair and in the 1570s was
said to 'lacke water'. The need to conserve the water supply led to
restrictions on the use of the Conduit. In 1578 it was decreed that no
one should bring to the Conduit any kind of vessel of greater size 'then
one woman is able to beare full of water and but one of every howse at
one tyme' and that the water bearers were to have their 'cale' or turn
'as hathe bene acustomed'. Three years later it was laid down that no
water should be drawn from the Conduit between 9 p.m. and 6 a.m.
To ensure obedience to this order the Conduit head was apparently
fitted with a lock and key. In 1586 John Witton was to 'kepe the kayes
of the Condite' and to unlock it at 6 p.m. and lock up at 9 p.m.
between 29 September and 25 March; for the rest of the year the
Conduit was to be open only between 6 a.m. and 9 a.m. and between
3 p.m. and 6 p.m.[16] It was an unsatisfactory system but it may have
been supplemented by other public sources of water. At her death in
1591 Alice Pendleton owed not only £1 12s to 'the Cundite in Manchester', but also £2 7s 7d 'to the pumpe in Deanesgate', which suggests
a public pump maintained by a levy on householders. There was also

a pump in Hanging Ditch for in 1602 the Court Leet ordered the inhabitants 'within the Circuite of Hangingdiche' to 'amend and cover and sufficientlye repaire the pompe in the Queenes Highwaie theire standinge so as yt be not hurtfull and dangerous not onlye to horses and other cattle but also to everye passenger and especiallye to children'.[17] Finally there was a 'well and wasshing place' near the wheat mill at which the leather dressers were, not surprisingly, forbidden to dress their leather.[18] It is impossible to tell how far these public water supplies were supplemented by private supplies to individual houses. The references in the Court Leet records to gutters, streams and water courses show that there was plenty of water about, but this surface water would not be fit to drink even by sixteenth century standards. The tapping of springs and the sinking of wells were possible sources of private supply, but there are no references to the former and only one reference to the latter. Robert Bridghouse's inventory valued 'the hovell over the well and the frame' at 10s.

Sanitation was as primitive as the water supply. Half a dozen inventories record the possession of chamber pots, but more may be concealed under the general heading of pewter. Ten people were given as owning close stools. Even these indoor conveniences do not solve the problem of disposal. Sanitation depended on the privy or 'lytle howse'[19] which was regarded as a fixture, though in one case, that of John Wharmby, the appraisers valued his privy along with his firewood and 'odd tymber'. Privies were sometimes placed next to the middens into which they drained; they were sometimes placed next to the street onto which they overflowed; they were sometimes built directly over a water course into which they discharged, thus forming a primitive sort of water closet. These methods were not regarded with favour by the Court Leet which found their effects noisome and which waged a perpetual war against them. The official view was that privies, especially those over gutters or near the street, should be provided with barrels which could be removed and emptied. Thus in 1562 the Court Leet ordered John Partington or his tenant to 'make the pryvey in the gutterr at the boothes end so that yt come not down to the earthe but be kept close in a barrel that yt be not noysome'. Forty years later John Fletcher was ordered either to remove his privy 'or sett a closse stoole under it'.[20] There were many such orders about privies, especially those which were noisome to neighbours or to the general public. Even the provision of barrels did not solve all the problems, for the barrels had to be emptied somewhere. They were emptied into the river Irwell, in theory between 10 p.m. and 4 a.m.[21] In theory again they should have been carried down the river-side steps to the water, but in practice they were often carried onto Salford Bridge from which the night soil was tipped into the stream below where it had 'a better chance of being carried out of the town, to spend its strength upon the desert air of Trafford or Barton'. [22]

These sanitary conditions were not peculiar to Manchester for they were found in any Elizabethan town. It is very difficult to judge their effects on the people who had to live with them. Those effects can hardly have been psychological; a man is not scarred for life, nor is his soul seared, because he has to use an outdoor privy, especially when he had never heard of, still less seen, a more salubrious alternative. Even at the end of the sixteenth century it is doubtful whether any Manchester householder had heard of, still less seen, John Harington's primitive water closet of 1596;[23] He can hardly have realised that his jakes could be metamorphosised. The effects of bad sanitation were physical and showed themselves in the pollution of drinking water and so the spread of disease. Both bad sanitation and a deficient water supply were hazards to health that could affect all urban dwellers. These adverse conditions should neither be forgotten nor exaggerated when trying to assess the physical environment in which the Elizabethans lived whether in Manchester or elsewhere. Within that physical environment the quality of life was much influenced by wealth; life was more tolerable in Elizabethan Manchester for those who had sufficient money to buy such comforts as were available. Survival too was affected by wealth; the poor men and women whose burials were recorded in the register of the Collegiate Church may have died because they were poor. But survival was also a matter of luck; in 1605 the same register recorded the burial of 1053 men, women and children from the parish of Manchester. Most of the dead had died of plague. Among them the old names appear: Pendleton, Haughton, Birch, Gee and so on. Bubonic plague was not a great respecter of wealth or status.

NOTES

[1] *C.L.R.*, i, pp. 54, 77, 153; ii, pp. 83, 108.

[2] Some pictures of early buildings are reproduced in A. Redford and I. S. Russell, *The history of local government in Manchester*, i.

[3] *Registers*, p. 266.

[4] Treen ware was wooden ware such as platters, dishes, spoons etc.

[5] *C.L.R.*, i, p. 153.

[6] Phillip Stubbes, *The anatomie of abuses*, ed. F. J. Furnivall (New Shakspere Society), i, pp. 50–9, 75.

[7] William Harrison, 'Description of England', in R. H. Tawney and E. Power, *Tudor economic documents*, iii, pp. 69–70.

[8] In this period brass was the general term applied to alloys of copper and tin

(bronze) or copper and zinc (brass). The brass of the inventories was almost certainly bronze.

[9] Harrison, *op. cit.*, ii, pp. 69–70.

[10] J. Hatcher and T. C. Barker, *The history of British pewter*, p. 1.

[11] Excluding his farm stock, apparel, yarn etc.

[12] L. Boynton, *The Elizabethan militia 1558–1638*, pp. 10, 299.

[13] *C.L.R.*, i, pp. 100, 123.

[14] *Ibid.*, i, pp. 155, 177; J. Tait, ed., *Lancashire Quarter Session Records*, i, pp. 24, 50. Ch.S. n.s. lxxvii (1917).

[15] *C.L.R.*, i, p. 205. The game was 'tipcat' in which a small piece of pointed wood was placed on the ground, struck on the end to make it rise and then hit in the air. It seems to have died out in Manchester, but it was still played in Westmorland in the 1920s.

[16] *C.L.R.*, i, pp. 160, 171, 202, 259.

[17] *Ibid.*, ii, p. 185.

[18] *Ibid.*, i, p. 114.

[19] *Ibid.*, i, p. 58.

[20] *Ibid.*, i, p. 73; ii, p. 178.

[21] *Ibid.*, i, p. 69.

[22] A. Redford and I. S. Russell, *op. cit.*, i, p. 110.

[23] Sir John Harington, *A new discourse of a stale subject, called the Metamorphosis of Ajax*, ed. E. T. Donno. The modern view that the use of outdoor conveniences is somehow demoralising seems to be exaggerated. The Willan family house in Yorkshire was very superior; it had two earth closets (including a two-seater), one in the garden and the other across the backyard. No one was noticeably demoralised by using them, but they were very cold in winter.

CHAPTER VIII

CONCLUSION

The emphasis that is usually laid on the agrarian basis of the Elizabethan economy has led to some neglect of towns and of their place in
that economy. This neglect is now declining with the increased interest in urban history and the increased awareness of the importance of
mobility, both of people and of goods. Yet much remains to be done.
The obsession with the gentry has produced exaggerated claims that
wealthy townsmen were forever seeking sanctuary and social advancement in the countryside, but little has been said about country people
who sought sanctuary and economic advancement in towns. The
Dick Whittingtons may have been as interesting as the scramblers
after rustic gentility. Migration is a reminder that towns were not
insulated from the countryside but were in many respects integrated
with it. The physical extent of that integration is difficult to assess,
whether it is expressed in terms of marketing areas or of catchment
areas for a surplus rural population or of 'debt bondage' areas where
surplus urban funds helped to finance agriculture, industry or conspicuous consumption in the countryside. The interplay between the
urban and rural economies must have affected the fortunes of towns,
and it is reasonable to assume that urban growth reflected in some way
a comparable growth in that part of the countryside with which a
town had economic links. Such a connection is not easy to demon-
strate. It is difficult to say how far the economic development of
Elizabethan Manchester reflected a similar development in Lancashire as a whole or in the south-eastern part of it.

It is often assumed that early Tudor Lancashire was an isolated
and an economically backward county. There may be some truth in
this, but it is easy to exaggerate the isolation. No doubt the trading
connections between Lancashire and the south were weaker and less
extensive in the first half of the century than in the second, but they did
exist then. The Kendal packhorse men who carried cloth to Southampton were joined by Lancastrians in their journeys south. Nor were
such commercial contacts limited to a single port. In the 1540s the

Bristol merchant, John Smythe, was getting Manchester cottons from Thomas Abeck of Manchester in return for wine, wool oil and woad, and also from Roger Taylor, a clothier of Bolton. The cottons were for export to Spain and Portugal. Smythe also sold iron and wine to James Webster of Manchester, who paid for them in part through Miles Wilson, a Kendalman.[1] Bristol's trading connections were reflected in the areas from which the port drew its apprentices. Between 1532 and 1542 some twenty-eight Lancashire boys went to serve their apprenticeship in Bristol. Most of these boys came from the west of the county, from Preston, Liverpool, Lancaster and Poulton, which rather suggests a greater contact by sea with Bristol than other sources reveal.[2] It is difficult to tell how far the movement of boys to the south-west was accompanied by a similar movement to London at this time. Certainly, Lancashire boys were going to London to be apprenticed to members of the Skinners Company between 1507 and 1509.[3] As apprenticeship was a formal legal matter it suggests some connection between the apprentice's father and his future master. The actual mechanism of this long distance apprenticeship has never been explored, but such apprenticeship is hardly compatible with the economic isolation of the county from which the apprentices came. Indeed the attraction of London may have been greater than the sources reveal, for in Elizabeth's reign, when the sources are fuller, it is clear that London relied heavily on the provinces for its apprentices.

That reliance on the provinces included reliance on the northern counties. Thus between 1558 and 1603 five Lancashire boys were apprenticed to London Skinners[4] and between 1580 and 1603 half-a-dozen such boys were apprentices to 'Writers of the Court Letter of the City of London', that is to scriveners.[5] The London Stationers Company was a greater attraction, for between 1562 and 1603 sixteen Lancashire boys were apprenticed to members of that Company.[6] The London Carpenters Company was a greater attraction still; no fewer than fifty-six Lancashire boys were apprenticed to members of that Company between 1573 and 1594. This number was exceeded only by the sixty-seven boys from London itself, the 104 from Yorkshire and the seventy-five from Northamptonshire.[7] Most of the Lancashire boys were the sons of husbandmen, and their average age at apprenticeship was just under twenty years. Very few of these boys ever became free of the Company. This is not the place to discuss the interesting problem of why these boys were so old or of what happened to them at the end of their apprenticeships. The very fact that boys sought apprenticeship in London suggests that the links between Lancashire and the capital were considerable and were not confined to the Lancashire cloth towns. Very few of the apprentices came from Manchester. Only one boy from Manchester was apprenticed to each of the four London companies here considered. This was natural enough. Most of the Lancashire boys were sons of yeomen or husbandmen and came from country districts or small towns. Thus no less than eight of the would-be carpenters were the sons of husbandmen from Furness and Furness Fells. The fact that a town sent few boys to London may be a sign, not of its isolation, but of its economic maturity. It may itself have been able to provide jobs for all but the most ambitious or restless of its young men. It may also have attracted country boys to itself as Bristol and Shrewsbury plainly did.[8] Whether Manchester acted as this sort of magnet cannot be established in the absence of any enrolment of apprentices, and indeed references to apprenticeship are surprisingly rare. The wills of Manchester men and women do not suggest by their bequests that the testators had been born outside the township. Such testators did not make charitable bequests to country places 'where I was born' as Londoners often did, but this is very negative evidence given the paucity of charitable bequests of any sort.

Manchester men may rarely have sent their sons to be apprenticed in London, but they often sent their cloth to be sold there. John Leake, in his familiar tirade of 1577, might declare that 'no true clothes' were made 'in the Northe partes',[9] but northern cloths, whether true or false, were being exported through London and other ports. The development of this export trade and of the domestic trade in both woollen and linen cloth was important for the growth of towns like Manchester which could act as centres for the manufacture or the collection and finishing of such cloth. This commercial connection between the cloth towns and their markets required a transport system of some sort, though little is known about it. Much of the carriage of cloth was by land. Manchester seems to have had a carrier service to London in the 1590s; in 1597 Dr John Dee was sending money and letters from Manchester to London 'by Bradshaw the carryer' and letters 'by the carryer Barret'. These things were sent in January and December, which shows that even a northern winter did not make road transport impossible.[10] Presumably the carriers brought back from London goods, puritan literature and perhaps plague. They may even have brought back copies of an anonymous Elizabethan play called 'A Pleasant Comedie of Faire Em, the Miller's Daughter of Manchester'.[11] Though the play was set in the reign of William the Conqueror, it had some local colour in the characters of Sir Edmund Trofferd (presumably Trafford) and Sir Thomas Goddard (perhaps an error for Gerrard) who was masquerading as 'the miller of faire Manchester' to escape the vengeance of the Conqueror. Unless Manchester appeared merely for alliterative purposes, the name should have had some significance for the audience, assuming the play was ever performed. It is doubtful, however, whether even its cloth trade made Manchester a household name to the groundlings; a clothier's daughter would have been more convincing.

It was certainly the cloth trade that enabled Manchester to play the role of a cloth town, to which it owed much of its importance and wealth. That role could only be sustained by contact with the cloth markets of London and elsewhere and by contact with the cloth producing areas of south-east Lancashire and perhaps also of north-east Cheshire. Woollen and linen cloth was produced within the town itself, but cloth making was a very labour intensive industry, which is one reason why so much of it was rural. The size of the population compared with the scale of the business conducted by the bigger clothiers strongly suggests that Manchester was a centre for the collection as well as for the manufacture of cloth. It was later to play this dual role, industrial and commercial, in the cotton industry. It was a role that made a town into something of a regional centre. As an entrepôt for cloth, Manchester established commercial links with its hinterland which were reflected in its market and shops and in the financial transactions, involving either credit or money lending, of its clothiers and traders.

A region can focus on a county capital like Norwich or Worcester, but Manchester was not such a capital. Situated almost on the southern border of its county, Manchester was prevented by geography, if by nothing else, from playing the role of a county capital even unofficially. In county administration it was simply one of the towns where the Quarter Sessions met. It was probably more important as a religious than as an administrative centre. Manchester was not 'the Geneva of Lancashire', a distinction reserved for Bolton,[12] but it was an important centre of puritanism, and as such had its attractions. In the 1580s John Bruen, esq., of Stapleford in Cheshire was travelling some thirty miles to Manchester to hear sermons there,[13] which suggests a wide market area for one commodity. In view of the puritan devotion to sermons, it is surprising that so few Manchester men made provision for even a funeral sermon in their wills. Only two did so. Richard Webster, the clothier who left 40s for a drinking after his burial, left 10s to Mr Andrew to make a sermon at his funeral, and the goldsmith, Robert Walshman, requested Mr Brigges to make his funeral sermon and left him 6s 8d for his pains.[14] Brigges was to receive what was the standard rate for a funeral sermon in London, where the provision for such sermons was much more common than in Manchester.[15] Whether the ardent protestantism of the deanery of Manchester, in contrast to most of the county, was a cause or an effect of the 'rise of capitalism' in that area, cannot be determined. It seems at least to have been nurtured by the clothiers' contacts with London.[16]

Elizabethan Manchester was not an isolated or an economically backward community, even if its administration had an archaic flavour. Though it was primarily a cloth town, it was not so dependent on a single industry as a nineteenth-century cotton or mining town might be. Moreover its cloth industry was really two industries, for Manchester made or handled both woollen and linen cloth. The two types of cloth were quite distinct, the one being based on animal and the other on vegetable fibre. There was no overlap as there was later to be when cotton and linen were combined into fustian. With very few exceptions men seem to have handled either woollen or linen cloth, but not both. To cloth must be added leather. Though the leather industry may have been more important than can now be determined, it never really rivalled the cloth industry. It was a natural second industry in a place which could draw its raw materials, hides and skins, from the animal husbandry of north Cheshire and south-east Lancashire, and could supplement them with imports from Ireland. Those who supplied the butchers' stalls with meat could supply the tanners with hides. The farmers within the township cannot have done this on their own; still less can they have supplied the millers with grain and the brewers with malt. Though Manchester combined agriculture with industry and trade, the agriculture was the least important element. The town must have been an 'importer' of food-stuffs, even if the sources of supply cannot now be traced. It is perhaps a sign of Manchester's urban economy that none of the corn dealers licensed by the Justices of the Peace in the 1590s resided in the township, though some lived in the parish.

The combination of agriculture, industry and trade implied a certain degree of diversification in Manchester's economy. This in turn may reflect a certain degree of diversification in the economic pursuits of individuals. It has been pointed out that, in 'Tawney's century', 'the more prosperous artisans tended to diversify their interests instead of ploughing back their profits into their basic activity'.[17] This seems also to have been true of those above the artisan level. Manchester clothiers often engaged in some farming. Shopkeepers extended their basic activity by owning two shops or by selling unrelated goods like mercery and grocery, but they also diversified into farming or as mercers supplemented their retail trade with the wholesale trade in cloth to London. A glazier kept a general store, and a saddler, a shoemaker and joiner dealt in linen yarn. The most common forms of diversification were farming, dealing in linen yarn and money lending. Not all forms met with approval. Shearmen objected to clothiers having cloth sheared on their own premises and dyers objected to unapprenticed dyers with other occupations engaging in their craft. Such objections seem to have been singularly ineffective. It is probable that the barriers between occupations were much less rigid in an unincorporated town than they were in an incorporated one. Manchester had no administrative machinery for supporting such barriers, and no gilds to enforce the old ideal of 'one man, one trade'. This relative freedom may have been more important in promoting economic growth than any alleged stimulus of the 'protestant ethic'. It may well have helped to create an urban economy resting on industry and trade, which produced most of the wealth and which by their nature made Manchester into a regional centre. As such a centre, Manchester had already developed into the regional capital of south-east Lancashire.

NOTES

[1] J. Vanes, ed., *The ledger of John Smythe 1538–1550*, Bristol Record Society, xxviii (1974), pp. 206–7, 215, 232–3, 279, 298.

[2] D. Hollis, ed., *Calendar of the Bristol Apprentice Book, 1532–1565*, Part I 1532–1542, Bristol Record Society, xiv (1949) *passim.*

[3] G. E. Cokayne, 'Skinners' Company apprenticeship', *Miscellanea Genealogica et Heraldica*, ed., J. J. Howard, Third ser., i, (1896), pp. 77, 151, 172.

[4] *Ibid.*, pp. 152, 172–3, 194, 247, 251.

[5] F. W. Steer, ed., *Scriveners' Company Common Paper 1357–1628*, London Record Society, iv (1968), pp. 39–41, 43.

[6] E. Arber, ed., *A transcript of the Registers of the Company of Stationers of London 1554–1640*, i. pp. 195–6, 259, 287–8, 325, ii. pp. 75, 91, 102, 135, 138, 158, 204, 248, 255, 261. Between 1571 and 1575 the records do not give the domicile of the apprentice's father (D. F. McKenzie, 'Apprenticeship in the Stationers' Company 1555–1640', *The Library*, 5th series xiii (1958), pp. 292–99).

[7] J. Ainsworth, ed., *Records of the Worshipful Company of Carpenters*, vi. *Court Book 1573–1594* (1939), *passim.* Anne M. Duffy, 'The structure and organisation of the Carpenters' Company of London in the sixteenth century', Manchester University B.A. thesis (1962).

[8] For Shrewsbury see W. A. Leighton, 'The Guilds of Shrewsbury', *Trans. Shropshire Archaeological and Natural History Society*, viii (1885), pp. 269–412.

[9] R. H. Tawney and E. Power, eds., *Tudor economic documents*, iii, p. 214.

[10] J. O. Halliwell, ed., *The private diary of Dr John Dee*, Camden Society xix (1842), pp. 57–8, 60.

[11] K. Warnke and L. Proescholdt, eds., *Pseudo-Shakespearian Plays*, i. (1883). I am indebted to the late Professor J. D. Jump for this reference.

[12] R. C. Richardson, *Puritanism in north-west England. A regional study of the diocese of Chester to 1642*, p. 142.

[13] *Ibid.*, p. 9.

[14] Brigges was probably Ambrose Briggs, described as curate in 1598 and minister in 1601 (*Registers*, pp. 108, 333). 'Mr Andrew' may have been Lancelot Andrewes.

[15] T. S. Willan, *The Muscovy merchants of 1555*, p. 61.

[16] R. C. Richardson, *op. cit.*, pp. 11–12.

[17] F. J. Fisher, 'Tawney's century', in *Essays in the economic and social history of Tudor and Stuart England*, (ed., F. J. Fisher) p. 7.

APPENDIX 1

RENTAL OF THE MANOR OF MANCHESTER 1599–1600[1]

Colihurste 1599. Rentale manerii de Manchester et pro herbagio de
Colihurste incipiens   3 die Maii 1599

Imprimis Received of Roberte Cloughe for one cowgate	6s	8d
Item of John Bordman for one cowgate	6s	8d
Item of Roger Ryder for his horsegate	13s	4d
Item of Thomas Morrisse for a cowgate	6s	8d
Item of James Rodley for a cowgate	6s	8d
Item of Mr Anthonye Mosley for 4 kyegates and one horsegate	40s	
Item of Wm. Leese for a cowgate	6s	8d
Item of Roger Smythe for a coltes grasse	10s	
Item of John Myles for a cowgate	6s	8d
Item of Roger Rodley for one cowgate	6s	8d
Item of Adam Bowker for 5 calves	16s	8d
Item of Edw. Hollande gent. for 2 geldings	26s	8d
Item of Rychard Rothwell one cowgate	6s	8d
Item of Wm. Glover for a cowgate	6s	8d
Item of John Soundiforthe one cow	6s	8d
Item of Henry Ryle one cowgate	6s	8d

Summa huius paginae   £9

Colihurste 1599

Item of Roberte Willson and his mother for 4 calves and one cowe	20s
Item of Hughe Ryder for 4 calves	13s 4d
Item of Roger Ryder for 3 kye	20s
Item of Fr. Pendilton for 2 calves	6s 8d
Item of Rychard Bryddocke for 2 calves	6s 8d
Item of Edw. Bryddocke for 8 calves	26s 8d
Item of James Rydinge for 2 calves and two kye	20s
Item of James Rodley for 2 calves	6s 8d
Item of Roger Rodley for an horse	13s 4d

Summa huius paginae   £6 13s 4d

[List of payments for winter pasture deleted]

This wynter pasture is putt downe after Manchester Michaelmas
Rents in fine libri.

Rente receyved after a ob. a weeke for everye Flesheborde of the

towne butchers for 6 weekes due on Whitsoneven 1599 and from
thence till Midsomer the nexte followynge beinge 4 weekes

2	Thomas Hultonn	6*d*	4*d*
2	James Hultonn	6*d*	4*d*
2	Roberte Potter		10*d*
2	Roberte Jackes	6*d*	4*d*
2	Fr. Wolsencrofte	6*d*	4*d*
1	Roberte Shelmerdenn	3*d*	2*d*
1	Thomas Hudson	3*d*	2*d*
2	Roberte Hudson	6*d*	4*d*
1	Henrye Siddall	3*d*	2*d*
1	Roberte Barlow	3*d*	2*d*
2	Uxor John Wharmebye	6*d*	4*d*
1	Rycharde Birtinshaw	3*d*	2*d*
2	Uxor Henrie Wharmebye	6*d*	4*d*
1	James Wolsencrofte	3*d*	2*d*
2	Roberte Goodyere	6*d*	4*d*
1	James Greneroade	3*d*	2*d*
1	William Lynney	3*d*	2*d*
1	Adam Syddall		5*d*
1	John Pilkingtonn	3*d*	2*d*
2	Alexander Potter		10*d*
1	Uxor George Greene		nihill
1	Uxor George Kirkall	3*d*	nihill
1	Adam Chorltonn		5*d*
1	William Dawson		5*d*

Summa receptorum huius paginae   13*s* 7*d*

Rente received of the foren butchers for the same tyme after
1*d* a weeke for every borde

1	Henrie Rydinges	6*d*	4*d*
1	Rychard Cooke	6*d*	4*d*
1	Peter Walworke agreed for 20*s* paid to the lord		
2	Thomas Peele agreed for one also		
1	Rychard Peake	6*d*	4*d*
1	Peter Walker	6*d*	4*d*
1	Rychard Walker the younger		10*d*
1	Rychard Walker the elder	6*d*	4*d*
1	John Houghe	6*d*	nihill
1	William Bradshawe	6*d*	4*d*
1	Robert Syddall	6*d*	4*d*
1	Henry Wood	6*d*	4*d*
1	Nicholas Syddall		nihill
1	William Dawson	6*d*	2*d*
1	George Chaderton	6*d*	4*d*
1	Rychard Coppocke	6*d*	nihill
1	Roberte Potter of Stoport		10*d*

Summa receptorum huius paginae   10*s* 10*d*

Towne butchers	1599 Michaelmas rente	1599 Christmas rente
2 James Hulton	12d	12d
2 Roberte Potter	12d	12d
2 Fr. Wolsencrofte	12d	12d
1 Roberte Shelmerden	6d	6d
1 Thomas Hudson	6d	6d
2 Roberte Hudson	12d	12d
1 Henrye Syddall	6d	6d
1 Roberte Barlow	6d	nihill
2 Uxor John Wharmebye	12d	12d
1 Rycharde Birtinshaw	6d	6d
2 Uxor Henrie Wharmebye	12d	12d
1 James Wolsencrofte	6d	6d
2 Roberte Goodyere	12d	12d
1 James Grenerode	6d	6d
1 William Lynney	6d	6d
1 John Pilkinton	6d	6d
1 Adam Chorlton	6d	6d
1 William Dawson	6d	6d
2 Thos. Hulton's sonne	12d	12d
1 Adam Syddall	nihill	nihill
2 Alexander Potter	negat	negat
1 Widow Greene	Rychard Birtinshaw	nihill
1 Wydow Kirkall	nihill	nihill
Roberte Jackes	12d	12d

Summa   28s 6d

Foren butchers	Michaelmas 1599 Rente	Christmas 1599 Rent
1 Henrye Rydinge	12d	12d
1 Rycharde Cooke	12d	12d
1 Peter Walworke and	agreed with the lord for one	
2 Thomas Peele	borde a piece	
1 Rycharde Peake	12d	12d
1 Peter Walker	nihill	12d
1 Rychard Walker the younger	12d	12d
1 Rychard Walker thelder	12d	12d
1 John Houghe	nihill	nihill
1 William Bradshaw	12d	12d
1 Robert Sydall	12d	12d
1 Henrye Wood	12d	12d
1 Nicholas Sydall	nihill	nihill
1 George Chaderton	negat	negat
1 Rychard Coppocke	12d	12d
1 Robert Potter de Stoport	nihill	nihill
1 Anthony Bery als Carpenter		12d

Summa   20s

Rente due by the towne butchers at Thannunciacion 1600

2	James Hulton	12*d*
2	Roberte Potter	12*d*
2	Fra. Walencrofte	12*d*
1	Roberte Shelmerdenn	6*d*
1	Thomas Hudson	6*d*
2	Roberte Hudson	12*d*
1	Henrye Syddall	nihill
2	Roberte Jackes	12*d*
1	Roberte Barlowe	6*d*
2	Uxor John Wharmebye	12*d*
1	Rycharde Birtinshawe	6*d*
2	Uxor Henrie Wharmebye	12*d*
1	James Wolsencrofte	6*d*
2	Roberte Goodyere	12*d*
1	James Greenerode	6*d*
1	William Lynney	6*d*
1	John Pilkinton	6*d*
1	Adam Chorltonn	6*d*
1	William Dawson	6*d*
2	Thomas Hulton's sonne	12*d*
1	Adam Sydall	nihill
2	Alexander Potter	negat
1	Rychard Kirshawe	nihill
1	Wydowe Kirkall	nihill
1	Roberte Syddall	6*d*
1	Raphe Peele pro tempore a principio	22*d*

Summa   16*s* 4*d*

Foren butchers pro Annunciacione 1600 Rente

Henry Rydinge	12*d*
Rycharde Cooke	12*d*
Rycharde Peake	12*d*
Peter Walker	12*d*
Rycharde Walker	nihill
Rycharde Walker younger	nihill
John Houghe	nihill
William Bradshawe	12*d*
Henrye Wood	12*d*
Nicholas Sydall	nihill
George Chadertonn	negat
Rycharde Coppocke	12*d*
Roberte Potter de Stockport	nihill
Anthonye Berye	12*d*

Summa   8*s*

Summa totalis receptae de le butchers   £4 17*s* 3*d*
Chetham 1599 Midsomer 1599

Imprimis received the 21 Julye 99 of Edwarde Bryddocke
for one halffe yeares rente due at Midsomer last paste   £13 19s 7d
Item received more of hym for the arrerage of Samuell
Chetham's rente for one halfe yere   5s 9d
Item received of John Fletcher the 1 of September 1599 for
parte of his fyne   £10
Manchester. Item received the 25 Maye 1599 of Rycharde
Moreton for one yeres arrerage of his rente due at St Michaell 1598   2s 1d
Item of Roberte Hulton for one yeres rente in arrerage then due also   9d
              Summa huius paginae   £24 8s 2d

Manchester   Rentes due at Midsomer 1599
Imprimis received of Mrs Prestwich and Adam Smythe for one
halffe yeres rente due at Mydsomer 1599 for Aldporte parke   26s 8d
Item of Sir John Byron knighte for one quarters rente then due
for Blakeley Blakeley fieldes and Bothomley   £8 6s 8d
Item of Alexander Reditche esquier for his halffe yeres rente
then due for the hamell of Cromsall   10s
Item of John Hunte for his quarters rente then due for the toll
tolboothe &c.   20s
Item of Sir Rychard Houghton knighte and George Boothe esquier
for theire holle yeres rente then due for the hamell of Assheton
under Lyme the patronage of the same and 2 cotages and 2
roodelande per annum a red rose and a penye I saye   1d
Item received of Wydowe Hoape for one halffe yeres rente due at
Mydsomer 1599 for the house in the Hangingdiche wherein she
dwelleth   21s 8d
              Summa huius paginae   £12 5s 1d

1599   Rentes due at St Michaell 1599
William erle of Derbye. Of his honor for a holle yeres rente due
for 3 tenements or burgages in Manchester nere the north-easte
parte of the churcheyarde in the Fennel streete and Mylnegate
beinge Chauntrie landes   22d
Item of hym for one wholle yeres rente then due for the hamell of
Pilkinton holden by the 4th parte of a k.fee²   2s 8d
Item of hym for one yeres rente then due for a tenement in
Milnegate in the tenure of Olyver Digle conteyninge one orcharde
and gardyn 12d one fielde on the eastesyde of the same the
Rydingebancke 20d and a parcell of grounde called Blakelache 4s,
in toto 6s 8d whereof 4d is denyed and the rest payde being   6s 4d
Item of hym for 2 lytle croftes nere Barlow Crosse parcell of
Mylnegates landes late in the tenure of John Holte and his wyffe
sometime Marlers per annum   3s 2d
Item of hym for 2 litle meadoes parcell of Mylnegates landes in
the tenure of Tho. Bamfford per annum   3s
Item of his honor for the Colledge barne per annum   18d
              Summa huius paginae   18s 6d

F

Item due for halffe yeres rente for Overalport at St Michael 1599   20s
Summa totalis huius paginae   38s 6d

St Michaell 1599

Sir John Bironn knighte. Item of hym for one quarter rente
then due for the hamells of Blakeley, Blakeley fieldes and
Bothomley   £8 6s 8d
Item of hym for the hamells of Gorton and Grenlomarshe for
one halffe yeares rent then due by the handes of Mrs Samsonn   £15 5s 8d
Item of hym for a tenemente in Ancotes as tenante in common
with the Feoffees of the Free Schoole in Manchester per annum   3s 4d
Sir John Radclyffe knighte Item of hym for one holle yeres chieffe
rente then due for the moitie of Flixton   20d
Leonarde Ashall gen. Item of hym for certen landes and
tenementes within the hamell of Flixton called the Shawe
per annum   8s 2d
Thomas Bamfford. Item of hym for one tenemente and lande
in his occupacion in Ancotes per annum   3s 4d
Summa huius paginae   £24 8s 10d

St Michaell 1599

Tenants of Mostonn. Of Rycharde Sydall 21d Edwarde Shaclocke
4s Roberte Jepson 2s Rychard Nugente 4½d Geffrey Bowker 12d
her[3] George Streete 9d her Rychard Streete 9d Kenyon pro
Nicolson 11d Anthony Bowker, Frithe and Sydall 11d and Oswold
Mosley 6½d in toto per annum 13s whereof paid to the lords of
Nuthurste 3s and the rest beinge 10s to the lord of Manchester
I say received   10s
Edmunde Prestwich ar. Of hym for one holle yeres rente due for
the moitie of Hulme nexte Manchester 5s for the tachement of his
mylne and 2 gardyns 5s 6d for a burgage conteyninge a house and
a barne and a parcell of lande in the Ackers 12d and for a burgage,
2 houses, one stable and 2 gardyns at the south gate of the Colledge
12d in toto per annum 12s 6d whereof he denieth 12d and the rest is
paide beinge   11s 6d
More of hym by Adam Mosse exec. for halffe a burgage in the
occupacion of Raphe Hawes per annum   5d
Roberte Cleyden his coheires. Of theym for the hamell of Cleyden
5s and for halfe a burgage in the Fenel streete sometyme parson
Cleydens in toto per annum   5s 6d
Summa huius paginae   27s 5d

St Michaell 1599

The heires of Edward Tildesley ar. Of theym for theire landes and
tenementes in Chorleton late Entwissells landes per annum   3s 4d
Rycharde Holland ar. Of hym for his holle yeres rente then due
for his burgages and landes in Manchester and a little croffte nere
to Alporte parke   5s 6d

The heires of John Boothe of Bartonn ar. defunctus. Of theym by
the handes of Roger Bexwicke for one burgage in Deanesgate
sometyme in the tenure of Katherin Ferrar per annum   12*d*

The heires of Adam Hultonn gen. Of hym for his holle yeres rente
then due for the hamell of Harperhey 26*s* 8*d* and for Gotherswicke
12*d* by the hands of his mother Mrs Alice Hultonn in toto
per annum   27*s* 8*d*

John Haughtonn gen. Of hym for a burgage in Marketstidlane
late Roberte Hardies per annum   12*d*

more of hym for certen burgages and landes in the Hangingdyke
parcell of Hultonn of Ferneworthes landes per annum   18*d*

Raphe Haughtonn. Of hym for one holle yeres rente then due for
one oxegange of lande in Dentonn sometyme one Wm. Hultons
landes   13*s* 4*d*

Summa huius paginae   53*s* 4*d*

St Michaell 1599

Wm. Dantesey esquier. Of hym for one wholle yeres rente then due
for 3 tenementes in the west end of the Fenel streete in the
occupacion of wydoe Radclyffe, Tho. Birche and widowe Barlowe   12*d*

Jo. Culcheth esquier. Of hym for his landes and tenementes in the
Mylnegate, late parcell of Roberte Oldegreves landes in the tenure
of Roberte Langley per annum   4*s* 1*d*

George Chouretonn. Of hym for one tenemente and gardyn in the
Mylnegate late parcell of the saide Oldgreves landes per annum   6*d*

Richarde Choureton. Of hym for one tenemente and gardyn in the
Mylngate also late parcell of the saide Oldgreves landes per annum   8*d*

Roberte Rodley. Of hym for his house and gardyn nexte Chouretons
parcell also of the saide Oldgreves landes per annum   6*d*

James Buckley. Of hym for 2 tenementes and 2 gardyns in the
Mylngate parcell of the said Oldgreaves landes per annum   6*d*

William Barlowe. Of hym for his house and gardyn in the Mylngate
in his own occupacion parcell of the said Oldgreves landes per annum   4*d*

Summa huius paginae   7*s* 7*d*

St Michaell 1599

William Glover. Of hym for one tenemente and gardyn in
Deanesgate late Tetlowes per annum   3*d*

Robert Glover. Of hym for one other tenemente and one gardyn in
Deanesgate late Tetloes per annum   3*d*

Edwarde Charleton. Of hym for one house and gardyn in the
Marketstidlane late his uncle Charletons per annum   6*d*

Alexander Radclyffe. Of hym for 3 tenementes and gardyns in
Deanesgate late Tetlowes per annum   6*d*

James Hulme ar. Of hym for his landes and tenementes in
Manchester per annum then due   2*s*

The heires of Wm. Holland late of Clyffton. Of hym for his landes
and tenementes in Manchester beinge 2 tenementes and one lytle

meadow in the upper end of the Marketstidlane nexte the
watringe place per annum then due   3s
George Birche gen. Of hym for one tenemente conteyninge 40 acres
in Gorton called Milkenslade sometyme Bamffords 12d and for the
moitie of three burgages in Fenel streete sometyme Chadwickes
landes 12d in toto per annum then due   2s
George Leighe ar.[4]   12d
Oswold Mosley   2s
Summa huius paginae   11s 6d

St Michaell 1599
George Typpinge et Isabell Wyllott. Of theym for the moitie of
Gaticote fieldes 12d and for Dodge meadoes 2s parcell of the Garret
landes per annum   3s
John Hunte gen. Of hym for one quarters rente then due for the
toll, tolboothe and stallage in Manchester 20s for one holle yeres
rente due for his landes and burgages beinge his aunciente inheritance 7s 6d and for one halffe yeres rente then due for three fieldes
in Marketstidlane and two fieldes at Sudehill 14s 0½d in toto   41s 6½d
Wm., Thomas and Ed. Pilkinton. Of theym for the new
buyldings in Mylnegate and the land upon bothe sydes the
streete there per annum   12d
Richard Shalcrosse de Lymehurste. Of hym for one quarter of
the burgage in Marketstidlane late Adam Hollands   3d
Wm. Radclyffe. generosus. Of hym for his auncient inheritance
per annum   9s 6d
More of hym which he holdeth per lease for yeres for an intacke
in Marketstidlane, inclosed betwene the highe waye and
Barkehouse field per annum   6d
More of hym for his porcion of Cowpes landes per annum   3s 10d
Summa huius paginae   59s 7½d

St Michaell 1599
George Chadertonn gen. Of hym for one yeres rente then due
for one burgage in Deanesgate with one croffte nexte Alporte
parke one other burgage in Deanesgate one other burgage in
Marketstidd one parcell of the field lyenge on the southe parte
of the Marketstidlane   11s 8½d
John Marler gent. Of hym for one halffe yeres rente then due for
the third parte of the burgages and landes late his grandfather
Berdisleys and for halfe a burgage late Roberte Marler wyves
grandfathers   8s 2d
Margaret Sharlocke wydowe. Of her for one holle yeres rente
then due for one barne and 2 closses in Marketstidlane called
Hobcroftes parcell also of Berdisleys landes per annum   3s 8d
James Baguley. Of him for a lytle closse parcell also of the saide
Berdisleys landes on the west parte of the little lane entringe in
Sousehills per annum   12d

More of hym for the closse called Fayrestidde per annum   12*d*
Feoffees of the Freeschole. Of theym for the Mylnes the Walker
croffte, certen landes in Ancotes late in the tenure of Hugh
Travys £9 13*s* 4*d* and for one burgage beinge the ushers house 12*d*
in toto per annum   £9 14*s* 4*d*

Summa huius paginae   £10 19*s* 10½*d*

St Michaell 1599

Tho. Walker. Of hym for a burgage in Marketstidlane   12*d*
Roberte Langley gen. Of hym for one yeres rente then due for one
burgage in Milnegate conteyninge two tenementes and 2 gardyns
late Buckleys lande 12*d* for one intacke buylded in Mylngate 3*d*
for 2 intackes in the Withingreve late Chaloners 8*d* for a chamber
at the nether mylne late Sir Hughe Bexwickes 6*d* and for Clemente
crofte 2*s* in toto per annum   4*s* 5*d*
Samuell Hardye. Of hym for halfe a burgage at the Smythiedoare
late Galleys land 6*d* and for parcell of Bulders tenemente 4*d*
in toto per annum   10*d*
Henrie Hardye. Of hym for one other parcell of the saide
Bulders tenemente per annum   6*d*
James Lancashyre. Of hym for the other parte of the saide
Bulders tenemente per annum   8*d*
Nicholas Harteley. Of hym for halfe a burgage in the Mylnegate
conteyninge two tenementes and two gardyns late Kenyons
per annum   6*d*
Richarde Mooretonn. Of hym for his porcion of certen landes
and burgages in Todelane and Withingreve late Hartes landes
per annum   2*s* 1*d*
Roberte Hiltonn. Of hym for his porcion of the saide Hartes
lanes per annum   9*d*

Summa huius paginae   10*s* 9*d*

St Michaell 1599

Thomas Kenyonn. Of hym for halffe a burgage in the Milngate
conteyninge two tenementes late in the tenure of Rychard Nugente
per annum   6*d*
Anthonye Mosley. Of hym for his holle yeres rente then due for
certen landes conteyninge 9 acres joyeninge on the south parte of
Colyhurste   7*s*
More of hym for his porcion of certen landes and tenements in
Mylnegate late parcell of Mylnegates landes per annum   13*d*
Edmunde Platte. Of hym for his porcion of the saide Milnegates
landes per annum   5*d*
Stephen Pendilton. Of hym for his porcion of the saide Mylnegates
landes per annum   3*d*
Henrye Adamson. Of hym for his porcion of the saide Mylnegates
landes per annum   5*d*
Rauffe Whitworthe. Of hym for one yeres rente for halffe an acre
lyenge betwene Newton lane and Colyhurste per lease   10*d*

The heires of Adam Oldam. Of theym for theire halfe yeres rente
then due for 2 tenementes and tenne acres of lande sometyme
parcell of the Heathes adjoyeninge upon Newton and latelye
purchased in fee   4s 5d

Summa huius paginae   14s 11d

St Michaell 1599

Seddon, Marcrofte and Sorocoulde. Of theym for certen tenementes
in the Hangingdiche in the occupacion of Steven Browne and
Edmunde Bowker one tenemente at the Smythiedoare in the
occupacion of Ed. Hardye and others, one tenemente and one
crofte in the tenure of George Proudlove per annum   8d
Adam Pilkinton gent. Of hym for an intacke at Sudehill 6d and for
the upper parte of the gardyne of Samuell Chetams heires nihil   6d
Uxor Hughe Shacklocke. Of her for a parcell of grounde in which
are certen lymepittes adjoyninge to the walke mylne   8d
More of her for the house in which she dwelleth beinge
thinheritance of Edmunde Platte gen.   12d
Geo. Sydall Intacke. Of hym for a burgage conteyninge a shoppe
and a chamber at the southe doare of the Boothes late Adam
Hollandes per annum   6d
Tho. Byrom Intacke. Of hym for a burgage in the Marketstidlane
conteyninge 3 tenementes with gardyns per annum   12d
Adam Byrom gen. Of hym for a house and one acre of lande in the
Nether Acres sometyme the Ladye Breretons per annum   12d

Summa huius paginae   5s 4d

St Michaell 1599

Amos Chetam and John Gillyam. Of theym for the moitie of halfe
a burgage in the upper end of Marketstidlane 3d and for a house
and gardyn in the netherend of Mylngate 5d per annum   8d
Tho. Harysonne alias Salter. Of hym for the other moitie of the
saide halffe burgage per annum   3d
Roberte Cloughe Intacke. Of hym for his house, orcharde and
gardyn in the upperend of the Marketstidlane per annum   10d
Roberte Becke thelder. Of hym for the burgage wherein his
mother dwelled late John Garnets 12d, for the intacke at the doare
4d and for a doale of lande in the Acres 6d in toto per annum   22d
Roberte Becke the younger and his mother. Of hym for two fieldes
and a barne nexte Emontoutlane late Mr Strangewayes landes 5s,
for 4 acres adjoyninge to Newton lane 12d for a halffe a burgage in
the Marketstidlane late Adam Hollandes 6d for halffe a burgage
in the Acres 6d for a tenemente and 14 acres called Hopwood-
clayden 12d for Keys burgage 9d for halffe a burgage in the
Marketstid in the tenure of George Sydall 6d in toto per annum   9s 3d

Summa huius paginae   12s 10d

St Michaell 1599

Uxor Richard Hoape. Of her for certen landes and burgages in

the Withingreve and Hangingditche late Typpings per annum	18*d*
Adam Hall. Of hym for two tenementes and a gardyn nexte the	
pynffolde by the lordes grante per annum	2*d*
Stephen Browne. Of hym for a burgage and the new buyldinges	
and gardyn on the backesyde the house wherein he dwelleth late	
Glovers landes per annum	12*d*
Rychard Shalcrosse senior. Of hym for certen burgages in the	
netherend of the Mealegate late Rychard Galleys per annum	3*s*
Rychard Shalcrosse junior. Of hym for the corner [house][5] late	
Henrye Gees per annum	2*s*
Thomas Tetlowe. Of hym for 4 tenementes and 4 gardyns in the	

tenure of Wydowe Croxtonn, one house and gardyn and one acre
of lande in the tenure of Rychard Foxe, the corner house in the
tenure of Henrye Hardye, one house at the Smithie doare in the
tenure of Samuell Typpinge the Fayrestids the house where
Mrs Hilton dwelleth and 6 moe tenementes in Deanesgate with
theire gardyns in toto per annum   5*s* 6*d*

Summa huius paginae 13*s* 2*d*

St Michaell 1599

Wm. Elloure. Of hymn for the house and gardyn in the Hanging-
ditche 10*d* and for lymepitts now converted to a dungehill on the
easte parte of Salford bridge 4*d* in toto per annum   14*d*

Edwarde Rillstonne. Of hym for a shoppe and chamber in the
Marketstid late Thomas Silles lande per annum   12*d*

Henrye Chetam. Of hym for 2 tenementes and a gardyn in the
Mylnegate late Wm Radclyffes   4*d*

Henrye Aynesworthe. Of hym for ½ a burgage in Marketstidlane
late Roberte Cannockes 6*d* and for the intacke on the south parte
of Salford bridge 1*d* in toto   7*d*

Roberte Goodyere. Of hym for one tenemente and a fielde
abuttinge uppon Hodgkynfield of Hulton on the west parte and
the lane leadinge from Barlow Crosse to Ancoates on the northe
the halfe yeares rente then due   3*s* 10*d*

More of hym for a barne in the Withingreve per annum   8*d*

More of him for ½ a burgage conteyninge two tenementes in
Mylnegate per annum   6*d*

George Birche mercer. Of hym for his holle yeres rente then due
for his moitye of Cowpes landes   4*s* 7*d*

More of hym for an intacke at the dore of Rychard Cleytonn on
thissyde Colyhurst whereon is buylded parte of a baye of a
chamber ad voluntatem domini per annum   1*d*

Summa huius paginae 12*s* 9*d*

St Michaell 1599

Edw. Marler. Of hym for the house in Mealegate late Roberte
Marlers, one house in the occupacion of the saide Edward Marler
and all the rowe to the house in thoccupacion of John Cowpe   12*d*

Jo. Holte. Of hym for the toll of the otemeale and greates   3s 4d
John Ashetons heires. Of hym for a burgage in the Deanesgate and
one doale of lande in the Overacres by estimacion one acre of lande
late Devyas lande per annum   12d
Samuell Chetam his heyres. Of hym for a burgage with the lower
parte of his gardyn uppon the southe-west parte of the Hanging
bridge and the shoppes also per annum   12d
Tho. Brounsword and his nephewe Tippinge. Of theym for halffe
a burgage in the Hangingdyke conteyninge two tenementes
shoppes and gardyn late Rychard Brounswordes per annum   6d
Rycharde Smethurste. Of hym for a burgage on the northe parte of
the Boothes doare in the tenure of Henrye Houghton per annum   12d

Summa huius paginae   7s 10d

St Michaell 1599

Edmunde Hopwood ar. Of hym for Wynningtons burgages in the
Marketstidde and Smithiedoare per annum   6s
Jerom Whitworthe. Of hym for his burgages and shoppes in the
netherend of the Mealegate sometyme Utleys landes and late
Roberte Harysons per annum   12d
Michaell Dickonson. Of hym for two tenementes sometyme a
barne and halffe an acre of lande in the Overacres and sometyme
Worsleys lande per annum   6d
Fraunciscus Pendletonn. Of theym for a tenemente and gardyn
in Deanesgate late Tho. Tetloes 6d, for a barne in the Marketstidlane
and his yarne crofte on the backsyde thereof 6d for a tenemente,
barne and gardyn at the Withingreve called Clayepittes by deede
9d and for halffe a yeres rente for the landes and tenementes
adjoyninge to Grundylane 12s 8d in toto per annum   14s 5d
Adam Hollande. Of hym for halffe a burgage in the Mylnegate
sometyme Ferrars and late William Bradshawes and Wm Leese
tenante to the same per annum   6d

Summa huius paginae   22s 5d

St Michaell 1599

Uxor George Wyrrall. Of her for certen tenementes latelye
buylded by her husbande in the Mylnegate and purchased of
Sir Edmunde Trafforde knighte per annum   12d
Thomas Radclyffe. Of hym for parcell of Raphe Hopwoods lande,
which he holdeth in the righte of his wyffe one of the daughters of
Rycharde Gee per annum   6d
Raphe Hopwoods heires. Of the heires of the saide Raphe
Hopwoode for the rest of the moitie of his landes per annum   5d
Geo. Birche clerke. Of hym for certen burgages in the Mylnegate
in the tenure of George Warde and Adam Hall per annum   2s 11d
Randull Hultonn. Of hym for two tenementes and gardyns and
two new buyldings on the southeast parte of the Churchestyle
parcell of Mr Hulme of Devehulme landes per annum   12d

George Birche sonne of John. Of hym for halffe a yeares rente of
the Smithie fielde and Deanesbancke bothe conteyninge fyve acres
or thereabouts   3s

Summa huius paginae 8s 10d

St Michaell 1599

William Ravalde. Of hym for certen burgages in the Mylnegate
in the tenure of uxor George Awynn and uxor Fletcher and the
cockefighte[6] and 2 tenementes adjoyninge per annum   22d
The heires of Henry Allynn. Of hym for 2 halffe burgages in the
Marketstidd betwene the house of Rychard Shalcrosse and
Rycharde Foxe per annum   12d
Roberte Robynsonn. Of hym for his burgage in the Mylnegate
called the stonehouse now newlye buylded 12d and for the
common oven 6s 8d in toto per annum   7s 8d
Richarde Foxe. Of hymn for his burgage in the Marketstid
wherein he dwelleth   12d
Geo. Tippinge et Isabell Willott. Of theym for halfe a yeres rente
then due for theire landes and tenementes in the Heathes late in
tenure of Massye Oldam and uxor Adam Buerdsall   10s 6d
John Marler gen. Of hym for his halffe yeres rente of 2 closses late
in the tenure of Rychard Galley and parcell of Shawes purchase 3s 4d
Thomas Pyecrofte. Of hym for a burgage in the Mylnegate in
the tenure of William Bennet and sometyme Corkers landes
per annum   12d

Summa huius paginae   26s 4d

St Michaell 1599

Thomas Birche als Orcharde. Of hym for 2 tenementes and a
gardyn in the Hangingedyke parcell of Mr Strangwayes landes
per annum   12d
Randull Massye. Of hym for his landes and burgages in the nether
end of the Mylnegate late parcell of Ruddes landes per annum   3s 8d
Uxor John Croxtonn. Of her for a lytle closse in the Sousehilles
sometyme Ruddes lande and late parcell of the said Massies lande 12d
John Gee. Of hym for his wholle yeres rente then due for the rest
of the saide Ruddes lands and burgages   4s 8d
George Proudlove. Of hym for his holle yeres rente then due for
the moitie of the landes and burgages late Hopwoodes 11d for
his halffe yeres rente then due for 2 fields in the Heathes as joynte
tenante with Shawe 3s 4d for a burgage in the Mylnegate in the
tenure of Mr Edwarde Hollande sometyme Whitworthes landes 6d
for a shoppe cellars and chambers late Thomas Sylles 12d for ½ a
burgage in Mylnegate late in the tenure of uxor Hughe Grene 6d
and for parcell of Haslomes lands 10d in toto   7s 1d
Henrye Adamson. Of hym for halffe a burgage an intacke
conteyninge a mylnestid upon Colyhurste to turne a grindlestone
ad voluntatem domini per annum   6d

Summa huius paginae   17s 11d

St Michaell 1599

Simon Malone. Of hym for a barne at the Withingreve for certen
yeres per lease from Mr Lacye beinge an intacke per annum   8*d*
Roger Bexwicke. Of hym for the dawbehill at the pinfold per
lease pro termino vitae Margaretae uxoris eius 6*d* and for his
porcion of Cowpes landes 9*d* in toto per annum   15*d*
Uxor Raphe Proudelove. Of her for 2 burgages or tenementes in
the Hangingdyke 18*d* and for halffe a burgage in the Withingreve
6*d*, bothe which were parcell of Steven Brownes landes, and for
parcell of Haslomes lands 10*d* in toto per annum   2*s* 10*d*
Ed. Knotte ad voluntatem domini. Of hym for one gardyn betwene
the 2 lytle lanes betwene Manchester and Hulmes bridge 4*d* and
for one gardyn thereto adjoyninge late in the tenure of Wm
Whiteheades wyffe 2*d* in toto per annum   6*d*
George Smethurst. Of hym for an intacke upon Colyhurste
conteyninge a house and garden per lease for yeres   6*d*
Roger Pendilton. Of hym for an intacke upon Colyhurst
conteyninge a house and a gardyn per lease for yeares   6*d*
Jo. Asheton draper. Of hym for an intacke conteyninge a house
and gardyn at Redbanke per lease for yeres per annum   3*s*
Summa huius paginae   9*s* 3*d*

St Michaell 1599

John Cowpe. Of hym for the hovell or penthouse anendste the
Smythie ad voluntatem domini per annum   4*d*
William Bowker. Of hym for an intacke in the higher end of the
Withingreve ad voluntatem domini per annum   12*d*
Richarde Pendiltonn. Of hym for one ½ yeres rent then due for a
parcell of waste uppon Tillhill nere Colyhurste whereon he hathe
buylded a house and made a gardyn per lease for 21 yeres from
St Michaell Anno R.R.Eliz. 29   15*d*
Rauffe Hulme gent. Of hym for one yeres rente of a house,
2 barnes, 4 fieldes called Chowfieldes and 2 pastures lyenge on
the northe parte of Newton lane late Robert Labreys   45*s* 6*d*
Item of hym for one yeres rente then due for his inheritance   30*s* 4*d*
Jo. Strangewayes gent. Of hym for one holle yeres rente then due
for certen landes and burgages in Nether Acres Deanesgate and
Mylngate   6*s* 2*d*
Roger Smythe. Item for a lytle mylnestid decayed upon
Colyhurste sometyme Harysons per annum   6*d*
Summa huius paginae   £4 5*s* 1*d*

St Michaell 1599

Regina Elizabetha
Manschantrie. Of her Majestie by the hands of Raphe Asheton
esquier her highnes receyvour for certen tenementes and gardyns
in the Mylnegate and Tode lane conteyninge 8 houses called
Manschauntrie late in the tenure of Robert Buckley per annum   18*d*

Manchestre Chantrie. More of her Majestie for one tenemente in
Deanesgate, one acre of lande in the Overacres and three fieldes
lyenge betwene Marketstidlane and Aldporte called Blackeacres,
certen tenementes with gardyns in the southe parte of the
Hangingdyke one tenemente with an orcharde and gardyn on
the southeast parte of the Marketcrosse late in the tenure of
Fr. Pendiltonn. Two tenementes with fyfftie acres of lande to
theym belonginge at Grenloecrosse which premisses were called
Manchester Chauntrie per annum   27s 7d
Ladies Chauntrie. More of her Majestie for certen tenementes in
St Mary gate which belonged to the late Chauntrye of oure Lady
per annum   3s
                    Summa huius paginae   32s 1d

                        St Michaell 1599
William Orrell esquier. Oh hym for his landes and tenementes in
Dalton sometyme one Ellyn Tarbuttes landes holden by the
8th parte of a knightes fee et reddit per annum   12d
More of hym for other landes in Dalton purchased of the Erle of
Derbye per annum   [6d][7]
More of hym for the manor of Turton holden of the lorde by the
8th parte of a knightes fee et reddit per annum   18d
Richarde Warde. Of hym for his landes and tenementes in
Sharpulls per annum   18d
The heires of Sharpulls. Of the heires of Sharpulls for theire landes
and tenementes in Sharpulls per annum   10d
Rycharde Holland esquier. Oh hym for his landes and tenementes
in Sharpulls per annum   10d
John Bradshawe esquier. Of hym for his landes and tenementes
in Bradshawe and Harwood late Robert Hollands and John
Davies holden of the lord by the 8th parte of a k. fee per annum 9d
James Anderton of Lostocke esquier. Of hym for his landes and
tenementes in Heaton sub foresta holden of the lorde by 10th parte
of a knights fee et reddit per annum   20d
More of hym for the manor of Lostocke holden by the third parte
of a knightes fee, et reddit per annum   11d
                    Summa huius paginae   9s

                        St Michaell 1599
James Worthingtonn gent. Of hym for his landes and tenementes
in Snydle late Roger Pendilburyes pro omnibus servitiis unum
esperverium[8] vel redditum per annum   12d
George Hulton ar. Of hym for his landes and tenementes in
Farneworthe and Rumworthe per annum   9s
Rycharde Leyver gen. Of hym for his landes and tenementes in
Lytle Leyver per annum   4s
Edwarde Chisnall ar. Of hym for his landes and tenementes in
Lytle Leyver also sometyme George Darcyes rente per annum   18d

Adam Byrom gent. Of hym for his landes and tenementes in
Lytle Leyver beinge the other halffe of the said Darcyes rente
per annum   18*d*
Wm. Hultonn esquier. Of hym for his landes and tenementes
called the Parke, and a tenemente called Midlewood in Hultonn
holden of the lorde by the 20th parte of a knights fee et rente
per annum   4*d*
Rauffe Seddon and Tho. Marcrofte. Of theym for theire landes
and tenementes in Farneworthe rente per annum   6*d*
Assheton Nuttall and his coparceners. Of theym for theire landes
and tenementes in Farneworthe per annum   2*s*
            Summa huius paginae   19*s* 10*d*

St Michaell 1599

Rauffe Ashetonn esquier. Of hym for his landes and tenementes
in Farneworthe per annum   18*d*
Mr Hoarde. Of hym for his landes and tenementes in Brundehill
holden of the lord by homage fealtie and sute of courte and the
yerelye rente of   15*s*
Myles Gerarde esquier. Of hym for his landes and tenementes in
Aspull late one Rychard Inces landes which hamell is holden of
the lord by the 8th parte of a knights fee and rente per annum   9*d*
Roberte Hyndley and his coparceners. Of theym for their landes
and tenementes in Aspull sometyme Roberte Hyndleys as
coparcener with the saide Rychard Ince rente per annum   9*d*
Edwarde Worthingtonn gen. Of hym for the manor of Worthington
holden by halffe a knights fee sute of court at Manchester and
the yearlye rente of   3*s* 8*d*
Thomas Southworthe esquier. Of hym for his landes and
tenementes in Brockeholes holden of the lord by the 4th parte of
a knights fee and the yearelye rente of   4*d*
Rycharde Elston gen. Of hym for his landes and tenementes in
Brockholes holden of the lord by the 4th parte of a knights fee
and pro warda castri Lancastriae 9*d* rent per annum   4*d*
            Summa huius paginae   22*s* 4*d*

St Michaell 1599

Rychard Leighe gen. Of hym for his holle yeres rente due for his
landes in Prestall per annum   3*d*
Rycharde Lathom ar. Of hym for his landes and tenementes in
Parbalte and Wrightinton holden of the lord by halffe a knights
fee per annum   2*s*
Roger Kirkbye ar. Of hym for his landes and tenementes in
Wrightintonn, tenante in common with others by halffe a
knights fee rente per annum   2*s*
Coheres of Thome Caterall ar. Of theym for theire lands and
tenementes in Wrightinton the holle hamell holden of the lord by
halffe a k. fee et reddit per annum   8*d*

Thurstan Heskytt gen. his heires. Of hym for his landes there
per annum   2*d*
Sir Rychard Shuttleworth knight. Of hym for his landes and
tenementes in Lostock per annum   7*d*
Wm. Earle of Derbye. Of his honor for landes and tenementes
[in] Halywell per 10th parte feodi militis per annum   8*d*
More of his honor for landes in Tunley   8*d*
More of his honor for his landes and tenementes in Anlazargh   3*s*
Roger Ryder his intacke on Colyhurst   6*d*
   [page total deleted]
More of the sayde erle for landes in Dalton   6*d*
Randall Barton ar. Of hym for the moitie of Flixton   20*d*
                    Summa huius paginae   12*s* 8*d*

St Michaell 1599

Roberte Heskytte ar. Of hym for one holle yeres rente then due
for his freelandes and tenementes in Wrightinton late Sir Rycharde
Houghtons knighte per annum   8*d*
More for landes in Wrightinton jure uxoris beinge Mr Stopforths
landes   6*d*
Roger Smythe. Of hym for an intacke uppon Colyhurste per annum   6*d*
Widowe Barlowe. Of her for her house and sixe acres of lande
uppon Colyhurste per annum   4*s*
James Lancashyre. Of hym for an intacke anendst his house   12*d*
Rycharde Cleyton. Of hym for an intacke anendst his house   12*d*
Rycharde Pendilton. Of hym for ½ an acre of lande uppon
Colyhurste   6*d*
Roberte Jannye. Of hym for the hovell anendst his smythie per
annum   6*d*
Stephen Pendiltonn. Of hym for his parte of the quarrye due at
St Michaell 1599 per annum   30*s*
Rycharde Rothwell. Of hym for the lyke yeres rente for his parte
then due   30*s*
              Summa huius paginae   £3 8*s* 8*d*
        Summa huius quarterii de S Michaele 99   £65 18*s* 8*d*

St Michaell 1599

Colihurste winter pasture
Imprimis received of William Leese for his cowe a moneth   10*d*
Item of Rycharde Rothwell for a fortnighte his cowe   6*d*
Item of James Rydings for 3 beasts till Christmas   6*s*
Item of Edward Bryddocke for 4 beasts and ½ till Martinmas   4*s* 6*d*
Item for Roger Ryder his horse   4*s*
Item of John Deane for his horse a moneth   16*d*
Item of Thomas Chadwicke for his horse one weeke   4*d*
Item of Mr Edw. Hollande for 2 horses a moneth   4*s*
Chetham St Michaell 1599
Item receyved of Edwarde Bryddocke for one halffe yeres rente

due at St Michaell tharchangell 1599 for the lordshippe of
Chetham £13 18s 2d

Summa huius paginae £14 19s 8d

St Michaell tharchangell 1599

Perquisites &c.

Imprimis received of Rycharde Nugente bororeve the 21 Januarye
1599 in parte of his accompte and receite due at St Michaell 99 30s

Item for the perquisites of the 3 Weekes Courte due at
St Michaell 1599 26s 8d

Item received of Asheton Nuthall for his reliefe after the deathe
of Fra. Nuttall his father 2s

Item for reliefe upon Nicholas Harteleys purchase 6d

Item of Rychard Shalcrosse and Margaret his wyffe for reliefe
after the deathe of her brother Edw. Gee 2s

Item of Wm Dawson for the charges of his privie seale 6s 8d

in estraye Item received of Henrye Holte for kepinge his nagge at
the Houghe 2 dayes 6d

Summa huius paginae £3 8s 4d

Manchester   Christmas 1599

Of theym[9] for one halffe yeares rente due at the feaste of the byrthe
of our Lord God 1599 for Nether Alporte commonlye called
Alporte Parke 26s 8d

Sir Jo. Byron knighte. Of hym for one quarters rente then due for
the hamell of Blakeley Blakeley fieldes and Bothomley by the
hands of his servante James Travys £8 6s 8d

More of hym for Faylesworthe per annum 7s

Jo. Hunte gen. Of hym for one quarters rente then due for the
toll &c. 20s

Wydowe Hoape. Item of Widowe Hoape for her half yeres rente
the due 21s 8d

Nicholas Harteley. Item of hym for his halffe yeres rente then due 20s

Summa huius paginae £13 2s

Rentes due at the Annunciacion of the blessed virgin Marye 1600

Imprimis for one halffe yeares rent then due for Overalporte[10] 20s

Sir John Byron knighte. Of hym for one quarters rente then due
for the hamells of Blakeley Blakeley fieldes and Bothomley
£8 6s 8d and for one halffe yeares rente then due for the hamell of
Gorton £15 6s 8d by the handes of his servante John Samon
in toto £23 12s 4d

John Hunte gent. Of him for his quarters rente then due for the
toll tolbooth and stallage in the towne of Manchester by the
handes of his servaunte Thomas Purseglove 20s

More of hym for his halffe yeares chieffe rente then due for fyve
fieldes whereof 3 lye in the Marketstidlane and two at Sudehill
the summe of 14s 0½d

Summa huius paginae £26 6s 4½d

Annunciacion 1600

Roberte Goodyeare. Of hym for one halffe yeares rente then due
for one tenemente and one closse now devided into severall
closses on the righte hande of the waye above Barlow Crosse
which leadeth to Ancotes sometyme Slades   3s 10d
Frauncis Pendilton. Of hym for the halffe yeres rente then due
for two tenementes and 18 acres of lande lyenge on bothe sydes
Grundielane within Manchester latelye purchased   12s 8d
George Tippinge et Isabell Wyllotte. Of theym for the halffe
yeres rente then due for their landes and tenementes in the
Heathes parcell of Roberte Shawes purchase conteyninge 13 acres
or thereabouts   10s 6d
Jo. Marler gent. Of hym for two closses in the Heathes parcell
also of Roberte Shawes purchase for one halfe yeares rente then due   3s 4d
The heires of Adam Oldham. Of theym for theire landes and
tenementes in the saide Heathes for one halffe yeares rente then due   4s 5d

Summa huius paginae 34s 9d

Annunciacion 1600

George son of Jo. Birch. Of hym for his halffe yeares rente then
due for two fieldes the one called Smithiefield and the other
Deanesbancke lyenge on the east parte of the Asheleis   3s
George Proudlove. Of hym for his halffe yeres rente then due for
2 closses in the saide Heathes parcell of Shawes purchase   3s 4d
John Marler gent. Of hym for one halffe yeres rente then due for
the thirde parte of the burgages and landes late his grandfather
Edmunde Berdislys and for halffe a burgage sometyme his father
Marlers   8s 3d
Richarde Pendiltonn. Of hym for his halffe yeares rente then due
for a parcell of waste uppon Tillhill nere Colyhurste uppon which
he hathe latelye buylded a house and made a gardyn and holdeth
the same by lease for 21 yeres from St Michaell Anno R.R.Eliz 29
15d and for his halfe yeres rente then due for ½ an acre lately
ymproved on Colyhurst 6d in toto   21d

Summa huius paginae   16s 4d
Summa huius quarterii   £28 17s 5½d

Summa totalis omnium receptorum et recipiendorum hoc anno
finito apud festum Annunciationis Mariae 1600
£183 9s 11½d

A brieffe note of all my receiptes this yere ended Thannunciacion of
Marye the blessed virgin 1600 as before appeareth at large in this booke.
Imprimis received for the summer pasture of Colyhurste in
Maye 1599 besydes Barlow and Pendletons allowance   £15 13s 4d
Item received of the butchers in parte   £4 17s 3d
Item for one halfe yeres rente due at Mydsommer 1599 for
Chetam and other money as appeareth by this booke   £24 8s 2d
Item for one quarters rente due at Midsommer 1599 for
Manchester   £12 5s 1d

Item for one quarters rente due at Michaelmas 1599 for Manchester	£65 18s 8d
Item for one halfe yeres rente due at Michaelmas 1599 for Chetam and for the wynter pasture of Colihurste prout patet at large before in this booke	£14 19s 8d
Item for one quarters rente due at Christmas 1599 for Manchester	£13 2s
Item for one quarters rente due at Thannunciacion 1600	£28 17s 5½d
Item for perquisites of courtes and reliefes	£3 8s 4d
So that my holle receipte as apperes on the page next before is juste	£183 9s 11½d

The saide accomptante Charles Leighe desyreth allowance for money by hym paide as followeth	
Imprimis paide to your lordship the 10th of May 1599	£15 10s 9d
Item paide more to your lordship the 16th daye of Julye 1599	£13 2s 6d
Item paide to Edwarde Chorltonn by your lordships appoyntment the 21 Julye 99 £4 and the 4 of August 1599 53s 4d in toto	£6 13s 4d
Item paide to the colyer and for worke aboute the colepitte	£3 6s 8d
Item paide the 1 of September 1599 to Mr Anthonye Mosleys wyffe for your lordships use prout patet per acquietance	£10
Item paide the 8 of September 99 for one to goe to Mr Heaton for Mr Traffordes fyne	8d
Item paide to Thomas Heaton which he paide to Mr Davemporte for counsell at the drawinge of Mr Byroms office the 12 Sept. 99	10s
Item paide on the fayre daye 99 for 2 quartes of wyne and suger 2s to the halberdmen 12d and to the waytes 12d in toto	4s
Item paide to Edw. Bryddocke which he layde downe for the colyer	18d
Summa huius paginae £49 9s 5d	

Item paide to the Queenes Majesties baylief for her highnes rente due at Michaelmas 1599	£6 15s
Item paide for one yeres rente then due to her Majestie for the lordship of Chetam	13s 4d
Item paide to your stewarde Mr Swingelhurste for his holle yeres fee due at St Michaell 1599	£10
Item for respyte of homage	36s 8d
Item paide to Thomas Heaton your feodarye his holle yeres fee due at St Michaell 1599	£4
Item paide for the yeres fee then due for the clerkshippe of your Courte	13s 4d
Item payde for Mr Stewards dynners at Michaelmas 1599 and Easter 1600	13s 4d
Item for the waytes and for wyne	2s 10d
Item payde to your sester Hollande at St Michaell 1599 20s	

at Christmas 1599 20s and at the Annunciacion of Mary 1600 20s
in toto   £3
                    Summa huius paginae   £27 14s 6d

Item paide the 6 of November 1599 to your brother Mr Anthonye
Mosley for your lordships use   £48
Item paide for mendinge yates and rayles to Hughe Barlow
Rychard Pendilton and others 2s for a staple for Colyhurste
yate 2d for mendinge the yrons 6d and for pitch 1d in toto   2s 9d
Item paide to Mr Davemporte when he rode to Newton about
Mr Byroms office the 10th of December 1599   20s
Item for shooinge my horse the same tyme and for my horse,
Thomas Heatons mans and my owne charges prout patet
per billam at Leaghe, Newton and Warington 2 dayes and
2 nyghtes   7s 2d
Item paide to olde Mr William Radclyffe for keepinge 2
younge swyne taken upp by hym as estrayes the seconde daye
of December 1599 and delyvered to me the 13th of the
same moneth 2s and for keepinge one of theym a weeke after
to Woollens wyffe 5d in toto   2s 5d
Item bestowed uppon the poore in Manchester at
Christmas 1599   40s
Item paide to your brother Mr Anthonye Mosley to your
lordships use the 21 Januarye 1599   £20
Item charges to Wigan doubtinge the office wolde have bene
sytten there in the begynninge of Marche for supper haye
and provander over nighte, for breakfast, haye and provander
in the morninge   23d
                    Summa huius paginae   £71 14s 3d

Item paide for Mr Davemportes beinge at Leaghe the 28 of
Marche 1600 and for his advyse the daye before touchinge
Mr Byroms office and perusinge the bookes   20s
Item for makinge two yron plates for the sadle of your dun
nagge and mendinge the same sadle 8d for provande and
haye the first nighte and in the morning 8d for naylinge hym
2d and for fetchinge and bringing the horse 4d in toto   22d
Item for Mr Davemportes dynner his mans and myne at
Leaghe and for horsemeate   18d
Item the receyvors fee due for one yere ended at
thannunciacion of the virgin Marye 1600   £6 13s 4d
Item paide for one to goe to Tho. Heatons to procure hym
to come with the bookes the 4th of Marche to Manchester
where Mr Byroms office shoulde have been sitten   8d
Item to Mr Escheters man 2s whereof I paide 12d and
Tho. Byrom 12d to procure Frydaye in Easter weeke for the
sittinge the office at Leagh   12d
Item my horse hyre and charge at Stopporte the 10th of

March 99 when Mr Leighe sealed his obligacions   8d
Item for a new yron per anno 1600   6d
        Summa huius paginae   £7 19s 6d

Summa expositorum hoc anno finite apud festum Annunciationis
beatae Mariae 1600 £156 17s 8d and besydes the arrerages and
remayns which is as followeth
Item this Accomptant ys to be allowed for certen arrerages of
rentes not yet receyved
Imprimis for one yeres arrerage due for the rente of Alport
fielde at Thannunciacion of the blessed virgin Marye 1600.
Whereof 20s was due at St Michaell before in anno 1599   40s
Item one yeres rent due by John Strangewayes gen. at
Michaelmas 1599   6s 2d
Item for Adam Byroms rent then due   2s 6d
Item for Tho. Haryson als Salters rent then due   3d
Item for George Allyns rent then due   12d
Item for Roberte Becke the younger for rent then due   9s 3d
Item for Mr Tildesleys heires rent then due   3s 4d
Item for George Hulton ar. his rent then due   9s
Item for Mr Candishe or Mr Horde theire rente then due[11]   15s
Item for Wydowe Barlow her rent then due   4s
Item Mr Oswold Mosleys rent then due   2s
Item Roger Pendilton his rent then due   6d
Summa totalis omnium arreragiorum hoc anno   £4 13s
Maii 1600 Item paide in money to your sister Mr Anthonye
Mosleys wyffe the remaynder of this accompte beinge £21 19s 3½d

So reste I cleare for this yere ended at Thannunciacion of Marye 1600
and desyre my quietus est the holle summe being discharged
viz. £183 9s 11½d
Item I have delyvered also to your lordships sester in lawe
Mrs Alyce Mosley in money and that she is to paye for me for
the pasture of Colyhurste over and besydes the sayd £21 19s 3½d
the summe of £15 I saye   £15
So that in all you are nowe to receyve of her   £36 19s 3½d
This last £15 is for the pasture of Colyhurst this yere 1600

NOTES

[1] M.C.L. MS.f.333 M 45. Arabic numerals have been substituted for the roman
numerals of the original.
[2] Knight's fee.
[3] heir.
[4] This and the following entry were added after a deleted page total. No details
are given, but the corresponding entries in the Rental for 1598–99 read 'Geo.
Leigh de Highlee ar. Of hym for the other moitie of Gatiecote field per annum
12d' and 'Oswolde Mosley gen. Of hym for his porcon of the Garret landes per
annum 2s'.

⁵ House is omitted but it is given in the Rental of 1598–99.

⁶ The Rental for 1598–99 has 'cockpitte'.

⁷ No sum stated; 6*d* was the amount in the Rental for 1598–99.

⁸ A sparrow hawk.

⁹ No names are given; at Midsummer they were Mrs Prestwich and Adam Smythe.

¹⁰ No name given; at Michaelmas the rent was payable by William Earl of Derby.

¹¹ 'pd in anno 1600' in the margin.

APPENDIX 2

LIST OF INVENTORIES

The status or occupation of a testator has been derived from either the will or the inventory; where it is given in brackets it has been conjectured. The total value of the personal property includes debts owed by or owing to the testator whether these were recorded in the will or in the inventory; only desperate debts have been excluded. The inventories are in the Lancashire Record Office at Preston.

1570	John Nabbs	clothmaker	£89	0s	6d[1]
1573	William Baguley	clothier	£584	16s	0d
1573	John Davie	occupier	£104	11s	4d
1574	Francis Pendleton	merchantman	£218	8s	10d
1581	Henry Burrows		£16	13s	4d
1581	John Shaw	mercer	£113	3s	1d
1582	John Cowopp	(yeoman)	£51	12s	6d
1582	Joan Edge	widow	£109	13s	5d
1583	Robert Birch	linen draper	£470	15s	2d[2]
1584	George Barlow	baker[3]	£15	18s	1d
1584	Edward Hanson	(mercer and grocer)	£391	17s	5d[4]
1584	Thomas Hardman	mercer	£451	6s	9d[5]
1587	Richard Hunt	gentleman	£137	3s	2d
1588	Thomas Beck	gentleman	£84	16s	4d
1588	John Billing	glazier	£325	9s	11d
1588	James Bradshaw	saddler	£460	0s	0d
1588	Thomas Brownsword	clothier	£1109	5s	5d
1588	Ottiwell Hodgkinson als Johnson	shoemaker	£87	13s	0d
1588	Thomas Holme	tailor	£27	0s	8d
1588	William Hunt	tanner	£146	12s	10d
1588	Arthur Kershaw	yeoman	£1	13s	0d
1588	Adam Oldham	yeoman	£164	17s	4½d
1588	Elizabeth Orred	(widow)[6]	£6	8s	3d
1588	William Pycroft	linen occupier	£57	15s	6d
1589	Margaret Hurlestone	widow	£123	7s	3d
1590	William Awyn	(draper)	£39	18s	1d

1590	John Dickenson	linen weaver	£15	7s	8d
1590	John Glover	singing man	£132	13s	7d
1591	Margaret Bowker	widow	£19	1s	3d
1591	Robert Clough	linen weaver	£100	4s	6d
1591	Adam Hope	whittawer	£135	0s	1d
1591	Alice Pendleton	widow	£586	6s	1d
1591	John Pycroft	linen weaver	£13	9s	5d
1591	Andrew Renshaw	(shoemaker and yarn dealer)	£111	13s	2d[7]
1591	Grace Whitworth	widow	£2	12s	6d
1592	Ellen Radley	spinster	£10	12s	3d
1592	Robert Wharmby	butcher	£12	9s	3d
1593	Joan Newall	widow	£101	18s	4d[8]
1593	Robert Bridghouse	joiner	£102	11s	2d
1593	John Buckley	preacher and minister	£35	19s	5d
1593	Francis Hough	clothier	£241	13s	2d
1594	Isabel Barlow	widow	£92	12s	9d
1596	Edward Ellor	(clothier)	£323	10s	0d
1598	Hugh Chadkirk	linen weaver	£79	0s	8d
1598	Edward Dyson	butcher	£34	0s	0d
1598	John Leese	clothworker	£272	9s	0d
1598	William Sandforth	linen draper	£77	10s	8d
1598	Robert Walshman	goldsmith	£128	15s	10d
1598	John Wharmby	butcher	£223	1s	9d
1598	Francis Wirrall	tanner	£93	6s	3d
1599	Margaret Bexwick	spinster	£8	13s	4d
1599	Roger Bexwick	yeoman	£110	1s	1d
1599	John Postells	(shearman)	£2	2s	9d
1599	Isabel Tipping	widow	£1526	0s	0d[9]
1600	Thomas Shalcross	(linen weaver)	£16	3s	2d
1602	John Marler	gentleman	£176	16s	3d
1602	Robert Radley		£44	3s	10d

NOTES

[1] The inventory is printed in Lowe, pp. 102–3.

[2] The inventory is printed in Lowe, pp. 103–5, but with the omission of the debts Birch owed.

[3] He was described as a baker in his will of 26 July 1583 and as a shoemaker in his inventory. The inventory implies that he was a baker, not a shoemaker.

[4] Some entries in the inventory are missing or illegible.

[5] Excluding desperate debts of £90 14s 11½d.

[6] She was described as the wife of Richard Orred in her will, but she was in fact his widow (*Registers*, p. 266).

[7] Not including 6s 8d in desperate debts.

[8] Not including £30 in desperate debts.

[9] Some entries in this inventory are illegible; the real total would be rather higher than £1526.

INDEX